DEVELOPMENT DYNAMICS OF A HIMALAYAN STATE

DEVELOPMENT DYNAMICS OF A HIMALAYAN STATE

VOLUME - II

SOME WAY FORWARD FOR A HIMALAYAN STATE

Edited by
R. R. Nautiyal
Rajlakshmi Datta

KALPAZ

First Published 2018

Published by

Kalpaz Publications
C-30, Satyawati Nagar,
Delhi - 110052
E-mail: kalpaz@hotmail.com
Ph.: 9212142040

Printed at: G. Print Process, Delhi

Cataloging in Publication Data—DK
Courtesy: D.K. Agencies (P) Ltd. <docinfo@dkagencies.com>

Development dynamics and way forward for an Indian Himalayan state / edited by R.R. Nautiyal, Rajlakshmi Datta.
volumes cm
Contents: vol. I. Sustainable development and development discourses for the Himalayan state of Uttarakhand — vol. II. Reflections on some significant dimensions of Himalayan character of development.
ISBN 9789386397348 (set: HB)
ISBN 9789386397881 (Vol. 1: HB)
ISBN 9789386397898 (Vol. 2: HB)

1. Economic development—India—Uttarakhand. 2. Sustainable development—India—Uttarakhand. 3. Natural resources—India—Uttarakhand. I. Nautiyal, R. R., editor. II. Datta, Rajlakshmi, editor.

LCC HC437.U88D48 2018 | DDC 338.95454 23

Contents

VOLUME - II

Section - V
Some Forte for the State

Section - VI
Human Development

Section V:
Some Forte for the State

15

A Conceptual Framework on Tourism of Uttarakhand through Alternative Approaches

Kavita Bhatt

Introduction

The economic potential tourism holds, for many – although not all - mountain communities, is quite clear: in most mountainous regions of the world, people have limited possibilities for generating income. Agriculture, forestry and animal husbandry form the backbone of local economies, but these contend with shallow soils, harsh weather conditions, and low market competitiveness. Therefore, diversification of livelihoods is often not a choice, but a necessity for mountain household. Mountain ranges offer possibilities to all kinds of tourists: sport fans come for hiking, climbing or skiing. Others come simply to appreciate beautiful landscapes. In remote valleys and on mountain peaks, many endemic plants invite visitors to discover unique biodiversity. Those interested in cultural heritage find compelling destinations.[1] The mountain state of Uttarakhand adds another dimension in tourism by pulling spiritual tourists from all over the world in search of bliss and to experience oneness with the Almighty in the serene environment.

This spiritual journey gets a momentum with yoga learning which attracts visitors worldwide to this *Devbhoomi.* India; as well as Uttarakhand has a worldwide popularity for yoga and its origin. UNESCO has decided to celebrate international yoga day every year on 21 June from 2015. And people are visiting Uttarakhand for the yogic practices beyond the boundaries of religion, caste, communities and countries. A huge proportion of tourists both foreigners and Indians move here for physical health, mental peace and spiritual bliss by yogic practices. It is argued in this paper that Uttarakhand's tourism sector has a huge potential given the nature of environment, resources required for almost all forms of tourism but to add impetus to the development of tourism in the state some alternative approaches in commercial level with public private partnership are in need. The argument has been justified by presenting some facts and figures and identifying the weaknesses in tourism sector for the state.

Tourism and Development

Economic development is primarily about enhancing a nation's factors of productive capacity, i.e., land, labour, capital and technology, etc. by using its resources and powers to reduce the risks and costs. It is helpful to develop the labour force, infrastructure, business and community facilities, work-environment, economic structure and institutional capacity to support economic growth. Economic development covers a broad and magnanimous set of activities and tools that assists communities in growth and prosperity. The best economic development practitioners strive to bring quality jobs, new business and increased services to communities through inventive approaches and result driven strategies.

The term economic development is generally a collective reflection of various financial aspects of a country/state/region; which reflects through the income and life standard of persons of that particular phenomenon. Nature provides basic resources for the concerned development; but the proper management and skills of the persons are also the basic requirement of economic development. Specially, in case of Uttarakhand; the present scenario needs a revisit to understand where the state is heading to. The people of Uttarakhand dreamt for a healthy progress and economic development through the constitution of separate state; but the scenario is not all very encouraging if the larger part of the state, the hills are considered. No doubt that the per capita income in this state is one of the highest but it does not conform that the hilly districts are the beneficiaries. The state is also facing the problems like natural disaster, various kinds of migration, imbalanced population, human animal struggle, forest fire, unhealthy healthcare system, poor transport and communication, unemployment, lacking appropriate education and many more. These problems can be divided in two major categories: natural and manmade. Whatever they may be, the people of Uttarakhand especially in the hills are facing a crisis. Being a Himalayan state; tourism is an immense source of income and livelihood and the people directly and indirectly rely on it largely.

Tourism as an activity is not a new phenomenon; but in recorded history there have been instances whereby one is able to know that man has been travelling throughout the age. In nineteenth century people have seen travelling for the purpose of trade and commerce. Throughout history, traders and merchants have travelled to far off lands in order to trade with other nations and tribes. People have started journeys to seek knowledge and to explore the unexplored land. During the middle ages, the practice for travelling for religious purposes became a well-established custom in many parts of the world. It served as a powerful means of shaping unity and understanding between people from widely different regions. India is a country which is known for its generous treatment to all visitors, no matter where they come from. It is entertaining its visitors with its varied attractions which include beautiful river and sea beaches, forests, wild-life, landscapes, snow, river, mountain peaks, technological parks, science museums, centres of pilgrimage, heritage trains, hotels, yoga, *ayurveda* and natural health resorts etc.

Tourism protects and maintains the natural and cultural resources of the country, helps in avoidance of migration of the local population, and brings about improvement in the economic and socio-cultural level and increases their economic importance and raise awareness regarding environmental values. Social interaction between tourist and host community enhances the mutual appreciation, tolerance, understanding, awareness, family bonding, learning, respects and likings. Tourism for an economy has significant contribution by providing an increase in foreign exchange earnings, creating more employment opportunities and infrastructure development. Thus, the linkage of tourism with development cannot be underestimated.

Tourism in Uttarakand : Facts and Figures

Tourism has been flourishing and growing since ancient time in Uttarakhand, but it has been in the last few years that explicit forethought has started to be given to this industry. Tourism has appeared as an imperative as well as planned industry which spread its benefits over large sector of the population. Uttarakhand, the 27th state of India, known universally as the territory of Gods, is one such state of India which offers variety of experiences to the tourist. Tourism needs vary and Uttarakhand has diverse tourism opportunities which has a potential to satisfy the wishes and demands of approximately every class of visitors.

Uttarakhand, as a Himalayan state attracts tourists for various kinds of tourism activities. Religious, yogic, health tourism or wellness tourism, ecotourism, adventure tourism, entertainment tourism etc are the main kinds in the state.

Table 15.1: Strength of tourists during the period 2000-2015 (Lacs)

Year	*Indian tourists*	*Foreign tourists*	*Total*
2000	110.79	0.57	111.36
2001	105.49	0.55	106.04
2003	116.52	0.56	117.08
2004	138.30	0.75	139.04
2005	162.82	0.92	163.73
2006	193.58	0.96	194.54
2007	221.54	1.06	222.60
2008	230.64	1.11	231.76
2009	231.54	1.18	232.72
2010	309.72	1.36	311.08
2011	266.65	1.42	268.98
2012	282.92	1.40	284.33
2013	288.64	1.35	225.24
2014	219.9	1.02	220.37
2015	293.74	1.11	294.85

Source: Compiled from UK Tourism Board and Ministry of Tourism.

Table 15.1 reflects the arrival of Indian and foreign tourists in Uttarakhand. From 2000 to 2015 the number of Indian tourists have increased 2.65 times while that of foreign tourists have increased almost two times. Total tourists in these fifteen years have also increased 2.64 times.

The 24 per cent fall in Indian tourists in 2014 was largely because of the grave and devastating disaster of 2013. Tourists all over the world were traumatised by the effect of disaster and the domestic and foreign visitors reduced in large numbers in the year.

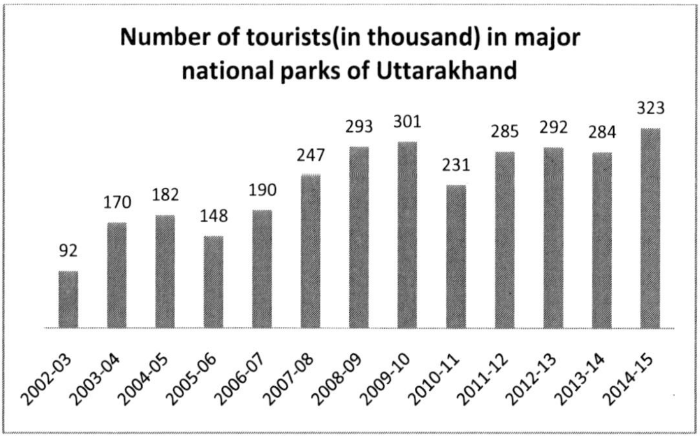

Source: Awasti, Uttarakhand Socio-Economic Mirror, Government of Uttarakhand, Vol. 1, No. 2, 2016.

Figure 15.1: Tourist arrival in major National Parks of Uttarakhand.

Uttarakhand is a land of flora and fauna with home to some rare species. In Uttarakhand, travellers get to see some most endangered and rare species in the world. Uttarakhand also is an attractive destination for bird watchers over the world. Figure 15.1 shows the number of tourists in national parks since 2002. It is very interesting to note that compared to 2002-03, in 2014-15 the arrival of tourists in national parks have increased 3.5 times.

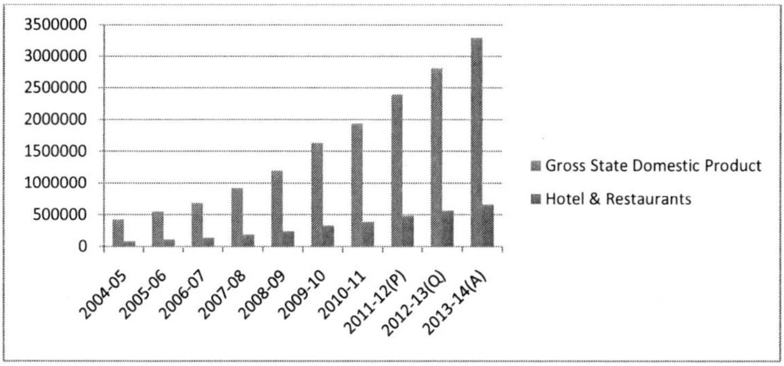

P: Provisional, Q: Quick Estimates, A: Advance Estimates

Data Source: Table 39 Estimates of State Domestic Product of Uttarakhand (2004-05 to 2013-14 With Base Year, 2004-05), DES, Uttarakhand.

Figure 15.2: State Domestic Product From Hotel and Restaurants at Current Prices [Rs Lakhs].

Figure 15.2 shows the GSDP at current prices and GSDP from Hotels and Restaurants for the state. It is very clear from the figure that the contribution of hotels and restaurants increased with increase in SGDP over the years which is a welcome sign but the growth has not been very significant compared to the tourism potential in the state.

Table 15.2: Percentage distribution of tourists by mode of travel

Mode of travel	*Percentage of tourist*
Air	9.0
Train	39.3
Taxi	16.0
Tourist Bus	24.3
Bus	9.9
Others	1.5

Source: Report on UK Tourism Development Master Plan 2007-2022.

It is observed from Table 15.2 that majority of the tourists reach Uttarakhand by train and tourist bus. Since Haridwar and Dehradun are the two main destinations for travelling by train from other states, tourists have to travel on road after that to move to higher terrains especially in the Garhwal Himalayas and most regions of Kumaon. Hence road infrastructure and related sanitation facilities on road, food joints, clean drinking water, health facilities are very much associated with it. These are the areas that needs to be prioritised in planning process. With all weather roads, the problem of seasonal tourism can be solved to some extent. Government has initiated the process but unless such infrastructure are developed in a time bound manner, many things get diluted over time.

Table 15.3: Percentage distribution of tourists by age group and gender

Age group	*Male*	*Female*	*Total*
15-24 years	4.98	3.48	8.46
25-34 years	20.90	15.92	36.82
35-44 years	11.44	11.94	23.38
45-54 years	7.46	6.97	14.43
55-59 years	3.98	6.97	10.95
60+	3.98	1.99	5.97

Source: Report on UK Tourism Development Master Plan 2007-2022.

Table 15.3 clearly shows that Uttarakhand attracts a lot of young tourists especially in the age group 25-34 and 35-44. This indication is very promising for the state as these tourists are usually a mixed bag of tourists which includes tourists for spiritual tourism, adventure tourism, cultural tourism, sight seeing etc. Hence there is a huge scope to link yoga with tourism to promote healthy life. *Ayurveda*, *unani* and *yog* along with tourism can be the core mantra and a niche for this hill state. This age group may be attracted more towards 'safari tourism' and 'adventure tourism'.

Table 15.4: Percentage distribution of tourist by source of information

Sorce of information	*Percentage*
Newspapers/ Magazines	4.5
Travel Magazines	21.4
Travel Books	40.3
Advertisement in print media	9.0
Advertisement in electronic media	9.4
Websites	28.9
Tour Promotion Exhibitions	0.5
Tour Promoters	14.9
Indian Tourist Office	4.0
Embassy of India	2.0
Friends and Relatives	37.8
Others	17.9

(Percentages do not add up to 100 due to multiple responses)
Source: Report on UK Tourism Development Master Plan 2007-2022.

It is observed from Table 15.4 that majority of the tourists get information regarding Uttarakhand from travel books. With digital revolution worldwide, it is expected that the majority of the tourists should get information from websites.

The websites for different forms of tourism for Uttarakhand along with regular updates and information on unexplored tourist spots can give a boost to Uttarakhand tourism and thus Uttarakhand economy. The websites developed even for the lesser known tourist destinations can also be a source of employment for educated local youths. It should incorporate village tourism in it and on line bookings should be facilitated for home stay in villages.

The expenditure on tourism for all departments combined is shown in Table 15.5. It shows that the percentage is not very significant compared to the huge tourism potential that the state has. However, a welcome sign is that it has increased by 0.26 percentage points from 2011-12 to 2014-15.

Table 15.5: Expenditure on tourism by all departments combined

(Figures in ₹ Lakh)

Year	*Total expenditure*	*Expenditure on tourism*	*Percentage Expenditure on Tourism*
2011-12	1746352.00	5520.00	0.32
2012-13	1926226.00	6172.23	0.32
2013-14	2208854.00	8688.17	0.39
2014-15	2719840.00	15664.83	0.58

Source: Budget Documents of UK, Department of Finance.

Table 15.6: Evaluation of tourist facilities in Uttarakhand by domestic tourists

(Figures are in percentage)

Facilities	**Grade given by domestic tourists**			
	Very good	*Good*	*Average*	*Poor*
Transport to Uttarakhand	18.46	**67.69**	12.54	1.30
Transport within Uttarakhand	13.06	**59.34**	24.17	3.44
Accommodation	33.96	**42.11**	23.09	0.84
Food and Beverage	26.59	**48.39**	21.13	0.89
Tourist Attractions	**66.80**	26.24	6.74	0.21
Maintenance of Tourist Attractions	8.11	42.63	**45.94**	3.31
Facilities around tourist attractions	6.94	41.55	**44.21**	7.29
Guide Service	5.44	15.61	38.95	**40.00**
Shopping Facilities	3.45	28.21	**43.57**	24.76
Entertainment Facilities	2.76	15.92	**46.05**	35.26

Source: Report on UK Tourism Development Master Plan 2007-2022.

As seen from Table 15.6 that while larger portion of the tourists consider transportation to the state and within the state, accommodation and tourist attractions good, majority of the tourists rate it as average as far as maintenance of tourist spots, facilities around tourist spots, shopping facilities and entertainment are concerned. A very interesting fact noticed here is that guide service has been marked poor by 40 per cent of sampled tourists.

There are many states in India with scarce resources but booming with the help of tourism. Perhaps Rajasthan is one of them. If anyone visits even the lesser known tourist destination of Rajasthan, one can find local guides. In Uttarakhand, if this area is given attention, then local youths can be trained as guides with proper knowledge and background of the area. This can not only increase employment but also promote tourism.

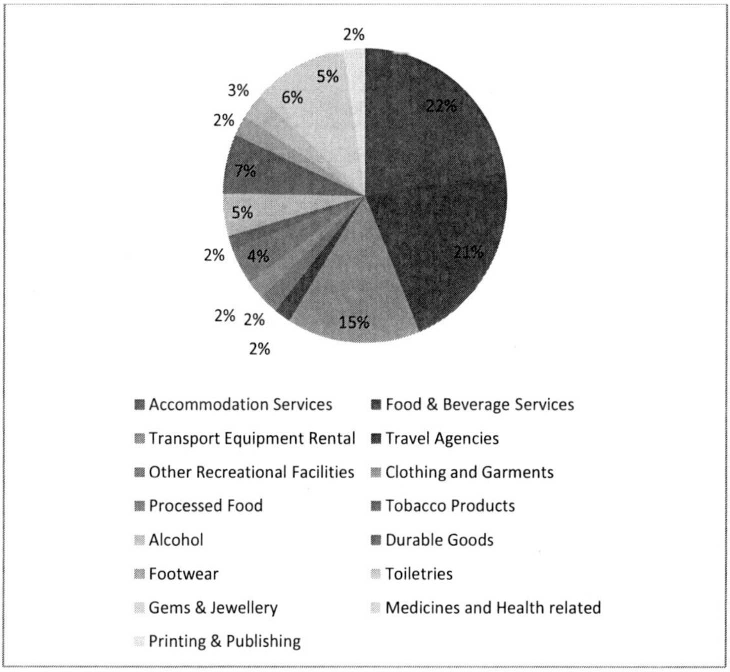

Source: Compiled from the collection of tourism statistics for the state of Uttarakhand by A AC Nielsen ORG -MARG Pvt Ltd.

Figure 15.3: Percentage Distribution of foreign tourists expenditure on different items.

The inflow of majority of foreign visitors, as observed in the state is primarily for adventure, trekking and yoga. It is seen from Figure 15.3 that while they spend 22 per cent of expenditure on accommodation, 21 per cent on food and beverages and 15 per cent on transport, equipment and rental, the other categories are not very significant. It is clear from the figure that necessary attention needs to be placed by the government as far as accommodation, food and transport are concerned so that firstly the foreign tourists are not exploited, secondly, quality is not compromised and thirdly, safety of the foreign tourists are prioritised.

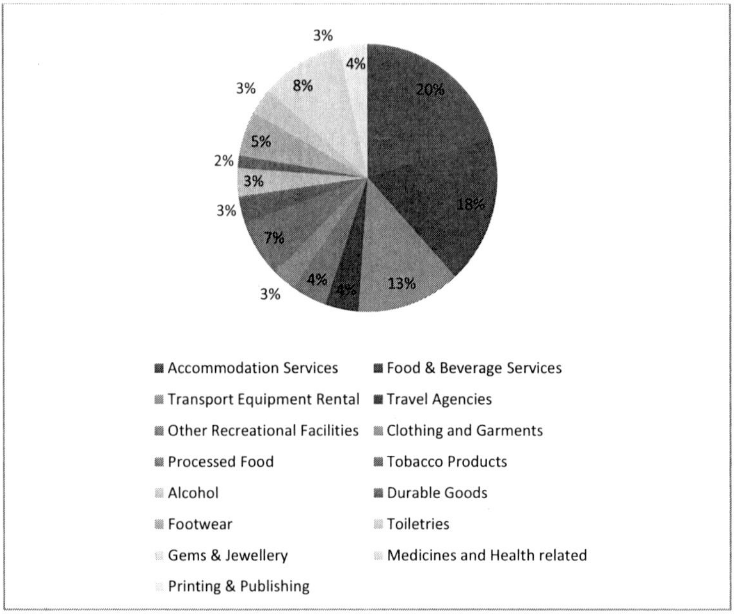

Source: Compiled from the collection of tourism statistics for the state of Uttarakhand by A ACNielsen ORG -MARG Pvt Ltd.

Figure 15.4: Percentage Distribution of domestic tourists expenditure on different items.

Figure 15.4 gives a glimpse of domestic tourists' expenditure. The majority of the expenditures are on accommodation and food followed by transport and equipment rental. It is seen that tourism in Uttarakhand has very little expenditure of tourists on local made products like woollens, *pankhis*, handicrafts, brassware, woodencraft etc. The situation demands a massive level production, promotion and marketing of such products and linkage with tourism. Websites with kind of products, photographs of products, prices, weight of the product and special products of different tourist destinations needs to be developed along with branding and proper certification. This will attract a part of expenditure of domestic tourists on such products. Tourists nowadays prefer to come to a destination with proper homework and hence such websites can be of immense help.

A NCEAR Report of 2002 however shows that tourists spent 10.74 per cent of the total expenditure on miscellaneous textile products in the state; even more than what they spent on food products (9.82 per cent). However, since these figures are debatable as the nature of sample, their socio-economic status, methodology of sample selection etc are not very clear, a very firm conclusion cannot be drawn.

It is worth mentioning here that as per the NCAER survey in 2002, only 11 per cent of the tourists reported that they were visiting the place due to media (TV, newspaper, magazines etc.) indicating a poor media exposure. A lot can be done to promote the destinations in Uttarakhand through the media. There could be advertisements in TV and newspapers highlighting "Destination Uttarakhand" with the catche words 'Simply Heaven' and all on the lines of the campaigns brought out by states like Kerala, Kashmir, Rajasthan etc. [Based on Uttarakhand Development Report 2009, pp. 59].

Some alternative approaches for tourism and a sketch for road ahead

The geographical and environmental peculiarities of Uttarakhand are most suitable for yogic practices and mental peace. Most of Yogis came here for spiritual growth in ancient time. According to Hath Yoga Pradeepika, the qualities[2] of the place where the yogic practices can be developed well, all those qualities are present in peaceful environment of Uttarakhand. Religious and spiritual tourism in the form of yoga; meditation, *ayurveda, unani,* etc. could be a niche for the economy.

To know the implementation of Yoga in Tourism Policy, it is necessary to understand the historical background of Yoga in special reference to Uttarakhand first. T.R. Anantharaman pointed out "the foundation of classical Yoga"[3] and historical roots of Yogic Tradition in Indian culture. He presented Yoga as the most ancient indigenous knowledge. According to his view, the beginnings of the Yoga tradition are no doubt shrouded in the mists of antiquity, but is universally recognised that Indian Yoga constitutes one of the oldest and most important scientific-spiritual legacies of humanity and has been preached as well as practised uninterruptedly since the dawn of human history.

The excavation of seals portraying deities in time-honoured meditative postures in the sites at Mohenjo-daro and Harappa of the Indus Valley period (3000-2000 BC) strongly suggests that the Yoga tradition is not only over 4000 years old, but was in fact given special recognition in the Indian society well before the Vedic period. Considering that any movement takes its own time to germinate and grow and that many, many generations of development are the chains for the wide acceptance of any concept or practice, today's promoters of Yoga all around the world may be fully justified in considering themselves as inheritors of a vibrant and glorious tradition that goes at least 5000 years back in human history.

In reference to Uttarakhand, history tells that in ancient time Uttarakhand was the capital of Yoga. The *Rishies*, *Munis*, seers and spiritual persons came here. They permanently lived here with mental and spiritual flourishing environment for their absolute well-wish. It is a well known fact that statues of Shiva and Parvati with various other Devatas in their Yogic postures are in the ancient temples of Uttarakhand. Shiva is recognised as the *Mahayogi* and *Yogeeshwar* according to our classical Vedas, Puranas and Yogic literature. According to A.K. Sinha[4], "Some of the Siva Lingas are found spontaneously formed in nature. Such naturally formed Siva Lingas are found in Somanath of Saurastra, Mahakala of Ujjain, Kedarnatha in the Himalayas, and Vishvanath in Varanasi." The presence of *Kedarnatha* in Uttarakhand is a boon for the state and a reason to attract spiritual tourists from all over the world. It is also complemented with the other spiritual *dhams* like Badrinath, Yamunotri, Gangotri and Gomukh, Tungnath, Baijnath and many more.

The word Yoga originates from the Samskrit Dhatu Yuj,[5] which means to be united or combined two essences with each other. The united essence could be in form of mind and body or soul and God. A blend of perfect health with the flavour of spirituality can be found with Yogic discipline. There are eight practices[6] of Yoga (called Yam, Niyama, Asana, Pranayam, Pratyahar, Dharana, Dhyan and Samadhi).[7] Asana, Pranayam and Dhyan (Meditation) are the most popular steps[8] of Yoga in present time for good physical and mental health. Thus, adequate facilities with some identified places as yogic hubs can add value to tourism sector. Yoga and ayurvedic related literature should be prepared for Indian and foreign tourists and universities in the state should encourage research for foreign students also to explore these areas. These in long-term will have a spillover effect to attract foreign tourists and boost the economy.

In order to attract more and more foreign tourists, advertisement in foreign journals, magazines and newspapers should be given in foreign languages. Besides, translation of tourist's literature in foreign language through different government bodies is another positive step that may be taken in this direction.

In Uttarakhand, Champawat is the lowest preferred destination of tourists (Uttarakhand Development Report 2009). But the picturesque district with very soothing climatic condition round the year can be explored for wellness and spiritual tourism. There should be a blend of *ayurveda* and yoga in such places with proper ecofriendly infrastructure, trainers, *ayurvedic* doctors, spas and most importantly branding of such practices in the district with time bound packages for tourists so that the tourists are very clear about the expenditure that they have to incur to avail such facilities.

Since tourism is a labour intensive industry, tourism related courses in higher education can accommodate a huge amount of labour force and restrict migration from the hills.

Health resort tourism is another activity which has a huge potential in the state considering the high market demand in world market. A large mass of foreigner (as has been seen) visit Rishikesh for the purpose of yoga and meditation. This activity should not only be promoted among the foreign tourists but also be promoted among the domestic tourists, so that they could be motivated to visit Garhwal and Kumaun region not only for pilgrimage but also for other purposes like- physical and mental health, peace, spirituality, cultural attraction and to have oneness with the nature and have a wonderful opportunity to de-stress themselves.

Development of centres for providing the facilities of Yoga, spiritual lessons, *ayurveda,* naturopathy and psychotherapy etc., and such revitalising courses can be incorporated into Tourism Policy.

Eco-tourism is another potential for the state. While for some sectors, the terrain of Uttarakhand acts as a constraint, it is an asset for eco-tourism. Jungle safari, trekking, forest trail, nature walks all can be exploited in nook and corner of this heavenly state. There are many trekking routes and *bugyals* that are no more tourist destination after disasters and many more unexplored. Such destinations have huge scope for boosting tourism sector. However, village **tourism** and **cultural tourism** should be promoted along the routes. Regional cuisine, regional culture like traditional dresses, song and dance to entertain tourists can provide livelihood to many and attract tourists.

Uttarakhand has also huge scope of **historical tourism** which is yet not explored at commercial level. Maintenance of places of historical and archaeological importance which are many in numbers can make Uttarakhand an attractive tourist destination. Research on such places and tourism facility is a prerequisite.

Moreover **aerial tourism** can be promoted for economically well to do and foreign tourists. Scenic 'Mountain Flights' to various destinations with continuous commentary during the journey and possible sources of Uttarakhand culture's taste during the flight can be a huge attraction. It can attract elderly high valued tourists who are constrained to visit the state due to health status, partial immobility due to age etc from different parts of the world. Such tourist crowd needs to be given special care by tourism department with all sorts of facilities and they can be offered to take the advantage of yoga and *ayurveda* blended tourism. The promotion can use taglines such as "visit as an aged tourist and leave as a cheerful healthy soul" or 'Just to rejuvenate in the heaven.'

Since the state was cut out from its parent state, the state government has already constituted autonomous institutions such as the Uttarakhand Tourism Development Board, Special Committee for Pilgrimage, and Adventure Tourism Committee. It is expected that these institutions work towards a common goal to provide sustainability to the tourism sector. The state government has also hired consultants to frame master plans for eco-tourism. But there is still a long way to go as far as this sector is concerned especially when the state is a mine of almost all forms of tourism. However, badly managed tourism policy can have unnecessary pressure on land, water, flora, fauna, environment etc. Proper garbage management in hills, traffic control in the hills, pre- and post-monsoon special fund for road maintenance are of great need in the state. With Global Sustainable Tourism as the base, tourism planners, environmentalists, historians, disaster experts, sociologists and culture experts, ayurvedic doctors, yogic gurus, therapists all should be brought together in a platform to give an acceleration to tourism sector of the state.

Acknowledgement: The author is thankful to Dr Rajlakshmi Datta for her comments and discussion on the first and second draft of the paper.

Bibliography

Anantharaman, T.R., (2007), Ancient Yoga and Modern Science, PHISPC, Centre for Studies in Civilisation, New Delhi, 2007, p. 7.

Collection of tourism statistics for the state of Uttarakhand by A ACNielsen ORG -MARG Pvt Ltd.

Datta, Rajlakshmi (2016) "Joining tourism and livelihood through banking: Some facts and figures for Uttarakhand"; Socio Economic Mirror, Govt. of Uttarakhand, DES Vol. 1, No. 2.

Directorate of Economics and Statistics, Uttarakhand.

Husain, Tarannum, (2007), Promotional Strategies of Tourism Industry in Uttaranchal State of India, In the abstract of a thesis guided by Prof. Mohd. Altaf Khan, Dept. of Commerce and Business Studies in Jamia Millia Islamia University, New Delhi, p. 56.

International Journal of Advanced Research in Management and Social Sciences ISSN 2278-6236, Vol. 1, No. 3, p. 12, September 2012.

Martin Dahinden, (2014), Tourism in Mountain Regions, Hopes Fears and realities; Published by the Department of Geography and Environment,

University of Geneva, the Centre for Development and Environment, University of Bern, and the United Nations Environment Programme.

Patanjali, Maharshi, Translated by G.L. Verma, Patanjali Yoga Sutra, Chaukhamba Surbharati Prakashan, Varanasi, 2010, in introduction.

Patanjali, Maharsi, (2005), Patanjal Yoga Sootra, Chapter 2, Kaivalyadham, Srimanmadhav Yogamandir Samiti, Lonavala, Pune.

Sinha, A.K., (1981), Science and Tantra Yoga, Vishal Publications, Kurukshetra, 1981.

Swatmaram, Swami, (2001), transelaters Swami Digambar, Dr Pitamber Jha, Hath Pradeepika, Kaivalyadham, Srimanmadhav Yogamandir Samiti, Lonavala, Pune, I chapter.

Translated by Panchamsinh, Swami Swatmaram, Hathyogapradipika, chapter 1, shloka 12-14, Chaukhamba Sanskrit Pratishthan, Delhi, 2003, pp. 5-6.

Uttarakhand Tourism Board.

Notes

1. Martin Dahinden, Tourism in Mountain Regions, Hopes Fears and Realities; Published by the Department of Geography and Environment, University of Geneva, the Centre for Development and Environment, University of Bern, and the United Nations Environment Programme 2014.
2. Swatmaram, Swami, (2001), transelaters Swami Digambar, Dr Pitamber Jha, Hath Pradeepika, Kaivalyadham, Srimanmadhav Yogamandir Samiti, Lonavala, Pune, I chapter.
3. Anantharaman, T.R., Ancient Yoga and Modern Science, PHISPC, Centre for Studies in Civilisation, New Delhi, 2007, p. 7.
4. Sinha, A.K., Science and Tantra Yoga, Vishal Publications, Kurukshetra, 1981, p. 28.
5. Patanjali, Maharshi, Translated by G.L. Verma, Patanjali Yoga Sutra, Chaukhamba Surbharati Prakashan, Varanasi, 2010, in introduction.
6. Patanjali, Maharsi, 2005, Patanjali Yoga Sootra, Chapter 2, Kaivalyadham, Srimanmadhav Yogamandir Samiti, Lonavala, Pune.
7. *Ibid.*
8. *Ibid.*

16

Water Resource and Mineral Resource Utilisation in Uttarakhand: A Dream Becoming Increasingly Elusive

A K Biyani

Every country or part of the land is gifted with some kind or other natural resources. Literature shows that (S. V. Ciriacy-Wantrup 1969[1], Gylfason *et al* 2001[2], Gavin Wright Jesse Czelusta 2005[3] etc) the natural resources play a very important role in the economic progress of the region or state. From the time immemorial, in increasing prosperity of individual to state, utilisation of natural resources were involved. With more knowledge about material properties and possible utilities, materials are now utilised in unbelievable domains and every material is finding new uses with every passing days and once thought free resources by earlier economists like water, sun, air have now become economically marketable commodities and one has to pay the dear price for what once free or abundantly available throw away cast resources. Once resources were divided in simple category : natural or manufactured one. This simple classification has been modified elaborately but the essence of the old terms remained unchanged.

The term natural resource is a comprehensive one. Natural resources are materials provided by the earth that humans can use to make more complex products. This includes anything either present in or on the earth or produced by the earth. In calling a material natural resource, the involvement of the earth is must. Humans cannot make the natural resources but by modification can make them more beneficial.

Natural resources include rocks and minerals, water, soil, air, sunlight, forest, plants and animals. These resources are differentiated in many ways using criteria of origin, utility, organic vs. inorganic, productability vs. reproductability, geological vs. non-geological, free vs. with cost etc. Natural resources are classified in the biotic and abiotic category, renewable and nonrenewable. These resources are recyclable, reusable as well as uncycleable or unusable. Some resources have inherent tendency to refresh themselves like air and water.

This paper will examine status of two natural or precisely geological resources namely, rocks and minerals and water resources of Uttarakhand, a state predominantly mountainous in character.

The characteristics of natural resources can be jotted down as follows:

- they are made by the nature or earth,
- human beings cannot make or create them,
- they are renewable and nonrenewable,
- some of them are perpetually available like wind, some show tendency of the periodic availability, for example sunlight, rainfall,
- some are available free of cost and despite the free availability cost has to be paid viz. water is free in rain but for a bottled water even in rain cost has be paid. During foggy days many people go in the area of sunshine for that cost has to be incurred.
- natural resources may have tendency to refresh themselves,
- misuse or overexploitations of the natural resources affect economy badly,
- nonrenewable natural resources once exhausted would have very faint chances of regeneration in near future,
- natural resources may be the cause of fight between individuals to countries, for example individuals often fight for small pieces of lands, for water, states fight over water rights and countries fight over control of natural resources beyond their territories e.g. South China Sea which contain petroleum deposits. China is trying hard to grab that sea,

- natural resources lose their strength/magnitude due to over exploitation or over application of pressure,
- regenerative resources grow or evolve with differential rate,
- natural resources are God given entities hence they their ownership lies in the hand of state,
- use of natural resources are regulated by state policy,
- sustainability of natural resources are now burning concern of right thinking citizens and UNO,
- resources are unevenly spread and everyone is entitled to use them as long as they are gifted by nature,
- same natural resources can be used in raw or processed form e.g. wood twigs can be used for burning but trunk can be used as timber after simple dressing,
- processing enhances the economic worth of the resource e.g crude petroleum is not of much use but by processing many products can be made from the same crude,
- origin and distribution of natural resources though is scientific but for every resource a complicated set of conditions work,
- substitute of the some resource may be developed but not all can be substituted,
- a single principal category may include hundreds of different kinds in that category viz. we have 4000 minerals and over one thousand different variety of rocks.

Uttarakhand is one of the natural resources rich state endowed with several perennial rivers, glaciers, springs, thermal water, lakes, ground water, industrial minerals and rocks, minor minerals, forests, fertile soil of Gangetic plain, human resource, unpolluted air in the hills, sunlight and varieties of flora and fauna. These resources could play very important in development of the state keeping in mind their sustainability.

Natural Resources of Uttarakhand

Uttarakhand state is well endowed with variety of natural resources. These resources are area specific viz. rocks, minerals etc. as well as widely distributed such as forest, water, sunlight etc. The natural resources can be utilised with or without processing. The natural resources have potential to become backbone of state's economy. The contribution of these resources in creating or generating the job is also huge if they are utilised optimally.

Water and rocks/minerals resources are taken up for further analysis as these are geological resources.

Water Resources of Uttarakhand

Uttarakhand gets nearly 40 per cent more rain than long-term average of the country which hovers around 112 cm/year. The country gets around 4000 ckm (cubic kilometer) water annually and in Uttarakhand receives around 85 cubic kilometer ckm water every year (Biyani and Gupta, 2004). Here water occurs in the form of ice and snow in glaciers and in rivers, springs, lakes and ground waters.

Rivers

The state is land of perennially flowing major rivers. These rivers are huge asset in the economy of the state. These rivers source water from the rain, glacial and snow melt, springs and lakes. The major water contributors are rain and underground spring waters. Uttarakhand annually receives 85 ckm rainwater and snow. The famous rivers of Uttarakhand are Alaknanda (Dhauliganga, Vishnuganga, Pindar, Mandakini, Nandakini), Bhagirathi (Bhilangana), Ganga (Hunil, Song), Tons (Rupin, Supin), Yamuna (Untagad, Rishiganga, Saurigad, Hanumanganga, Kamal), Goriganga and Mahakali. These rivers carry huge amount of waters in them that flow down in turbulent form in the narrow valleys due to steep gradients of the rivers.

The river water can be used for power generation, bringing sand-*bajri* in plain areas, adventure tourism, aquatic food, transportation etc. When the state was formed only a small part of water was used for power generation and there were no other use of flowing water except running *gharats (kind of traditional flour mill)* for milling purpose. In last few years, large number of river beach site resorts came up along the Ganga River providing gainful employment to large number of person and cultivating entrepreneurship in the state but owing to order of the National Green Tribunal majority of them have been closed down as they were affecting the environment. Rivers or lakes behind dams could be used for adventure tourism in a big way and a plan is prepared for the Tehri dam reservoir but environmentalists opine that it might be hazardous for environment. Sand-bajri, a highly valuable material bought by rivers from washing of the hill slopes, has been discussed in mining section.

Glaciers

Glaciers are relatively permanent and extremely slowly moving masses of ice and snow. The glaciers are formed above snowline whose height is variable and for Uttarakhand it is > 5000 m. At present the Himalayan glaciers are in general recession phase which means their dimensions are decreasing. This is geologically a common fact that size of a glacier is fluctuating; alternating increases and decreases which in geological parlance is called glacial and interglacial periods respectively in which glacier's volume always changes in a considerable range. The interglacial period in Uttarakhand started about 10000 years ago (Biyani, 2006).

The glaciers are located in extreme northern part of the state. They were formed few millions years ago and once occupied a considerably large area than the present. The important glaciers of the state are Arwa, Banderpunch Baspa, Bhagirathi, Chaturangi, Jamdar Kharali, Khatling, Gangotri, Jagin, Khulia, Lambar, Mana, Nandadevi, Pindari, Ratiaraj, Raktavarna, Arun, Swargarohni, Panchachuli, Milam and Pindari.

According to Raina and Srivastava (2008), glaciers of Uttarakhand can be divided in four major river catchment areas viz. Yamuna, Bhagirathi, Alaknanda and Ghaghra and these catchments of the state has 968 glaciers, occupy 2857 sq km area and are holding 209.37 cubic kilometer (ckm) ice (Table 16.1).

Table 16.1: Basin-wise glaciers in Uttarakhand, their area spread and volume of ice

Name of the Basin	*No. of Glaciers*	*Area in sq km*	*Volume in ckm*
Yamuna	52	144	12.2
Bhagirathi	238	755	67.02
Alaknanda	407	1229	86.38
Ghaghra	271	729	43.77

Source: Raina and Srivastava, 2008.

The glaciers of Uttarakhand, in summer season, feed all major rivers with their melt waters. The contribution of glaciers in rivers originating from glaciers may be nearly hundred per cent near snouts but in descending journey when other rivers of non-glacial origins join, a major the percentage of glacially contributed water gradually declines and by the time rivers leave the state, per cent of glacial contributions come down to less than 20.

Since the state formation, dimensions of glaciers might have declined. The Gangotri and the Satopanth glaciers are receding in size with 10 m/year rate. If we consider decline of glaciers in Uttarakhand started 10000 years ago on geological evidences, which means the glaciers would have been present at least 100 km south of their present locations.

Therefore, the length of the Gangotri glacier would have been 130.2 km then the present 30.2 km. Geological evidences simply do not support this length. Glacial melting has little to do with present climate change hype as melting was started when climate was pristine. The fear that glaciers will vanish from the landscapes of Uttarakhand in near future is hypothetical from geological and meteorological reasons.

The contribution of glaciers in economic development of state is immense as they maintain rivers flow in dry season and support adventure tourism or trekking. Journey to glacial snouts is very excruciating as popular snouts are many tens of km from last transport destination. This increases number of days and expenses with added uncertainty of route blockades due to landslides. Lakes formed by glacial processes are a big tourist attraction in the state. To give big boost to glacial tourism, glaciers should be made easily accessible and safe.

Lakes

Lakes are narrated as enclosed water bodies. Lakes are described on the basis of size, location, origin, water quality, utility, ecological characters etc. Himalaya has large numbers of lakes of different size, shape and origin. Uttarakhand state is endowed with large number of lakes present in every nook and corner of the state. The important lakes of Uttarakhand are Nainital lake, Bhimtal, Sattal, Chorabari or Gandhi Sarovar, Dodital. A recent remote sensing based census (Sharma, 2016) revealed presence of 1392 lakes in 2015 in glaciated higher altitude area and are formed by various glacial process. Surprisingly, in comparison to last census that took place in 2000, number of lakes were 1056 which means 346 less on 1:50000 scale images. Author has attributed this increase is due to formation of depressions on glacial melted sites and the use of better technology. Recession of glacial snouts leave irregular and uneven debrised area, which in course of time becomes lakes by filing water in the depression (Sharma, 2016). The other mechanisms of lakes formations in Uttarakhand are natural and artificial damming of rivers, changes in course of rivers, internal deformation and breaking of mountains, accumulation of spring water etc.

Lakes may create problem like the devastating flood; water in Kedarnath in 2013 came from Chorabari Lake which is situated three km north of Kedarnath. The huge amount of debris sediments, that were probably lying on the lake floor, 6-7 lakh cubic meters, was brought by flood water. Lakes are good tourist attraction, however this potential is yet to be tapped in a significant way as most of the lakes are located in very remote areas and on high altitudes. The accessibilities to lakes need to be improved in the state.

Springs

Springs are surface discharge of underground water. Springs are formed by intersection of water with ground surface or slopes. Springs are classified on the basis of volume of water discharge, water availability duration, source of water, origin, water quality, temperature, utility etc. Spring waters of the Doon Valley have been examined chemically and found suitable for drinking and other purposes (Dudeja and Biyani, 2009).

Due to rapid urbanisation and population pressure, springs are facing gloomy future viz. the sulphur springs of Sahastradhara till few years back were discharging waters round the year but now water discharge is limited to half of the year. In many villages in the state, springs are the only source of water.

The state has more than 60000 springs and many of these are dried up, therefore, the Government of Uttarakhand has devised a plan ₹ 450 crores recently in July, 2016 to revitalise these springs. Action on revitalisation is likely to start soon.

Thermal springs

At present more than 350 hot water springs have been recorded in the country and 50[4] hot water springs are recorded in Uttarakhand. Scientists define hot water springs as those whose water discharge temperature is more than 10°C of average annual temperature of that area. In Uttarakhand, the temperature of water discharge varies between 24°C and 87°C. The hot water is used for many purposes from electricity generation to domestic heating, snow melting, poultry, agriculture, drying, tourism, pisciculture, bakery, minerals and chemicals extractions and dairy in different countries. The important locations of hot water springs in Uttarakhand are at Dehradun, Sahastradhara Wazri, Banas, Janakichatti, Yamunotri, Tapovan, Badrinath, Bhapkund Aungi, Bhukki, Jhyan, Gangnani, Joti, Junja, Kali, Manep, Moran, Rameri, Rapavan, Sera, and Madkot. There is good possibility that more hot water springs may be discovered in future when geological investigations of remote northern part would be initiated (Biyani, 2002).

The thermal springs of Uttarakhand has geothermal electric power potential of 2000 mega watt (Biyani, 2006). This vast potential is totally untapped so far, despite known to authorities before creation of the state and still there is no planning to use this energy for any meaningful purpose. The reasons of gross neglect are location in very remote areas, apparent low discharge, limited potential of each site in comparison to mega power projects, thrust on hydro power generation, lack of technology and also lack of initiative at national level. Even if a part of this potential is tapped; it would contribute in economic development of the state.

Ground water

Ground water all over the world is exploited through tube wells, hand pumps, dug wells. The contribution of ground water in development is overwhelming as it is a cheap and reliable source of water in areas which are far off from the perennial rivers. Ground water meets the most of the agricultural requirement in plain regions. In hilly tract of the state, utilisation of ground water is particularly low, however now hand pumps can be seen frequently along the roads and is meeting the requirement of in-house consumption. The percolation of rain, river and lake and reservoir waters enriches the ground water base and 15-20 per cent of rain water or utilisable water goes inside the earth in plain or gently sloping terrains, this percentage depends upon topography and geology of the area. In Uttarakhand this percentage would be much less as exceedingly large part of the state is of hilly nature due to which very little time is available for percolation.

The ground water is extracted through varieties of means as mentioned. The ratio between extracted water and percolated water is called ground water development. According to the Central Ground Water Board measurements, the state has 2.04 ckm annually replenishable ground water, of which available water for utilisation is 2.00 ckm and quantity of actually utilised water is 1.13 ckm. 1.0 ckm km water is utilised for irrigation and 0.03 ckm water is utilised for drinking and irrigation purposes. The ground water development of the state in 2014 was 57 per cent, while all-India figure is 58 per cent, in 2004 and 62 per cent in 2014, and district-wise it is 12 per cent in Dehradun, 56 per cent in Nainital, 43 per cent in Hardwar and 79 per cent in Udham Singh Nagar. CGWB has measured ground water development in plain part or in large valleys of the state. The ratio is increasing every year. As long as ratio remains below 70 per cent, area belongs to safe category. Thus, Uttarakhand belongs to safe category and has good potential to exploit groundwater without adverse consequences.

Hydropower

The electric power is key to economic development of any state or nation. This power is obtained mainly through various sources like hydro, thermal, atomic, solar and wind. Merits and demerits are associated with each source of power generation. Hydropower can be generated either by run off of the river scheme or by the storage scheme. In case of former, strength of running water is used and in later case stored water in dam is used for power generation. The perennial rivers of Uttarakhand are huge source of electric power. Almost all rivers can be harnessed for power generation.

An exhaustive survey has already been conducted about the power potential of river. It is estimated that 27039 MW power can be generated if all investigated sites (Figure 16.1) are tapped (Tables 16.2 and 16.3) and in addition to this large number of sites of few KW to few MW do also exist of substantial potential. When this state was formed, the overall capacity was about 1000 MW that now stands to 3971 mega watt (ujvnl.com) nearly four times increase in capacity in last 15 years. This capacity would have increased far rapidly had the policies being different. Many projects which were half way in completion state or work had started, were forced to be closed down owing to environmental or litigational reasons.

Harnessing of the rivers for reliable power generation state will have to launch an ambitious programme for large dams sooner or later. The work on the dams have been stopped on the issues of poor compensation, loss of livelihood, rehabilitation, environmental impact, seismic threats to structure. None of these issues are unresolvable. These problems can be solved amicably through discussions and for environmental damage corrective measures can be taken up in nearby affected areas. Large dams are must for the state as they would provide assured and controlled power supply, meet the demands of irrigation, drinking and industry in water stressed areas, protects from flood and draught, provides safety net against earthquakes, create job, traps sediments, promote tourism, adventure sports, inland water navigation, massive thrust to aquatic fauna particularly pisciculture. These activities except power generation and irrigation were non-existent when state was formed but now they are in emerging mode, once state resolved to promote this then quantum jump in job generation, economic development and revenue collection would occur. Small dams or runoff the river schemes are in no way substitute of major dams as none of the benefits are possible on large scale.

Source: ujvnl.com)

Figure 16.1: Map showing the locations of hydro power generation in Uttarakhand.

Table 16.2: Status of hydropower generation by various agencies in Uttarakhand. UJVNL- Uttarakhand Jal Vidyut Nigam Limited, CPSU- Central Public Sector Undertakings, IPP-Independent Power Producers, UREDA-Uttarakhand Renewable Energy Development Authority, ID-Irrrigation Department, PDA-Pancheswar Development Authority. UIPC-UIPC

Details of Hydro Power Potential in Uttarakhand

Project Particulars (MW)	UJVNL	CPSUs	IPPs	UREDA	ID	UIPC	PDA	Identified	Total (MW)
Under Operation	1290.10	1800.00	876.65	4.80	-	-	-	-	3971.55
Under Construction	173.50	2135.00	207.30	2.02	-	-	-	-	2517.32
DPR Approved, Clearances Obtained/ Under Process	818.50	2217.00	646.00	-	-	23.35			3704.85
Projects for which DPR Prepared	1486.50	159.00	296.00	-	178.50	17.00	6620.00		8757.00
Under S&I Stage	877.20	1890.00	540.00	29.76	-	2706.15		2045.00	8088.11
Total	**4645.80**	**8201.00**	**2565.95**	**36.58**	**178.50**	**2746.50**	**6620.00**	**2045.00**	**27039.33**

PDA -Pancheswar Development Authority   ID - Irrigation Department

Table 16.3 Locations of the hydropower projects on rivers in various districts of Uttarakhand and capacity and current status (as on Oct., 2016)

S.NO.	NAME OF THE PROJECT	CAPACITY in MW	DISTRICT	RIVER	NAME OF CO.	STATUS
1	Taluka Sankri	140.00	Uttarkashi	Tons	UJVNL	
2	Sidri Deori	80.00	Uttarkashi	Tons		Govind ghat Secn.
3	Nattwar Mori	60.00	Uttarkashi	Tons	SJVNL	
4	Mori hanol	63.00	Uttarkashi	Tons		
5	Hanol Tuini	60.00	Dehradun	Tons	Sunflag	
6	Tuini Palasu	66.00	Dehradun	Tons	Irrigation Dept.	
7	Kishau Dam	600.00	Dehradun	Tons	UJVNL	
8	Chibro	240.00	Dehradun	Tons	UJVNL	Commisioned
9	Khodari	120.00	Dehradun	Tons	UJVNL	Commisioned
10	Supin	11.20	Uttarkashi	Tons	UJVNL	Identified
11	Jakhol Sankari	51.00	Uttarkashi	Tons	SJVNL	
12	Arakot Tuini	70.00	Uttarkashi	Tons	Irrigation Dept.	
13	Rupin -IV	10.00	Uttarkashi	Tons	Tons Hydro	
14	Rupin -V	24.00	Uttarkashi	Tons	Himalaya	
15	Hanuman chatti-Saina chatti	40.00	Uttarkashi	Yamuna	UIPC	
16	Ganganl	8.00	Uttarkashi	Yamuna	Regency yamuna Energy	Under Const.
17	Saull -Barnigad	10.00	Uttarkashi	Yamuna	UIPC	
18	Barnigad	6.50	Uttarkashi	Yamuna	Ramamo Trans.	Allocated to IPP
19	Barnigad -Naingaon	10.00	Uttarkashi	Yamuna	UIPC	
20	Lakhwar Vyasi	420.00	Dehradun	Yamuna	UJVNL	Under Const.
21	Dhakrani	33.75	Dehradun	Yamuna	UJVNL	Commisioned
22	Dhalipur	51.00	Dehradun	Yamuna	UJVNL	Commisioned
23	Kulhal	30.00	Dehradun	Yamuna	UJVNL	Commisioned
24	Nilang	190.00	Uttarkashi	Bhagirathi		
25	Karmoli	140.00	Uttarkashi	Bhagirathi	THDC	
26	Jadhganga	50.00	Uttarkashi	Bhagirathi	THDC	
27	Gangotri	70.00	Uttarkashi	Bhagirathi		
28	Bhaironghati stage I & II	381.00	Uttarkashi	Bhagirathi	UJVNL	Rejected by GOI
29	Loharinagpala	600.00	Uttarkashi	Bhagirathi	NTPC	Rejected by GOI
30	Palamaneri	480.00	Uttarkashi	Bhagirathi	UJVNL	Rejected by GOI
31	Maneri Bhali stage -I	90.00	Uttarkashi	Bhagirathi	UJVNL	Commisioned
32	Maneri Bhali stage -II	304.00	Uttarkashi	Bhagirathi	UJVNL	Commisioned
33	Tehri dam	2000.00	Tehri	Bhagirathi	THDC	Commisioned 1000mw
34	Koteshwar dam	400.00	Tehri	Bhagirathi	THDC	Commisioned
35	Kotlibhel -IA	195.00	Tehri	Bhagirathi	NHPC	Under Const.
36	Kakora gad	12.50	Uttarkashi	Bhagirathi	Harsil Hydro P ltd.	
37	Jalandhari gad	11.80	Uttarkashi	Bhagirathi	Harsil Hydro P ltd.	
38	Assiganga - III	7.30	Uttarkashi	Bhagirathi	UJVNL	Under Const.
39	Kaldigad	9.00	Uttarkashi	Bhagirathi	UJVNL	Under Const.
40	Bhilangana top	11.00	Tehri	Bhagirathi	Self Id Catagery	
41	Bhilangana Kaldal HEP	25.00	Tehri Gharwal	Bhagirathi	Self Id Catagery	
42	Bhilangana Gangi HEP	25.00	Tehri Gharwal	Bhagirathi	Self Id Catagery	
43	Bhilangana Rosh HEP	25.00	Tehri Gharwal	Bhagirathi	Self Id Catagery	
44	Bhilangana Silagar HEP	25.00	Tehri Gharwal	Bhagirathi	Self Id Catagery	
45	Guttu HEP	25.00	Tehri Gharwal	Bhagirathi	Self Id Catagery	
46	Bhilangana - III	24.00	Tehri	Bhagirathi	Polyplex corporation	Under Const.
47	Bhilangana - II	63.00	Tehri	Bhagirathi	UJVNL	Divided into 3 projects
48	Bhilangana	22.50	Uttarkashi	Bhagirathi	Swasti Power	Commisioned
49	Kot Buda Kedar	6.00	Tehri	Bhagirathi	Gunsola Hydro	Commisioned
50	Bal Ganga -II	7.00	Tehri	Bhagirathi	UJVNL	Identified

(Contd…)

51	Jhalakoti	9.00	Tehri	Bhagirathi	Gunsola Hydro	Under Const.
52	Alaknanda	300.00	Chamoli	Alaknanda	G.M.R	Under Const.
53	Vishnu Prayag	400.00	Chamoli	Alaknanda	J.P. Hydro	Commissioned
54	Vishnugad Pipalkoti	444.00	Chamoli	Alaknanda	THDC	Under Const.
55	Bowla Nandprayag	300.00	Chamoli	Alaknanda	UJVNL	Under Const.
56	Nandprayag Langasu	141.00	Chamoli	Alaknanda	UJVNL	
57	Utyasu -VI	110.00	Rudraprayag	Alaknanda	UIPC	
58	Utyasu -IV	125.00	Rudraprayag	Alaknanda	UIPC	
59	Utyasu -II	175.00	Rudraprayag	Alaknanda	UIPC	
60	Srinagar	330.00	Pauri (G)	Alaknanda	GVK	Under Const.
61	Kotli Bhel - I B	320.00	Pauri (G)	Alaknanda	NHPC	Under Const.
62	Kotli Bhel - II	530.00	Pauri (G)	Ganga	NHPC	Under Const.
63	Chilla	144.00	Pauri (G)	Ganga	UJVNL	Commissioned
64	Pathari	20.40	Pauri (G)	Ganga	UJVNL	Commissioned
65	Mohammudpur	9.30	Pauri (G)	Ganga	UJVNL	Commissioned
66	Niti Ghamsali	32.00	Chamoli	Dhauliganga(G)		
67	Bampa Kurkuti	60.00	Chamoli	Dhauliganga(G)		
68	Maneri Jhelam	114.00	Chamoli	Dhauliganga(G)	THDC	
69	Jhelam Tamak	128.00	Chamoli	Dhauliganga(G)	THDC	
70	Tamak Lata	280.00	Chamoli	Dhauliganga(G)	UJVNL	
71	Lata Tapovan	171.00	Chamoli	Dhauliganga(G)	NTPC	
72	Tapovan Vishnugad	520.00	Chamoli	Dhauliganga(G)	NTPC	Under Const.
73	Kosa	18.00	Chamoli	Dhauliganga(G)	UIPC	
74	Rishiganga -I	70.00	Chamoli	Alaknanda	UJVNL	
75	Rishiganga -II	35.00	Chamoli	Alaknanda	UJVNL	
76	Rishiganga	13.20	Chamoli	Alaknanda	Rishiganga Power co.ltd	Commissioned
77	Kalpganga -I	6.25	Chamoli	Alaknanda	UIPC	
78	Pulna SHEP	25.00	Chamoli	Alaknanda	Self Id Category	
79	Bhuindar ganga	24.30	Chamoli	Alaknanda	Super hydro P.ltd.	
80	Nandakini -III	5.60	Chamoli	Alaknanda	Vishal Exports	
81	Vanala	15.00	Chamoli	Alaknanda	Him Urja	Commissioned
82	Raj Bhakti	3.60	Chamoli	Alaknanda	Him Urja	Commissioned
83	Devali	13.00	Chamoli	Alaknanda	Him Urja	
84	Gohana tal	60.00	Chamoli	Alaknanda	THDC	
85	Birahi ganga -II	5.20	Chamoli	Alaknanda	PES Engineering	
86	Birahi Ganga	7.20	Chamoli	Alaknanda	Bhiral ganga hydro	Commissioned
87	Balkhila -I	5.50	Chamoli	Alaknanda	UIPC	
88	Amrit ganga	6.00	Chamoli	Alaknanda	UIPC	
89	Rambara	76.00	Rudraprayag	Mandakini	Lanco Kondapali	
90	Phata -Byung	76.00	Rudraprayag	Mandakini	Lanco Kondapali	Under Const.
91	Chunni Semi	24.00	Rudraprayag	Mandakini	UIPC	
92	Singoli Bhatwari	99.00	Rudraprayag	Mandakini	L & T	Under Const.
93	Vijainagar Tilwara	30.00	Rudraprayag	Mandakini	UIPC	
94	Tilwara Rampur	25.00	Rudraprayag	Mandakini	UIPC	
95	Rampur Rudraprayag	25.00	Rudraprayag	Mandakini	UIPC	
96	Chaumasi	7.00	Rudraprayag	Mandakini	UIPC	Kedarnath Sanctuary
97	Kali Ganga -II	6.00	Rudraprayag	Mandakini	UJVNL	Commissioned
98	Kalimath	6.00	Rudraprayag	Mandakini	UIPC	Kedarnath Sanctuary
99	Madmaheshwar -II	8.00	Rudraprayag	Mandakini	UIPC	
100	Madmaheshwar	15.00	Rudraprayag	Mandakini	UJVNL	Under Const.

(Contd...)

101	Pinder Jawarpani	24.00	Bageshwar	Pinder	Self Id catagary	
102	Malayadaur HEP	26.80	Bageshwar	Pinder	UIPC	
103	Pinder Bhadung	20.00	Bageshwar	Pinder	Self Id catagary	
104	Khati - Lumi	19.20	Bageshwar	Pinder	UIPC	
105	Lumi - Tikh	11.40	Bageshwar	Pinder	UIPC	
106	Tikh - Kunwargarh	45.60	Bageshwar	Pinder	UIPC	
107	Kunwargarh - Choting	36.80	Chamoli	Pinder	UIPC	
108	Manmati -Malkhet	10.20	Chamoli	Pinder	UIPC	
109	Malkhet	15.00	Chamoli	Pinder	Malkhet Power	
110	Pinder - Bora gad	18.50	Chamoli	Pinder	Self Id catagary	
111	Devsari Dam	252.00	Chamoli	Pinder	SJVNL	
112	Ming -Naigaon	96.00	Chamoli	Pinder	UIPC	
113	Bagoli	60.00	Chamoli	Pinder	UIPC	
114	Thapli	44.00	Chamoli	Pinder	UIPC	
115	Bangri	24.00	Chamoli	Pinder	UIPC	
116	Sundardunga - I HEP	25.00	Bageshwar	Pinder	Self Id catagary	
117	Sundardunga - II HEP	26.00	Bageshwar	Pinder	Self Id catagary	
118	Sundardunga - HEP	23.70	Bageshwar	Pinder	UIPC	
119	Malayadaur - jatoli khati	38.10	Bageshwar	Pinder	UIPC	
120	Bilup gad - I SHEP	25.00	Bageshwar	Pinder	Self Id catagary	
121	Baum	7.00	Bageshwar	Pinder	UIPC	
122	Jogi Kothi SHP	8.60	Chamoli	Pinder	Self Id catagary	
123	Dhairandhar SHP	8.00	Chamoli	Pinder	Self Id catagary	
124	Dhura	8.80	Chamoli	Pinder	UIPC	
125	Dhura Debal	6.90	Chamoli	Pinder	UIPC	
126	Dungri -Tharali SHP	10.00	Chamoli	Pinder	Self Id catagary	
127	Sarju -I	7.50	Bageshwar	Sarju	Uttar Bharat	Under Const.
128	Sarju -II	15.00	Bageshwar	Sarju	Uttar Bharat	Under Const.
129	Sarju -III	10.50	Bageshwar	Sarju	Uttar Bharat	Under Const.
130	Balighat	5.50	Bageshwar	Sarju	UIPC	EDCL
131	Khutani	21.00	Bageshwar	Sarju	UIPC	Bidding Completed
132	Seraghat	11.10	Bageshwar	Sarju	UIPC	Bidding Completed
133	Nayar	17.00	Pauri	Nayar	UIPC	Ready for Bidding
134	Burthing -Purdam	6.50	Pithoragarh	E.Ramganga	UIPC	EDCL
135	Balgad	19.50	Pithoragarh	E.Ramganga	UIPC	Bidding Completed
136	Eastern Ramganga	15.00	Pithoragarh	E.Ramganga	UIPC	
137	Siligad HEP	10.20	Pithoragarh	Ramganga	Self Id catagary	
138	Ramganga	198.00	Pauri	Ramganga	UJVNL	Commisioned
139	Kumeria -Garjia (Bawas)	12.50	Nainital	Kosi	UIPC	Project in buffer Zone of Jim Corbett
140	Mapang Sirkari	340.00	Pithoragarh	Gorigenga	GVK Industries	
141	Sirkari bhayol - Rupsiyabagar	210.00	Pithoragarh	Gorigenga	UJVNL	
142	Rupsiya bagar - Khasiya	260.00	Pithoragarh	Gorigenga	NTPC	
143	Gauriganga III A&B	140.00	Pithoragarh	Gorigenga	NHPC	
144	Karmoli Lumti Talli	55.00	Pithoragarh	Gorigenga	NHPC	
145	Gauriganga IV	115.00	Pithoragarh	Gorigenga	UIPC	
146	Tankul	12.00	Pithoragarh	Gorigenga	UJVNL	
147	Madkini -V HEP	24.80	Pithoragarh	Gorigenga	Self Id catagary	
148	Madkini -IV HEP	23.50	Pithoragarh	Gorigenga	Self Id catagary	
149	Okhali -II HEP	25.00	Pithoragarh	Gorigenga	Self Id catagary	
150	Okhali HEP	25.00	Pithoragarh	Gorigenga	Self Id catagary	

(Contd...)

151	Pyunshani - Madkini	25.00	Pithoragarh	Goriganga	Self id catagary	
152	Madkini	13.50	Pithoragarh	Goriganga	Madkini Hydro	Under Const.
153	Kulka -Jimba	15.00	Pithoragarh	Goriganga	Self id catagary	
154	Jimba - Maran	24.00	Pithoragarh	Goriganga	Self id catagary	
155	Jimba - Saidip HEP	25.00	Pithoragarh	Goriganga	Self id catagary	
156	Jimbagad	7.70	Pithoragarh	Goriganga	Krishna Knitwear	Under Const.
157	Paina Sagu HEP	24.00	Pithoragarh	Goriganga	Self id catagary	
158	Paina Nathing HEP	21.00	Pithoragarh	Goriganga	Self id catagary	
159	Ralam Chharpu Udiyar	25.00	Pithoragarh	Goriganga	Self id catagary	
160	Ralam saba	25.00	Pithoragarh	Goriganga	Self id catagary	
161	Ralam Balsaini	25.00	Pithoragarh	Goriganga	Self id catagary	
162	Ralam Simpu	25.00	Pithoragarh	Goriganga	Self id catagary	
163	Poling HEP	25.00	Pithoragarh	Goriganga	Self id catagary	
164	Goshi HEP	25.00	Pithoragarh	Goriganga	Self id catagary	
165	Pittigad SHEP	15.00	Pithoragarh	Goriganga	Self id catagary	
166	Bokang Bailing	330.00	Pithoragarh	Dhauliganga	THDC	
167	Chungar Chal	240.00	Pithoragarh	Dhauliganga	NHPC	
168	Sela Urthing	230.00	Pithoragarh	Dhauliganga	UJVNL	
169	Urthing Sobla	280.00	Pithoragarh	Dhauliganga	Reliance	
170	Dhauliganga Intermediate stage	200.00	Pithoragarh	Dhauliganga	NHPC	
171	Dhauli ganga	280.00	Pithoragarh	Dhauliganga	NHPC	Commisioned
172	Mandab HEP	20.00	Pithoragarh	Dhauliganga	Self id catagary	
173	Sobla -I	8.00	Pithoragarh	Dhauliganga	UJVNL	Commisioned
174	Tijam HEP	14.00	Pithoragarh	Dhauliganga	Self id catagary	
175	Garbyang	131.00	Pithoragarh	Mahakali	UIPC	International border
176	Budhi	192.00	Pithoragarh	Mahakali	UIPC	International border
177	Malpa	138.00	Pithoragarh	Mahakali	UIPC	International border
178	Garba -Tawaghat	610.00	Pithoragarh	Mahakali	NHPC	International border
179	Tawaghat - Tapovan	105.00	Pithoragarh	Mahakali	UIPC	International border
180	Tapovan -Kalika	160.00	Pithoragarh	Mahakali	UIPC	International border
181	Kalika - Baluwakot	120.00	Pithoragarh	Mahakali	UIPC	International border
182	Pancheswar	7000.00	Pithoragarh	Mahakali	Govt. of India	International border
183	Tanakpur	120.00	Nainital	Mahakali	NHPC	Commisioned
184	Kuti SHP	6.00	Pithoragarh	Mahakali	UIPC	
185	Palang SHP	6.50	Pithoragarh	Mahakali	UIPC	
186	Najyang SHP	5.50	Pithoragarh	Mahakali	UIPC	
187	Simkhola SHP	6.75	Pithoragarh	Mahakali	UIPC	
188	Khatima	41.40	U.S.Nagar	Sharda	UJVNL	Commisioned

Source: ukvnl.com, 2016.

Mineral Resources in Uttarakhand

Uttarakhand is a part of Himalayan mountain terrain that confines between the rivers Brahamaputra in the east and Indus in the west. The Himalayan mountain range is also a part of the Alpine-Himalayan mountain system. The mountain range has evolved in last 50-55 millions years due to collision of the India and Asia. Since then mountain is growing in height and expanding in size.

The mountain is constituted by varieties of rocks that were as old as 2200 million years to youngest one are few thousand years old. In common parlance, rocks and minerals are considered as synonym but fact is minerals constitute the rocks. Minerals are categorised in two types one with significant economic value and are designated as *ores* and others of relatively less economic values like sand, clay etc. In nature, minerals are formed by varieties of processes those took place in certain specific conditions or set ups. Valuable mineral rich region like Jharkhand, Rajasthan etc. are testimony of operation of these processes in contrast the Uttarakhand region was not favoured by the nature to this extent owing to its geological set up. However, this paucity of high valued minerals is compensated by the abundant availability of relatively low value minerals like limestone, dolomite, sand, gravels etc.

Legally, all mineral resources are property of nation or government or all mankind. Their evaluation and exploitation is decided by the Central Government. Minerals are classified into atomic minerals (exclusive right of Central Government), major minerals (gold, silver, platinum, copper, iron ore, coal, petroleum etc. are controlled by the policy of Central Government) and minor minerals such as sand, *bajri*, stones are controlled by policy of state government. Thus, state governments constitutionally who owns the land have no or very little control over the mineral resources which are present on or in the land of the state boundary. To advance the process of liberalisation, the Central Government has divested its control on some major minerals and notified them in minor category in 2016, thus the power of granting license of prospecting, exploration and exploitation is vested in the state governments. The notified list (minerals in italics are present in commercially exploitable quantities in Uttarakhand) includes agate, ball clay, *barite,* calcareous sand, chalk, calcite, china clay, corundum, *dolomite*, diaspore, dunite/pyroxinite, feldspar, fuchsite quartzite, jasper, felsites, fire clay, *gypsum*, laterite, lime kankar, mica, *ochre*, *quartz*, *sand*, *silica sand, talc/steatite*, *pyrophyllite, quartzite, shale* and *slate.*

Minerals present or available in large volume and could be extracted profitably are called *deposits* while others do present in the area but cannot be mined economically are designated as *occurrences* or *show*. The occurrences of base metals like copper, lead, zinc, antimony and bismuth are plenty in Uttarakhand but none of the occurrence capable of sustaining large scale mining operation in the state. Many a times, media present exaggerated report of discovery of vast mineral deposits but later the so called discovery proved to be uneconomical; this happened with reporting of gold deposits in the Outer/Siwalik Himalaya.

Mineral Wealth in Uttarakhand

Economic minerals of Uttarakhand can be divided in three categories viz. occurring in great abundance such as limestone, dolomite, magnesite, talc, silica, bajri-sands, quartzite etc; in second category minerals occurring in small quantity but having high value and can be mined without cost like petroleum, natural gas, gold, uranium etc. and third category minerals have very scanty and nominal presence such as gold, silver, tin tungsten etc. Minerals of many varieties are reported from the several locations of Uttarakhand, the important minerals and location of worthy deposits (quantity is indicated by mt million tons or t in brackets) of Uttarakhand is as follows (Biyani, 2006, Valdiya, 1980, IBM, 2015):

Limestone – The limestone, marble, dolomite, magnesite and talc/ steatite/soap stone occur near to each other. It is most valuable resource of the state. It is found at Bashti- Naurala- Adhichaura and Garjia- Balmara to Jauljibi-Dhung Dharchula (178), Gangootal Balihat (94) and Rargaon (7.8) in Pithoragarh; Parkot-Darimkhet in Almora and Chaukhutia in Saryu valley having total deposits of several billion tons. Postala to Kulior deposit of (16), Bagaur-Chaunala Shuintola belt (60). Barkot-Nutiya (38.2), Lambidhar, Hathipaon (7.8), Song valley (307), Sahastradhara area and Deoban-Bajmara area in Dehradun district. Tehri Nagni in huge quantity. The indicated quantity in brackets is in mt is very small, in fact state possesses huge quantity in several billion tons.

Marble- Dehradun- Lambidhar (10 mt), Charpatti (3 mt), Kiarkuli (2 mt) and in Lansdowne area of Pauri Garhwal.

Dolomite - Dehradun Sahastradhara, Mussoorie, Nainital.

Magnesite - Bisabajer, Chandak, Dharigaon, Baste, Deopala, in Pithoragarh; Dol-tusrani, Rithait, Ganai, Tachhini, Phandiari, Bauri, Asaun, Salia, Dhuraphat of Gangoli area and of Jhirauli; Panthsera, Gaidali, Dundu, Dewalthal, Bora-Agar, Rain–Agar, Kanda, Pana, Bhurgaon, Dewaldhar, Bhaldeo, Chaugaonchhina, Chahana, Girichhina and Someshwar in Kumaun and in Bagoli, Bangthal-Kimotha, Latudhar-Laldhara and Kyunja, Gol, Kholi, Thal, Kirauli, Khunakilbara, Dolam, Wan, Durmi, Gulabkoti Tapowan-Dwin in Garhwal. Some of these deposits evaluated in detail showing potential of 280 mt (Valdiya, 1980, pp. 253) while taken together all magnesite deposits may have many billion tons value.

Talc – Jakher, Harap, Maulgar, Biskhal, Surag in Baijnath area, Agar-Girichhina of Someshwar, Khuna-Pachar and Dayali, Gairar, Masuli, Birkhal, Mailgar and Surag (0.66 mt) in Bageshwar, Maljhula, Painya-Pauri, Imkhola, of Balwakot, Dewalthal, Bora Agar, Rain Agar, in Gangolihat. Chamoli- Bhardarigaon, Bora, Gonai, Kimkhet, Phadyali Rein, Agar Agar, Barabesi, Bano, Dugal Agar, Kanoliekhira, Melapani, Mush gal, Kailganga, Torosi, Belakuchi, Hiuna in Garhwal. Total deposits are of more than 6.2 mt.

Gypsum– Nainital- Dhapila, Sonarmera (37503 t), Pauri- Khhararichatti (158500 t), Tehri- Garurchatti – (106658 t), Gugthani (5080 t), Mahipur (2032 t), Rangargaon (30841 t), Khemsar, Narendra nagar, Chhipaldi and in Sahastradhara area of Dehradun.

Pyrophyllite – Sayanachatti, Yamuna valley.

Phosphorite- Maldeota, Mussoorie, Durmala, Dubra, Mathet, Chamasari-Pari Tibba, Chaunpa-Kumali Mahrana, Kimoi, Jaikhal, Bhusti, 19 mt. length 120 km thickness 1 to 150 m in Mussoorie Syncline. Lansdowne, Kiurki-Mohanchatti, Kasani, Sot, Kakarwargad and Jabarsot in Nainital of poor quality.

Uranium- Chamethi-Pokhri-Tungia areas in the Chamoli district and Maldeota, Durmala in Dehradun (200-980 ppm).

Barite- Koti in Dehradun district (500 t, 20000 t are proven and inferred reserve).

Base metals – copper, lead, zinc, bismuth and antimony are grouped in base metals class as often these elements occur together because of chemical similarity. The important locations of base metals in Uttarakhand are Almora -Shishakhani, Chhanapani, Balaldeo (0.55 mt); Chamoli-Barmatiya, Dhanpur, Maloni, Mohankhal, Pokhri, Dobri, Lameri, Langasu and Ratura –all occurrences; Dehradun- Kwanu (0.3 mt), Amtiyargad (1.4 mt), Shallukhad atoll zone, Sahastradhara; Nainital – Amritpur, Galpakot, Khansyush; Pauri – Birgana, Bagosi, Dharkot all occurrences; Pithoragarh-Askot (1.4 mt), Baphila (fairly big deposit) and Baphila – only occurrences. Base metal deposits at some places occur along with magnesite.

Silica sand – Sathang-Deodhar, Jarmalu, Dharamandhar, Malap, Dhanku-Chantradhan. Sands contain SiO_2 99-99.77 per cent and FeO 0.02 to 0.36 per cent.

Gold – Pitoragarh- Ralam, Askot, Chalthi, Galakot. Durgapopal having concentration 0.2 to 13.2 parts per million and at Sona nadi in Siwalik rocks.

Silver – occurs at Birgana, in Pauri Garhwal and Askot and Shishakhani in Bageshwar and Chamri and Barmatiya in Chamoli.

Graphite – Almora- Kalimati, Persai, Siran; Pauri- Thailisen, Kaprauli, Garurchatti, Nainital- Betalghat-Jalu, Palsima and Palon in Pithoragarh district.

Ruby and Sapphire- north of Yamunotri.

Sulphur- Sutal in Nandakini.

Hard coal- Laldhang in Almora.

Granite – occurs abundantly in state as small to medium sized rock masses.

Sandstone- it is also occurring in vast quantity of variable quality.

Bajri and Sands- present in all river beds in large quantity.

Schist and gneiss building material used for walls and foundation present in the interior region of the state in very large quantity.

Slate- mainly used for roof and wall construction present in large quantity barring outer part of Himalaya.

Iron ore- Bhukanda, Ali, Pokhri Agar in Chamoli and Kala Agar in Nainital.

Other minerals asbestos, kyanite, tin, tungsten shilajeet, magnetite, stibnite, mica, alum and clay occur in minor quantity.

Potential of Mineral Deposits

The utility of minerals decides by the quantity of minerals in deposits, quality of minerals, impurities or gangue or waste minerals, mining method and cost, location, government royalty and taxation, methods of benefication and extraction, cost of transportation of and market price. Many good mineral deposits located in remote or far flung areas may not be commercially viable on account of some of these factors e.g. glass sand in Purola area is of good quality but because of high transportation cost it is unviable and same is the case of high extraction and transportation cost of phosphorite deposits of Maldeota and Durmala mines of Dehradun. These mines operated by the then Pyrites and Phosphate Chemicals Limited, employing more than 300 persons were closed due to high extraction and transportation costs as demand of phosphorite was mainly in southern states.

The limestone mineral deposits were known prior to independence of the country and before the creation of Uttarakhand a flourishing limestone and gypsum mining industry was present in the Dehradun. This industry was gradually closed after 1983 on the directive of the Supreme Court of India on the ground of pollution. Before closure, more than 55 limestone mines, two cement plants, one calcium carbide plant, many marble chips and lime kilns were operating in the area and were employing approximately 10000 persons directly or indirectly. Besides these, sand and gravels of Doon rivers were sent to distant destination of Uttar Pradesh. Frequent changes in mining policy by the state government and litigations in courts used to affect the mining operations in the state then as well as now.

At present mining operation in Uttarakhand is limited to few minerals only such as sand, bajri, loose boulders present in the river beds and Uttarakhand is second largest producer of magnesite and talc in India. These are very important construction and industrial minerals. Minerals used in construction industries are brought by turbulently flowing rivers from higher elevation to lower elevation particularly in rainy season and available in huge volumes. Few other minerals exploited illegally in small volumes. These two factors are very crucial in proper planning and utilisation of mineral resources.

Though Uttarakhand is not enriched with high value minerals and this short coming is compensated by abundant supply of low value minerals. Full potential of available minerals is yet to be established. If commercially viable minerals are mined at optimum level, taking care of environmental and other issues, the mining industry could strengthen economy to great extent. Sand bajri mining in the Gaula, Kosi, Dabra rivers alone generate huge employment as every year mining alone provides job to 10000 persons and 7000 vehicles and nearly 100 bullock carts have been registered to carry out excavated materials as reported by forest corporation. Almost all rivers of state when enter in plain regions, deposit their huge heterogeneous sized load on the river beds or in nearby flood plains, which is of immense economic value on account of basic raw material of construction industries. The systematic extraction from all feasible locations may provide ample revenue as royalty and would create huge numbers of jobs. The mining potential of other minerals like limestone, dolomite, talc/ steatite, white Berinag quartzite of fine grained nature have a huge potential to change the economic fortune of the state.

State may also have possibility of petroleum and natural gas either in south or north. ONGC has drilled an unsuccessful well long back in Mohand area, south of Dehradun since then no attempt has been made for exploration of oil and natural gas. The exploration activities should be revived in the Outer and the Tethyan Himalaya in suitable terrains. Stray coal layers are present in the Siwaliks, possibilities of coal or coal bed methane needs to be explored. Ruby and sapphire are present in north of Yamunotri and this region has not been investigated geologically yet (Biyani and Shah, 1999). A detailed exploration activity should be conducted here.

Opportunities in Mining Sector

The mining sector since very old time is considered as primary sector of economic activities that meet the basic requirement of the society. Uttarakhand has huge mineral resources that can be exploited for many millennia. The biggest problem related with mineral resources in Uttarakhand is of data reliability. This is on two counts: firstly, quantity of resources and mineral availabilities are precisely not known and second, is related with production, local consumption and revenue figures. There is wide disparity between data of different agencies dealing with minerals. For successful mining operation, the precise quantity of mineral should be known at least before mining plan is implemented. This requires intensive prospecting and exploration of mineral deposits. Whatever quantitative data are available are of very preliminary type and are under estimates. The geological setup of Uttarakhand is highly disturbed; therefore, it is not easy to assess the quantity of mineral deposits which is must for long-term exploitation planning. The mining industry provides jobs not only for mines but also both in upstream and downstream segments. Once the mineral reaches to destination, it is consumed by the industries and several products are developed. Mineral based industries would prefer Uttarakhand because of cheap hydroelectric power available here and good market potential as minerals based industries by and large are absent here. Thus, again ample job opportunities exist here if properly utilised. Mining and associated mineral based industries could solve the problem of unemployment to considerable extent. Three cement clinker crushing and two glass manufacturing units are operating in Roorkee region using raw materials produced in other states. Several cement, glass; marble, quartzite, slate and granite tiles, decorative stones magnesite-soap stone, plaster of paris processing/manufacturing units can be established in the state. Easily, lakhs of people can gain useful employment in this sector. Besides, this State and Central governments can earn valuable revenue from various taxes, cess and royalties.

Revenue Generation

Since time immemorial the mineral deposits were considered as important part of the state's economy as they are providing jobs to large numbered of people, supplying needed raw material to industries, generating royalty on extracted material, foreign exchange by export and also taxes on downstream products. India is fourth largest producer of minerals in terms of volume and ninth largest producer in terms of commercial value.

Locals of Uttarakhand used to mine iron and copper since ancient times but later the local mining industry vanished due to cheaper imported metals. The first systematic mineral survey was started by the Britishers in 1815 when they sent the copper ore samples of the Pithoragarh to Kolkata for analyses. The state is second leading producer of magnesite (25 per cent) and steatite or soap stone (10 per cent). More than 30 minerals are reported in production list of the state; however the substantial mining is done of magnesite, steatite, sands-bajri, limestone and dolomite.

At present except magnesite sands, bajri and stone mining and crushing, no other mineral is yielding revenue. This is a great loss to state's economy. When state was formed the royalty from mineral deposits was 16.8 crores in 2001-02 this amount rose to 35.6 crores in 2004-05, fell to 13.5 crores in 2008-09 and again jumped to 112.4 crores in 2011-12 (dgm.royalty, 2015). In 2016-17, it is expected to cross more than 500 crores. The contribution of minor minerals in total production is 88.2 per cent, 99.2 per cent and 85 per cent in 2010-11, 2011-12 and 2012-13 despite abundant availability of the industrial minerals like limestone-dolomite, magnesite, white fine grained quartzite, granite and rounded white colour quartzite stones of decorative value. Uttarakhand's contribution is 2.58 per cent in total production of minerals in nation.

In terms of value, in Uttarakhand's total value of mineral product is 85 crores of rupees in 2012-13 and in this contribution of minor minerals was 64 crores, it was eight per cent less than previous year (IBM, 2015). The assessed value of minerals is doubtful as state is earning far more amount as royalty from minor minerals alone.

The mines scenario is highly dwindling; there were 37 mines in 2010-11, reduced to 32 in 2012-13 and only 15 mines are in working state. Mineral production is also swing in wide limit, it was 137.7 in 2011-12 falls to 94.6 in following year and 78.6 in 2013-14 (base 2004-05=100) and before closure of mines in Dehradun, more than 50 limestone were working.

Criminal Loss

Due to various reasons, the state suffer mammoth loss in terms on money to exchequers and of unemployment viz. the Tehri dam of 1000 MW capacity is producing 300 crores unit of electricity annually. Our potential of minor and major hydro electric scheme is of 30000 MW which means state would be in a position to produce 9000 crores unit annually while at present the state is producing approximately 1100 crores unit. If the price of electricity is converted in terms of rupees, then amount would be mind boggling. The loss of geothermal energy can be used for numerous purposes. Tehri dam is quenching the thrist of nearly six million people in and around Delhi and irrigating the land of lakhs of acres and effectively controls the flood in UP and Bihar.

Similarly, minerals and rocks of economic utility if fully and judiciously exploited, then many cement plants, limestone based units, refractory bricks from the magnesite and dolomite, talc/steatite powder units, glass factories, granite/quartzite/ decorational slate tiles factory, minor base metal ores beneficiation plants could become strong pillars of state economy.

Search of New Mineral Resources

Since formation of Uttarakhand no new mineral deposits have been discovered. Perhaps the reasons for this are no concerted efforts for search were made by either central or state governments. There are number of central government agencies working for this purpose namely, the Geological Survey of India, Atomic Mineral Division, Indian Bureau of Mines, Oil and Natural Gas Commission and mineral specific agencies like Manganese Ore India Ltd., Coal India Limited etc. and research organisation like Wadia Institute of Himalayan Geology and the state government has its own geological wing named as Directorate of Geology and Mining. These organisations at present are focusing on their assigned tasks which is not necessarily search of new deposits. Besides these professional organisations, in the higher education setup of the state many universities and colleges have geology department which are engaged in other research activities. The onerous task of searching is also dissuaded by the topography as the northern part of the state is full of high mountains where no logistic facilities are available, frequent glaciers mask the underlying geology, emphasis on water resources development, environmental sensitivity of people, limited duration of working as high altitude regions get snowfall in September and the snow melts around May/ June making working conditions difficult, courts directives etc. Unless a long-term specific programme of discovery of mineral resource is launched particularly for northern region, the state will have to remain content with what is known.

Problems

Uttarakhand has huge possibility in mining sector and in mine-based industries. The important minerals which can be mined on sustainable basis are limestone, dolomite, talc, magnesite, gypsum, glass grade silica sands, quartzites of high purity, rounded decorative stones, granite and river brought sand gravels and boulders. The exploitation of these minerals may have potential to yield royalty in billions of rupees. Industries based on these minerals like cement, chemicals, tiles, refractory, stone crushing etc. may yield additional revenue by imposing tax/levies on finished products. Despite richness in sand, bajri and stones, at times the state is importing these materials from the nearby state due to policy problems and litigations in courts. The important problems in exploitation of natural resources are related with exploitation policy and regulating authorities, environmental problem, geological set up of state, topography, climate, quality, illegal mining, litigation, infrastructural bottleneck, quality, processing industry and market.

Advantage Uttarakhand

If stated hydropower plants and exploitation of natural resources are undertaken in full form, then every nook and corner would develop with a very rapid rate in the state. This will stop migration of people from hills to plain as they would get decent jobs in nearby areas of their living and thus remote areas would also get developed. Mineral resource exploitation remains unaffected from routine economic fluctuations hence they are dependable resources for economic development.

Road Ahead

The data indicates that state of Uttarakhand is richly endowed with minerals and water resources, however the utilisation of these resources are much below the expected level. State was created for the faster economic development of hilly regions as there was general feeling before creation of state that there were deliberate neglect in hill's resources and people which was considered a root cause of backwardness of the hill region of the undivided state. The state is able to harness only 15 per cent of hydro resource and in case of minerals, increase in revenue due to increase in tax and general inflation, a declining trend is discernible in mining operations. Thus, two precious resources are not only grossly underutilised but trend of either elimination or dismantling is rising in the horizons. A number of factors are responsible for this situation and feats are hailed as historic achievements but ultimately it is the state or public that is suffering silently and innocently. With booming economic activities, prosperity is elusive day dream.

The frequent intervention of the judiciary, National Green Tribunal (NGT), pollution control department, NGO is a matter of concern in environmental aspects particularly hype on eco-sensitivity and environmental fragility. The Tehri dam which became functional in 2008 would have become functional in at least a decade before if there was not frequent disruption by environmental and rehabilitation lobbies. Till now, neither Tehri nor 60 years old Bhakra dams have created any major environmental problems. In fact they are contributing handsomely in solving food and power problems of India, therefore, the fear of environmental issues need to be firmly addressed. Mining activities are totally banned in forested areas or in the interior areas and dams' construction have been stopped. With this kind of approach the state is slowly creating more problems rather than providing amenities to rising population of the state. Empty exchequer and burgeoning loan on state are unlikely to be sustained for long. To aver unpleasant future situation, right kind of policies with emphasis on revenue generation and societal development have to be put in practice. Environmental and social sensitivities should be freed from clutches of vested groups. In the matter of delaying the implementation of projects on environmental and social issues, the state government should adopt same line of actions as of the Central Government's action against foreign-funded NGO's who were deliberately misleading the masses or frivolous litigations or demonstrations or obstacles. Once the mining or engineering projects accorded permission for development, statuary provisions be made that the approved projects have to be completed in the stipulated time frame and for any shortcoming by investigating agencies detected in implementation stage should be heavily and exemplarily penalised. Growth without some amount of destruction is impossible. Hence the tradeoff between the loss and gain has to be understood by policymakers of the state for a booming Uttarakhand economy in the future.

Acknowledgement

Author is thankful to Dr. Rajlakshmi Datta, co-editor, for inviting to pen this contribution on appropriate occasion. Author expresses thanks to Dr. Harish Bahuguna for providing input in hydro power section. Thanks are also due to Dr. O. P. Kulshrestha, Principal of DBS PG college, Dehradun for providing congenial environment.

References

Biyani, A.K. (2006). Dimensions of Himalayan Geology. Satish Serial Publications House, Delhi, 330 pp.

Biyani, A.K. (2002). Hot springs of Uttaranchal: Science, utility, occurrence, potential, threat, development and conservational challenges. In: Verma, N.K. (ed.) Proc. Natural Wealth of Uttaranchal, Technological Publications, Kalidas Road, Dehradun, pp. 291-298.

Biyani, A.K. and Gupta, S.K. (2004). River linking. Curr. Sci. v. 87(3), pp. 277-278.

Biyani, A.K. and Shah, N. (1999). Geological resources of the Higher Himalayan Yamuna Valley. Spl. issue Himalayan Geoenvironment and Resources, Ashmica, V5, pp. 42-45 (Hindi).

Dudeja, D. and Biyani, A.K. (2009). Hydrogeochemical and quality assessment of spring water of Doon Valley, Uttarakhand. International Journal of Environment and Development, V.6 (2), pp. 93-115.

dgm.uk.gov.in/files/pdf/royalty 2015 accessed on Sept. 13, 2016

GoI (2006), Dynamic Groundwater Resources of India (as on March 2004), New Delhi.

GoI (2007), Report of the Steering Committee on Water Resources for Eleventh Five Year Plan (2007-2012), Planning Commission.

http:// www.ujvnl.com accessed on 10 Oct., 2016.

Indian Bureau of Mines (2015). Indian Mineral Year Book 2013. Part I State Reviews. Uttarakhand. p. 8 accessed on Sept. 13, 2016.

Mines.nic.in/writereddadata accessed on Sept. 13, 2016.

Raina, V K and Srivastava, D (2008). Glacier Atlas of India, Geological Society of India, Bangalore, p. 315.

Sharma, P. (2016). Inventory and monitoring of glacial lakes in Uttarakhand Himalaya. Unpublished dissertation submitted to HNB Garhwal University, Srinagar, pp.129.

Valdiya, K S (1980). Geology of Kumaun Lesser Himalaya. Wadia Institute of Himalayan Geology, Dehradun, p. 291.

Notes

1. S. V. Ciriacy-Wantrup 1969, Natural Resources in Economic Growth: The Role of Institutions and Policies; American Journal of Agricultural Economics, Vol. 51, No. 5, Proceedings Issue, (Dec., 1969), pp. 1314-1324.
2. http://www.bbk.ac.uk/ems/faculty/zoega/research/.PDFNatinvest31
3. Gavin Wright Jesse Czelusta February 2004; Mineral Resources and Economic Development, Conference on Sector Reform in Latin America Stanford Center for International Development.URL: http://ai2-s2-pdfs.s3.amazonaws.com/dc0f/dc264aeee4f5f3e 551fcb59863 ba9c07a4e2.pdf
4. V.P. Dimri Geothermal Energy Resources in Uttarakhand, India J. Ind. Geophys. Union (October 2013) v. 17, no. 4, pp. 403-408.

17

Animal Husbandry in Uttarakhand: A Potential Sector for Livelihood Generation and Economic Empowerment

Manoj Kumar Pant and Preeti Kathuria

Introduction

India is endowed with the largest livestock population in the world. Livestock rearing is one of the important economic activities in rural areas of the country providing supplementary income for most of the families dependent on agriculture. Apart from providing a subsidiary income to the families, rearing of livestock such as cattle, buffaloes, sheep, goats, pigs, poultry etc. is a source of protein supplement to the family members of the household in the form of milk, eggs and meat. Animal Husbandry and Dairying Programme have attained considerable importance in various Five Year Plans and several schemes/ projects have been taken up by the States and the Centre for the development of this sector. In order to make an objective assessment of these projects and evaluate their impact, the need for reliable and correct data is utmost essential. Timely availability of reliable and current data relating to various indicators is essential for monitoring, evaluating and evolving policies for various developmental activities in this sector.[1] As per 19th Livestock census, 2012 (GOI, 2014) India's livestock sector is one of the largest in the world with a holding of

11.6 per cent of world livestock population which consists buffaloes (57.83 per cent), cattle (15.06 per cent), sheep (7.14 per cent), goats (17.93 per cent), camel (2.18 per cent), equine (1.3 per cent), pigs (1.2 per cent), chickens (4.72 per cent) and ducks (1.94 per cent). India has huge livestock population of 512 million nos. which mainly includes cattle, buffaloes, goats, sheep and pigs. The total livestock population in India has decreased by 3.33 per cent over the previous census.[2] Realising the potential of animal husbandry sector various schemes and initiatives have already being taken in India like National Livestock Mission, National Diary Plan, National Programme for Bovine Breeding and Diary Development, National Kamdhenu Breeding Centres, etc. The purpose is to get improved germplasm, semen selection for cross-breeding technologies to create sturdy, resilient and productive progeny of cattle, to enhance the production of eggs, milk, silk and other animal products. Moreover the Blue Revolution in India is a very substantial step to give thrust to the fisheries sector.

Table 17.1: Position of Select Livestock population

Livestock population	*First rank country in world*	*India's position in world*
Cattle	Brazil	2nd
Buffalo	India	1st
Sheep	China	2nd
Goat	India	1st

Source: GOI 2014.

As far as livestock population is concerned, India ranks first [Table 17.1] in buffalo and goat population, while ranks second in cattle and sheep population with huge scope to utilise the animal wealth.

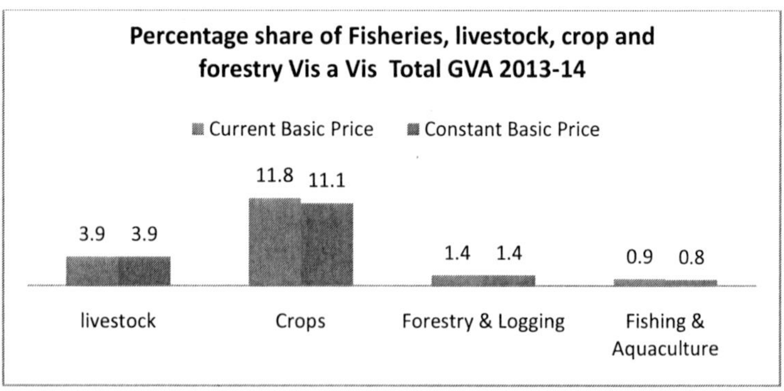

Source: Basic Animal Husbandry and Fisheries Statistics 2015.

Figure 17.1: Percentage share of Fisheries, livestock, crop and forestry Vis-à-Vis Total GVA 2013-14, India.

Figure 17.1 shows percentage share in the components of primary sector to Gross Value Added in 2013-14 at both current prices and constant prices. It is clear from the figure that the contribution of livestock, fishing and agriculture is not significant and hence given the nature of livestock population, has a huge scope of development.

Uttarakhand: Scope of Animal Husbandry

Uttarakhand lies in the Himalayan Region and has certain unique mountain characteristics specific to Himalayan states.The place of mountains, its people and resources are gaining importance in world agenda as it has been recognised the world over that sustainability in the mountain region will lend a hand not only for the upland but also the people lying down land. Livelihoods in mountains are constrained by various factors and hence livelihood options which are mountain friendly needs to have priority in economic planning process in a mountain state like Uttarakhand.

The people of the Indian Himalayan Region, like elsewhere in other mountain ecosystems, are heavily dependent for their livelihood on their immediate natural resources and production from primary sectors such as agriculture, forestry, livestock, etc. The dependency of the continually growing population on finite resources, lack of viable technologies to mitigate the mountain specificities and enhanced production to meet the demands are depleting the resources along with increasing marginality of farmers, ultimately promoting poverty.[3] In the context of Uttarakhand, these acts as a push factor for migration.

Uttarakhand has a total area of 53,483 km of which 86 per cent is mountainous and around 65 per cent is covered by forests. As per 2011 census total population of Uttarakhand state is 101.17 lakhs out of which 69.45 per cent is rural and 30.55 per cent is urban population. Livestock farming in Uttarakhand forms an integral part of the rural economy contributing in some form or the other to household income and family nutrition, besides producing the much needed biomass and draught power for agricultural operations. As per 19th livestock census 2012, in comparison to country, Uttarakhand has 1.05 per cent cattle, 0.91 per cent buffaloes, 0.57 per cent sheep, 1.01 per cent goats, 0.19 per cent pigs and 0.64 per cent poultry. There has been a significant increase in the population of crossbred cattle and decrease in indigenous cattle population. Overall, total population of cattle has decreased. Increase in cross-breed population reflects the direct influence of the Breed Improvement Programmes being carried out. There has been a decline in the population of buffaloes also. There was significant increase in population of sheep and goats, since 2007.

This has been totally market driven as the demand for meat has been ever increasing. Interestingly there has been a very significant increase in poultry which may be attributed to increasing consumption trends of poultry meat and eggs. Besides these, sheep and goat husbandry is deeply rooted within the rich cultural and traditional heritage of Uttarakhand and forms one of the major economic backbones of the marginal and landless farmers of the state. Annual growth rate was recorded maximum[4] in the state of Madhya Pradesh, Kerala, Delhi and Uttarakhand for the production of milk, egg, meat and wool, respectively. As per Directorate of Economics and Statistics the contribution of primary sector in the Gross State Domestic Product (GSDP) in year 2015-16 was 11.80 per cent in which the proportion of animal husbandry was 2.62 per cent.

The recent livestock census 2012 shows that the total population of the livestock in the state is 96.64 lakhs including poultry. The detailed species-wise breakup is as below:

Table 17.2: Species-wise Livestock Population in Uttarakhand (2012)

	Species	*Population (Lakhs)*		*Species*	*Population (Lakhs)*
1	Cattle	20.06	5	Horse/Pony/Mule/Donkey	0.45
2	Buffalo	9.88	6	Pig	0.2
3	Sheep	3.69	7	Others (Yak/Dog/rabbit)	2.27
4	Goat	13.67	8	Poultry	46.42

Source: Department of Animal Husbandry, Uttarakhand.

Methods and Data

The present paper is based on extensive perusal of secondary data from various published research articles, annual reports and data published by Department of Animal Husbandry Dairying & Fisheries (DAHDF) from time to time. Report of the Working Group on Animal Husbandry and Dairying for the Eleventh Five Year Plan (2007–2012) and Twelfth Five Year Plan (2012-2017) by Planning Commission, Government of India were also used as a source of information. Basic Animal Husbandry Statistics (BAHS) served as a major source of information. Report of National Accounts Division published by Ministry of Statistics and Programme Implementation, Annual Report (2011-12) of Ministry of Agriculture, Government of India and Directorate of Economics and Statistics Uttarakhand were reviewed for the present compilation. Moreover reports of Uttarakhand state government, Department of Animal Husbandry, etc were also collected to know state level prospects of animal husbandry in the state of Uttarakhand. All types of major livestocks available in the state except fisheries have been included in the paper for analysis.

INSTITUTIONAL SETUP AND SERVICE DELIVERY IN THE STATE

The responsibility of providing animal health services in Uttarakhand both prophylactic and therapeutic; farm advisory services; extension and communication; technical backstopping; animal breeding services; and all other inputs related to the livestock sector lie with the Department of Animal Husbandry. This it carried out through its vast institutional setup

Table 17.3: Institutional Setup for Animal Husbandry in Uttarakhand

S. No.	*Institution*	*Number*
1	Veterinary Hospitals	325
2	'D' Class Dispensaries	10
3	Veterinary Dispensaries	775
4	A. I. Centers (Deptt.)	686
5	Sheep Breeding Farms	11
6	Angora Goat Farm/Goat Farm	02
7	Cattle Breeding Farms	04
8	Poultry Farms	07
9	Angora Rabbit Farms	05
10	Intensive Poultry Development Project (IPDP)	08
11	Sheep & Wool Extension Centers / Stud Ram Centres	113
12	Disease Diagnostic Labs	08
13	No. of Hatcheries	07
14	Piggery Farms	02
15	Wool Grading Centre	01
16	Frozen Semen Production Centre	01
17	Frozen Semen Bank	02
18	SPVs	
	1- U.L.D.B.	01
	2- U.S.W.D.B.	01
	3- U.A.W.B	01
	4- Uttarakhand Gau Seva Ayog	01
	5- Registrar, Uttarakhand Vety. Council	01

The state has also setup Special Purpose Vehicles (SPVs) for addressing specific sectors within the livestock sphere.

Source: Compiled from Animal Husbandry Department, GoUK.

consisting of Veterinary hospitals, dispensaries, A.I. Centres, Livestock production farms; Training centres and other production support institutions etc. As per the Department, several institutions are spread over the state as shown in Table 17.3.

Uttarakhand Livestock Development Board (ULDB), is an automomous institution set up under the Centrally sponsored National Project for Cattle and Buffalo Breeding and is registered under the Societies Regn. Act 1860. The board is the sole agency for the production and supply of quality frozen semen doses (as per MSP norms of GOI); procurement and supply of Liquid Nitrogen through the establishment of a state LN2 grid; and all other inputs related to the successful field delivery of Artificial Insemination. In addition to this the board also procures and supplies buffalo and cow bulls for establishment of Natural breeding centres in an organised manner in the remote mountainous regions of the state. The board also looks after the various fodder development initiatives of the Department of animal husbandry. In line with the national objective of conserving and propagating the indigenous breeds of cattle, the board is using the Embryo Transfer Technology for conservation and propagation of Red Sindhi breed of cattle.

Uttarakhand Sheep and Wool Development Board (USWDB)'s basic objective is to intensify, manifest and create new opportunities in the field of sheep, goat and rabbit husbandry for increasing employment generation and enterprise development in the state.

Promotion of machine shearing for qualitative and quantitative improvement in raw wool, health coverage to sheep and goat, facilities like tent, solar lamp, mattress, tarpaulin, umbrella, shoes, rain coat and torch to shepherds on migratory routes, breed improvement through distribution of elite quality rams from the 05 Ram Raising Units (RRU) and providing facilities through 05 Mobile Veterinary Vans in 05 sheep dense populated districts viz. Pithoragarh, Bageshwar, Chamoli, Uttarkashi and Tehri are few pioneering activities of USWDB.[5] All these five districts lies in the hilly terrains of the state and has huge scope for sheep rearing due to its favourable climatic condition required for sheep rearing.

Uttarakhand Animal Welfare Board (UAWB) has been established with the motive of welfare and humane treatment of animals as per the recommendations of the GOI.The state of Uttarkhand [known as Dev Bhoomi] has a complete ban on the slaughter of cow and its progeny. A separate Ayog, the Uttarakhand Gau Seva Ayog has been constituted as per the directives of the central government for the same. Besides these the Uttarakhand Veterinary council has been set up under the Veterinary Council of India Act 1981.

Facts and Figures

Table 17.4 analyses the trend in milk production over the span of 13 years since the new state was formed. It is clear from the table that over the years the production of milk is increasing in all the 13 districts of the state except in year 2014-15 where the production has slightly declined in eight out of thirteen districts. Out of the 13 districts the maximum milk production in all the years was found in Haridwar district which is one of the plain districts of the state and is a pilgrimage hub of the Hindus. Though the minimum production of milk was recorded in Champawat district from 2001-02 to 2008-09, it was found to be rising gradually in later years. From 2009-10 to 2014-15 the minimum milk production was found in Rudraprayag district. It is noteworthy that both Champawat and Rudraprayag districts are located in hilly areas of the state. Hence milk production and associated livelihood option has not been optimally utilised in those hill districts. The probable reason may be two. Firstly, lack of marketing linkages of milk produced is constrained in the district which discourages production at commercial level, secondly, there is lack of technical knowhow on milk related products where such products may be stored for some time. There is a huge possibility to explore this avenue.

The Table 17.5 reveals the status of egg production in the state since its bifurcation. It is evident that there are huge inter-district variations with regard to egg production in all the years of reference. Udhamsingh Nagar occupies first position in the production of egg as compared to other districts. There is also significant difference in egg production in Udhamsingh Nagar and other district. However, the minimum production of egg was 3.240 lakh in Rudraprayag district in year 2001-02 which went upto 20.374 in year 2014-15. On the other hand the egg production was 314.0 lakh in US Nagar in year 2001-02 which rose upto 2603.53 lakhs in 2014-15. Both Udhamsingh Nagar and Rudraprayag occupied first and last positions in egg production respectively in all the years. It is to be noted that the district with maximum production of egg is a plain district and with minimum production is situated in hilly area of the state. There is scope in the hill districts for accelerating poultry farming as alternative livelihood options other than traditional agricultural practices.

Table 17.4: Milk Production in Uttarakhand over the years (in 000 MT)

District	*2001-02*	*2002-03*	*2003-04*	*2004-05*	*2005-06*	*2006-07*	*2007-08*	*2008-09*	*2009-10*	*2010-11*	*2011-12*	*2012-13*	*2013-14*	*2014-15*
Dehradun	75.220	76.620	93.046	97.865	97.865	99.018	99.949	101.367	108.338	110.107	113.219	120.849	130.708	147.19
Uttarkashi	49.200	49.540	45.400	46.654	47.239	46.891	48.850	53.762	53.855	54.005	55.953	58.662	61.214	58.597
Haridwar	166.210	168.090	206.728	206.016	206.174	207.347	209.863	209.942	225.054	226.124	229.638	236.412	245.393	259.93
Pauri	94.690	96.670	95.888	96.376	97.093	98.056	98.083	97.994	104.371	104.537	106.043	110.719	115.789	113.22
Chamoli	66.850	68.163	72.104	72.552	73.752	74.389	74.373	73.962	70.398	69.068	70.314	72.621	75.002	70.431
Tehri	100.340	100.970	100.624	102.571	104.366	104.698	104.274	105.430	109.399	110.702	112.559	116.837	121.464	112.88
Rudraprayag	35.820	36.550	42.105	42.487	42.861	43.143	43.100	42.691	46.498	46.129	48.080	50.146	51.89	44.909
Almora	113.380	144.120	108.255	109.569	109.674	110.427	111.149	110.791	150.954	151.753	155.081	160.705	163.907	146.64
Pithoragarh	83.090	83.710	92.373	93.561	94.467	95.369	96.179	96.289	100.706	99.532	100.896	106.749	112.332	117.33
Nainital	64.330	66.230	95.906	89.759	94.468	94.720	93.149	94.749	128.057	130.371	135.177	141.327	151.294	157.33
Champawat	30.520	30.730	39.817	40.306	40.721	41.147	41.505	41.548	48.400	48.635	50.563	53.705	56.506	54.47
Udhamsingh Nagar	139.000	140.410	147.540	147.952	148.261	149.274	151.136	152.930	176.008	177.079	182.355	190.387	203.471	223.96
Bageshwar	47.480	47.830	48.038	49.932	48.589	48.842	49.131	48.941	55.178	55.309	57.010	59.235	61.178	58.465
Maximum	166.210 (H)	168.090 (H)	206.728 (H)	206.016 (H)	206.174 (H)	207.347 (H)	209.863 (H)	209.942 (H)	225.054 (H)	226.124 (H)	229.638 (H)	236.412 (H)	245.393 (H)	259.93 (H)
Minimum	30.520 (C)	30.730 (C)	39.817 (C)	40.306 (C)	40.721 (C)	41.147 (C)	41.505 (C)	41.548 (C)	46.498 (R)	46.129 (R)	48.080 (R)	50.146 (R)	51.89 (R)	44.909 (R)

Source: Department of Animal husbandry, Uttarakhand;H= Haridwar, C=Champawat and R=Rudraprayag.

Table 17.5: Egg Production in Uttarakhand (in Lakh)

S. No	District	2001-02	2002-03	2003-04	2004-05	2005-06	2006-07	2007-08	2008-09	2009-10	2010-11	2011-12	2012-13	2013-14	2014-15
1	Dehradun	203.250	208.410	356.903	357.903	352.423	354.427	364.226	367.408	357.771	371.314	389.726	413.708	451.722	501.2211
2	Uttarkashi	8.610	8.930	22.140	20.714	22.733	22.888	23.027	23.137	26.049	26.601	28.186	31.536	35.997	40.603
3	Haridwar	49.340	49.730	25.275	25.390	24.444	24.646	24.768	24.897	29.980	31.656	37.552	52.456	80.946	78.452
4	Pauri	54.630	56.500	52.747	50.845	50.688	50.227	49.531	51.171	37.510	37.941	40.650	45.770	53.225	66.021
5	Chamoli	7.640	7.890	13.044	12.678	12.526	12.413	12.256	12.657	12.677	13.621	15.891	19.226	22.178	25.070
6	Tihari	30.650	31.770	20.941	21.215	21.506	21.652	21.785	21.889	33.057	34.020	38.660	41.827	46.093	51.784
7	Rudra-prayag	3.240	3.340	4.275	4.166	4.078	4.045	4.038	4.155	6.623	7.457	8.835	10.467	12.535	20.374
8	Almora	50.960	52.160	47.266	49.234	50.946	51.314	51.262	51.087	48.448	48.792	51.750	57.698	63.747	78.600
9	Pithoragarh	38.020	38.900	71.737	71.916	78.494	78.986	79.352	79.090	28.118	29.425	29.967	35.351	45.815	49.018
10	Nainital	105.970	108.700	63.474	61.189	59.542	61.713	66.998	70.167	69.241	70.222	75.299	89.583	102.582	108.024
11	Champawat	11.050	11.310	11.940	12.153	12.853	12.944	12.941	12.897	21.360	22.506	23.914	27.816	31.510	34.990
12	Udhamsingh Nagar	314.000	314.760	1141.197	1166.775	1171.019	1181.270	1188.165	1231.120	1846.267	1901.260	1949.721	2226.784	2391.92	2603.53
13	Bageshwar	16.320	16.690	11.153	11.383	12.058	12.143	12.144	12.103	18.610	19.030	21.769	26.942	33.468	39.752
	Maximum	314.000 (U)	314.760 (U)	1141.197 (U)	1166.775 (U)	1171.019 (U)	1181.270 (U)	1188.165 (U)	1231.120 (U)	1846.267 (U)	1901.260 (U)	1949.721 (U)	2226.784 (U)	2391.92 (U)	2603.53 (U)
	Minimum	3.240 (R)	3.340 (R)	4.275 (R)	4.166 (R)	4.078 (R)	4.045 (R)	4.038 (R)	4.155 (R)	6.623 (R)	7.457 (R)	8.835 (R)	10.467 (R)	12.535 (R)	20.374 (R)

Source: Department of Animal Husbandry, Uttarakhand, Here U=Udhamsingh Nagar, R=Rudraprayag.

Table 17.6: Wool Production in Uttarakhand over the years (in '000 Kg)

S.No	District	2001-02	2002-03	2003-04	2004-05	2005-06	2006-07	2007-08	2008-09	2009-10	2010-11	2011-12	2012-13	2013-14	2014-15
1	Dehradun	21.006	21.479	28.345	29.312	29.034	29.474	30.074	30.419	20.003	18.931	19.796	20.370	20.778	18.962
2	Uttarkashi	112.843	121.109	133.298	136.099	138.448	137.724	138.128	144.597	115.833	115.899	117.128	125.634	138.510	142.309
3	Haridwar	10.810	10.912	2.202	2.249	2.210	2.253	2.249	2.294	4.619	4.913	4.956	5.282	5.989	6.060
4	Pauri	68.911	72.639	27.419	29.504	30.335	31.943	30.891	30.711	20.386	19.935	19.963	22.207	24.928	25.545
5	Chamoli	53.782	57.302	37.496	37.794	40.180	40.040	41.301	41.477	57.321	65.531	67.510	77.150	90.384	107.043
6	Tehri	39.768	42.379	19.094	19.399	19.597	19.544	19.784	20.937	30.603	30.981	32.771	34.523	37.699	42.361
7	Rudraprayag	10.733	11.436	13.572	13.635	14.599	14.491	14.995	14.943	11.607	11.512	11.442	14.875	16.541	14.347
8	Almora	7.186	7.044	6.584	6.576	6.363	6.487	6.730	6.761	6.474	6.113	5.902	6.368	7.248	6.864
9	Pithoragarh	64.548	63.344	43.812	43.787	42.327	43.187	44.704	44.729	52.087	53.488	55.609	58.416	64.033	69.742
10	Nainital	3.606	3.973	0.160	0.165	0.151	0.145	0.148	0.139	0.113	0.117	0.088	0.136	0.158	0.121
11	Champawat	-	-	0.074	0.088	0.086	0.087	0.089	0.088	0.071	-	-	-	0.000	0.000
12	Udhamsingh Nagar	6.131	6.185	2.223	2.286	2.227	2.252	2.287	2.291	2.961	2.907	3.023	2.863	3.062	3.001
13	Bageshwar	27.146	26.864	28.049	27.906	27.316	27.814	28.691	28.594	31.129	31.875	32.342	32.114s	30.836	32.570
	Maximum	112.843 (U)	121.109 (U)	133.298 (U)	136.099 (U)	138.448 (U)	137.724 (U)	138.128 (U)	144.597 (U)	115.833 (U)	117.128 (U)	117.128 (U)	125.634 (U)	138.510 (U)	142.309 (U)
	Minimum	3.606 (N)	3.973 (N)	0.074 (C)	0.088 (C)	0.086 (C)	0.087 (C)	0.089 (C)	0.088 (C)	0.071 (C)	0.117 (N)	0.088 (N)	0.136 (N)	0.000 (C)	0.000 (C)

Source: Department of Animal Husbandry, Uttarakhand. Here U=Uttarkashi, N=Nainital, C=Champawat.

The Table 17.6 presents data on production of wool in various districts of the state of Uttarakhand over the years. It can be comprehended that out of 13 districts the maximum production of wool was reported in Uttarkashi district in all the reference periods. Though in year 2009-10 the production went significantly down but it again got momentum from year 2012-13. While the minimum production of wool was accounted in Nainital district in year 2001-02 and 2002-03, but from year 2003-04 to 2009-10 the minimum production was reported to be in Champawat district. It was less than one thousand kilo gram in the district. A huge difference between the production of wool in Uttarkashi district and other districts is clearly visible. While many other districts in the state have same geographical conditions, but the figures raise a question on why wool production has not been at par with Uttarkashi. One of the probable reasons for Champawat having very less production is that the density of population in the district is one of the lowest in the state. Since production of wool has a huge scope to generate employment in the state, the possibilities especially in the hill districts needs to be explored extensively. Wool production and woollen garments making can turn out to be a niche area for the hill areas of the state.

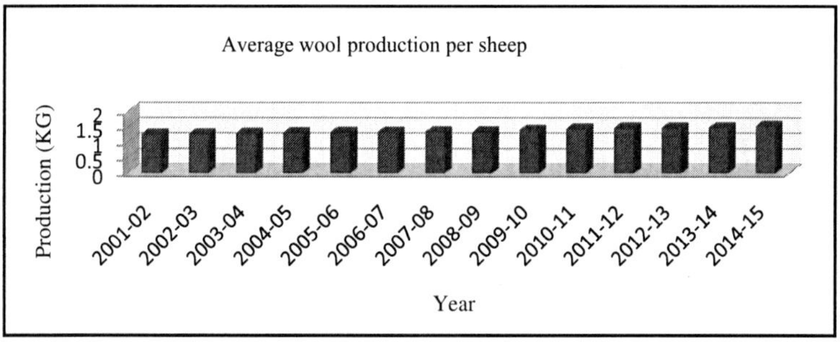

Data Source: Department of Animal husbandry, Uttarakhand.

Figure 17.2: Average wool production per sheep in the state over the years.

Looking over the prospects of employment opportunities through sheep and wool production in the state of Uttarakhand, the state government has established Uttarakhand Sheep and Wool Development Board (USWDB) in year 2003 and is registered under Societies Act. The aims of the board are to implement health programmes for curbing the mortality rate among sheep and goats, to improve the breed of sheep and goats, to support in getting the fair price of the produce, to provide information on new technologies through trainings; to make aware people about the work of sheep and goat rearing and lastly to support in formation of SHGs/

organisations and committees of sheep and goat rearers. Figure 17.2 gives a glimpse of average wool production per sheep in the state over the years which shows a growth over the years but not at a very high pace.

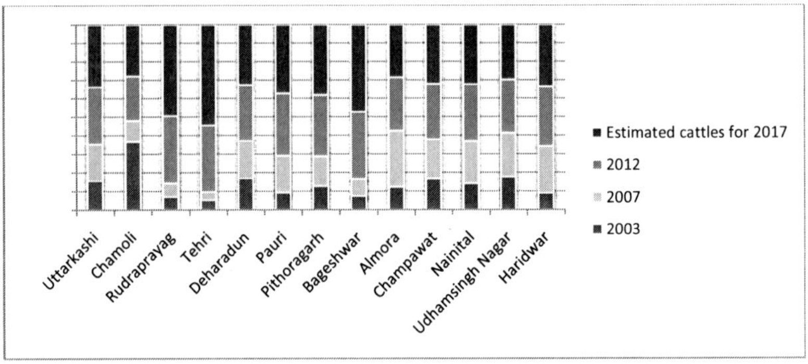

Source: Data from Animal Husbandry Uttarakhand.

Figure 17.3: Exotic and Crossbred Cattle[6] in Uttarakhand in the districts.

Figure 17.3 explains the number of exotic and crossbred cattle in various districts of Uttarakhand state. Starting with year 2003 it can be observed that highest number of these cattle is seen in Chamoli district followed by Udhamsingh Nagar, Uttarkashi, Dehradun districts and so on respectively. However, in year 2007 when the next animal census was undertaken the maximum number was accounted in that year at Almora and minimum was in Tehri districts respectively. Similarly in year 2012 the maximum number was in Rudraprayag, Tehri and Bageshwar district. It is to be noted that the minimum number was found in Tehri district in year 2003, but the number increased and became maximum in another census in the Tehri district. The estimates for year 2017 have been made. However, in year 2017 the maximum number of exotic and crossbred cattle

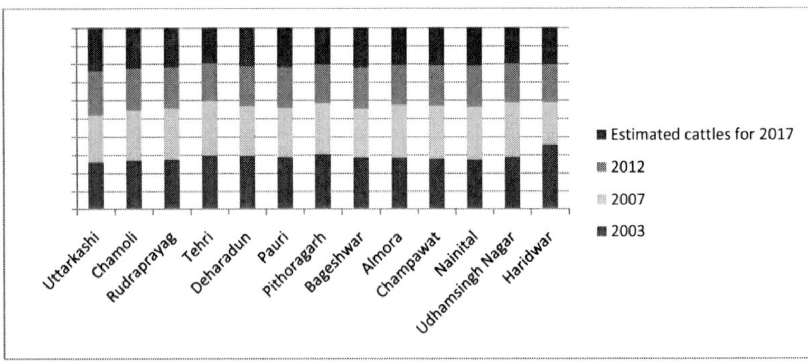

Figure 17.4: Indigenous[7] Cattle in Uttarakhand in the districts.

has been estimated in Tehri district and minimum in Chamoli district. The variation in exotic and wheat cattle in the different years points out a very significant finding. It shows that except Chamoli in all the districts those exotic and wheat cattle has shown a steady rise in numbers.

As far as number of indigenous cattle is concerned, the highest number in year 2003 was reported in Haridwar district which is one of the plain districts of the state. While minimum in the same year was observed to be in Uttarkashi district. In the second census i.e. in year 2007 the maximum of all was accounted in Tehri and Uddhamsingh Nagar where one of the districts i.e. Uddhamsingh Nagar falls in plain and Tehri in hilly area. On the contrary the minimum was in Haridwar district. This reveals the number of indigenous cattle declined in Haridwar district. The data of census 2012 reveals the fact that Uttarkashi district had highest number of indigenous cattle and it was found to be more or less same in other districts as well. However, the estimates have been made for year 2017 which states that maximum number was in Uttarkashi district followed by other district without much fluctuations.

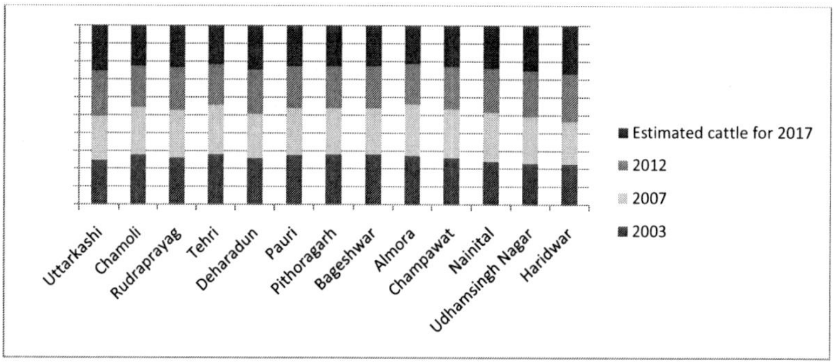

Figure 17.5: Total Cattle in Uttarakhand in the districts.

Figure 17.5 comprehends the total number of cattle in 13 districts of Uttarakhand state over the years. During the first census in year 2003 the maximum number of total cattle of all types was accounted in Chamoli district followed by Bageshwar, Pithoragarh and so on. Similarly in year 2007 the highest number of cattle of all breeds was found in Almora while lowest in Haridwar district in the same year. The analysis for year 2012 reveals that highest number of total cattle were in Dehradun district followed by Uttarkashi and lowest of all in Pithoragarh district. The estimated number of cattles in year 2017 reveals that it would be highest again in Uttarkashi district followed by Haridwar and minimum in Tehri district.

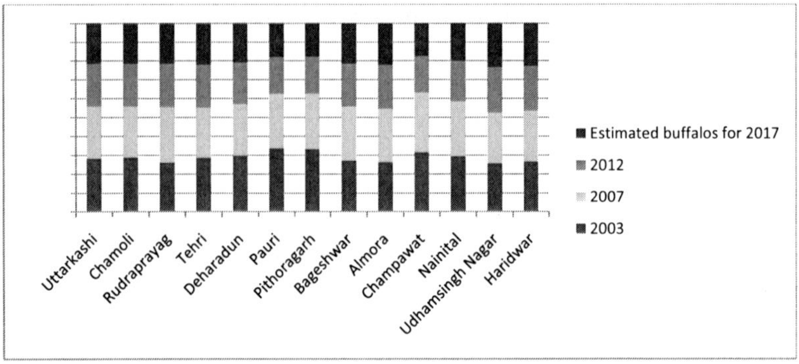

Figure 17.6: Buffaloes in Uttarakhand in the districts.

The number of buffalos in various districts of Uttarakhand state across the years has been illustrated in Figure 17.12. The figure explains that there is huge potential of buffalo rearing in the state. During year 2003 the maximum number of buffalos was calculated in Pauri followed by Pithoragarh and Champawat districts of the state. It is to be noted that all of these districts are located in hilly terrain. While on the other hand the lowest number was in Uddhamsingh Nagar followed by Rudraprayag district respectively. In the next census in year 2007 the higest number was accounted in Champawat and lowest of all in Udhamsingh Nagar and Haridwar district. Both the district with low population is located in plains. Similarly in year 2012 the district with utmost population was Rudraprayag followed by Bageshwar and other in descending order. The estimations made for year 2017 reveals the fact that Udhamsingh Nagar followed by Tehri will constitute highest population and lowest will be in Champawat and Pauri district. Champawat district is one of the district which was having maximum population of buffalos in year 2003 and the number became lowest of all in year 2017.

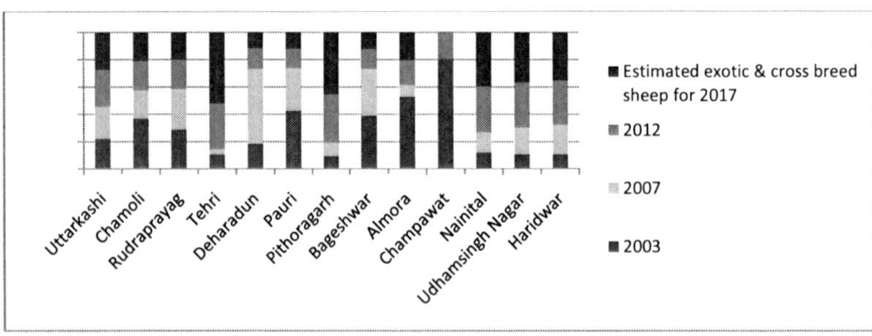

Figure 17.7: Exotic and Cross Breed Sheep in Uttarakhand in the districts.

The population of Exotic and Cross Breed Sheep in various districts of Uttarakhand state represents that there are huge fluctuations in the population over the years across districts. Starting with year 2003, the highest population was calculated in Champawat with massive difference from other districts and lowest in Pithoragarh followed by Haridwar, Uddhamsingh Nagar and Tehri districts of the state respectively. While in year 2007 Dehradun district occupied first position and Tehri fell to last position in terms of number of exotic and cross-breed sheep. In year 2012 the district with highest population was shifted from Dehradun to Pithoragarh and the lowest population was recorded in Pauri and Bageshwar districts respectively. Based on the the available data, the assumptions for year 2017 has been made for all the districts. The estimations reveal that Tehri will have largest number and leaving Dehradun on the lowest side as compared to all distrcts.

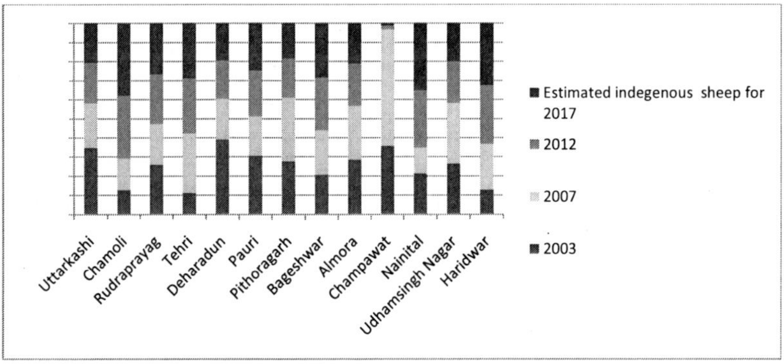

Figure 17.8: Indigenous Sheep in Uttarakhand in the districts.

The Figure 17.8 above elucidates the population of native sheep in 13 districts of the state across various years. During the first census in year 2003 the highest number of indigenous sheep was maximum in Dehradun district followed by Champawat, Uttarkashi and other districts in descending order. However, the minimum of all was in Tehri district. Moreover in year 2007 the district with highest number was Champawat and least population was in Nainital district. The available data for census 2012 discloses the fact that Chamoli district had largest population as compared to other districts and Champawat with minimum population. It is to be noted that in year 2007 Champawat district occupied first position in the number of indigenous sheep across the state and the number became lowest in years 2003 and 2017 respectively. Chamoli district has been estimated to have the maximum population in year 2017 leaving all other districts behind.

Table 17.7: Total Sheep in Districts of Uttarakhand State

S.No	*District*	*2003*	*2007*	*Change in Percentage 2003-07*	*2012*	*Change in Precentage 2007-12*
1	Uttarkashi	101268	89724	-11.40	93883	4.64
2	Chamoli	45651	53536	17.27	102353	91.19
3	Rudraprayag	15636	13199	-15.59	15453	17.08
4	Tihri	14811	24155	63.09	43323	79.35
5	Dehradun	22176	15485	-30.17	11721	-24.31
6	Pauri	33963	23376	-31.17	25523	9.18
7	Pithoragarh	32804	39043	19.02	47336	21.24
8	Bageshwar	19983	20040	0.29	17635	-12.00
9	Almora	4890	4721	-3.46	3732	-20.95
10	Champawat	58	57	-1.72	8	-85.96
11	Nainital	178	132	-25.84	293	121.97
12	Udhamsingh Nagar	2157	2656	23.13	1925	-27.52
13	Haridwar	2270	4287	88.85	5571	29.95
Total		295845	290411	-1.84	368756	26.98

In the above Table 17.7 district-wise number of sheep has been presented. The data reveals that during 2003 to 2007 there has been decline of -1.84 per cent in the number of sheep. While there has been growth of 26.98 per cent in the number during 2007 to 2012. If district-wise analysis of the available data is done, it can be comprehended that during 2003-07 there has been positive change in the number of sheep in Haridwar, Tehri,

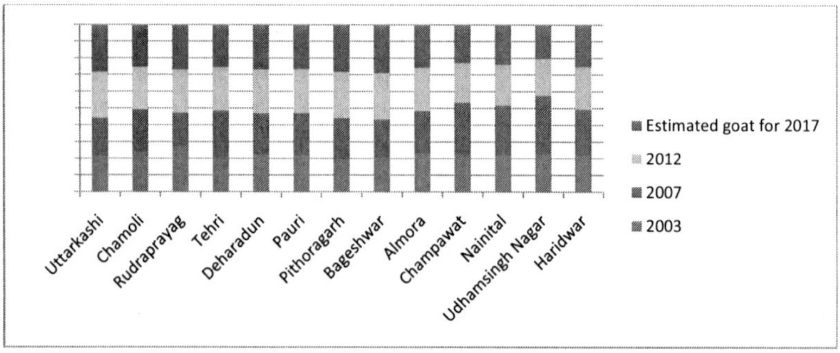

Fig. 17.8a: Total Goats in Uttarakhand in the districts.

Udhamsingh Nagar, Pithoragarh, Chamuli, Bageshwar districts while in Pauri, Dehradun, Nainital, Rudraprayag, Uttarkashi, Champawat and Almora districts the change was reported to be negative. On the other hand during 2007-12 there was an increase in the number of sheep in Nainital, Chamoli, Tehri, Haridwar, Pithoragarh, Rudraprayag, Pauri, Uttarkashi districts and decline in Champawat, Udhamsingh Nagar, Dehradun, Almora, Bageshwar districts of Uttarakhand state.

Rearing of sheep and goat has important role in the state economy. In the hilly regions of the state a section of population is engaged in rearing of sheep and goat. It acts as supplementary and regular economic activities for landless, marginal and small farmers. There has been significant increase in the number of goats in the successive years. The above graph explains the figures of goats district-wise. The data reveals the fact that there has been positive change in the number in 12 districts except Rudraprayag during the year 2003 to 2007. Whereas during year 2007 to 2012 there has been growth in the numbers in Nainital, Chamoli, Tehri, Haridwar, Pithoragarh, Rudraprayag, Pauri and Uttarkashi districts while in remaining five districts i.e. Champawat, Udhamsingh Nagar, Dehradun, Almora, Bageshwar the growth was calculated to be negative. However, for year 2017 there have been positive estimations in the number of goats in the sequence viz; Pithoragarh, Bageshwar, Dehradun, Tehri, Rudraprayag, Chamoli, Uttarkashi, Haridwar, Almora, Champawat, Nainital and Udhamsingh Nagar respectively.

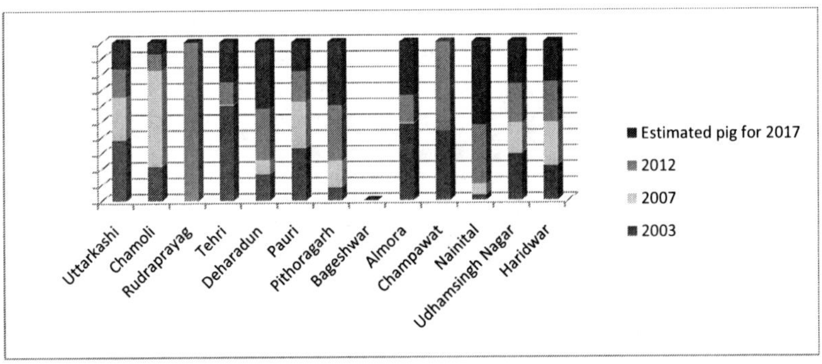

Figure 17.9: Exotic and cross-breed pigs in Uttarakhand in the districts.

Figure 17.9 presents data on population of exotic and cross breed pigs in various districts of newly formed Uttarakhand state over the years. The available statistics reveals that there is no exotic and cross-breed pigs in Bageshwar district of the state. In the year 2003 the highest number of exotic and cross-breed pigs were accounted in Tehri and lowest number in Nainital district. Similarly in year 2007 the maximum population was reported in Chamoli and lowest again in Nainital district. The number increased upmost in Rudraprayag district and Chamoli went to minimum of all in 2012. The estimated population in year 2017 was found to be maximum in Nainital and lowest in Chamoli district.

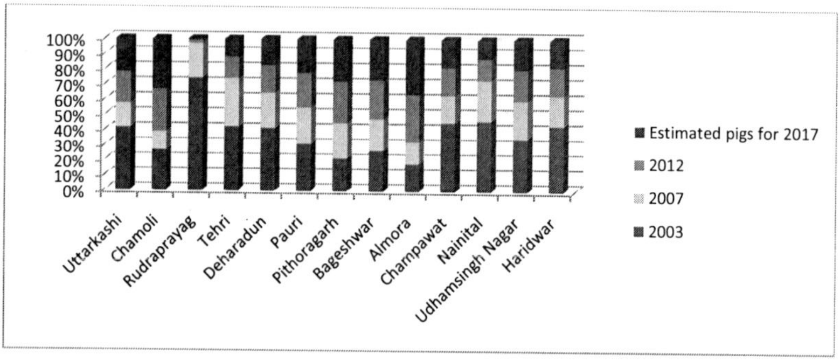

Figure 17.10: Indigenous pigs in Uttarakhand in the districts.

The state of Uttarakhand also consists of indigenous pigs in all the districts. However, in year 2003 the first census of animals after its bifurcation reveals that Rudraprayag district had largest population of native pigs and Almora district had lowest population. Moreover in year 2007 during the second census, the lowest population of indigenous pigs was found in Chamoli district with other districts above it. During 2012 and 2017 the district with maximum population was Almora and lowest estimated number in 2017 was Rudraprayag followed by Nainital district.

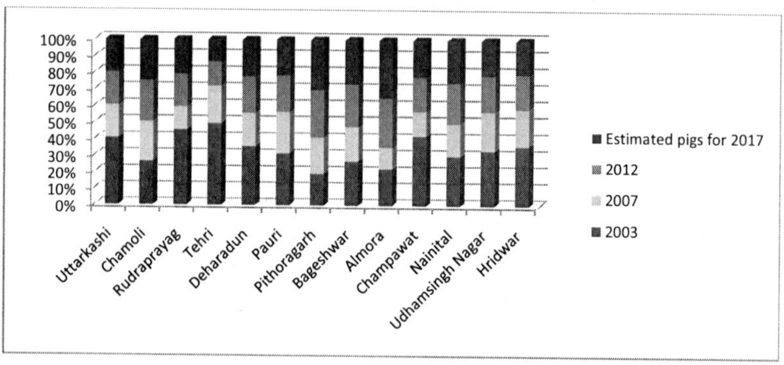

Figure 17.11: Total pigs in Uttarakhand in the districts.

The figure on total pigs states the population of pigs including exotic and indigenous pigs in various districts of Uttarakhand state. The chart presented above clears that Tehri had highest population of pigs in year

2003 while in year 2007 the population was more or less same in all the districts with minor variations. But in year 2012, Pithoragarh and Almora districts had maximum number while Tehri had minimum number of pigs in the state. The calculations have also been made to know the estimated population of pigs in next census which states that it be maximum in Almora and minimum in Tehri district. Nevertheless Tehri district had largest population of pigs as compared to all other districts in year 2003.

Bee Keeping and Sericulture

The state of Uttarakhand is extremely rich in bee forage plants, but proper use of this resource is not being made[8] (Gaur and Nawani, 1989; Gaur and Tiwari, 2000, 2001). The area is rich in plant species like Aesculusindica, Alnusnepalensis, Bassialatifolia, Berberis spp., Bombaxceiba, Citrus spp., Cotoneaster microphyllus, Cornuscapitata, Juglansregia, Lagerstroemia spp., Myricaesculenta, Ougeiniaoojeinensis, Phyllanthusemblica, Prunuscerasoides, Prinsepiautilis, Pyrus spp., Rosa spp., Rubus spp., Rhododendron arboreum, Terminalia spp., Toonahexandra, Zanthoxylumarmatum and numerous Asteracean, Crassulacean, Lamiacean members along with oil, vegetable, fruit and cereal crops which are good sources of nectar and pollen for bees[9]. Especially for the forest fringe areas of the state, bee keeping can act as a major livelihood measure. Bee keeping has the potential to act as a major livelihood option without destroying the habitat. As per National Bee Board figures, bee keeping has a huge potential to generate employment. Statistics shows that 3.75 lakhs man-days are required to maintain, 10,000 Bee colonies in hives. Thus, for employment generation especially in the hilly districts and forest based areas, this can act as a potential livelihood option.

The study by Tiwari *et al*[10] revealed that traditional beekeeping is a live heritage in the area. Besides using traditional bee keeping, there is a need to adopt modern beekeeping practices. Sectors like bee management, better extraction and storage practices with the potential of raising the quality and quantity of honey need to be strengthened. Reuse of honey combs after extraction by minimising the loss of bees labour, will help in rapid multiplication of A. carana colonies. Bee pollination results not only help in yield increase of various oilseeds or legume crops through pollination but also help in improvement in quality of produce.

Uttarakhand has excellent opportunity both for mulberry and tasar silk production as the state is rich in natural vegetation of oak and pine in the Central Himalayas. The agro-climatic conditions are suitable for mulberry silk production in terai and foothills. There is a good potential for rearing tropical tasar in Champawat and Pithoragarh districts. There are 72 mulberry farms in the state covering an area of more than 500 acres which also operate as Chawki Rearing Centres. There are one to four sericulture societies, nine research stations/units of Central Silk Board including two Technology Dissemination Centres and one Silk Seed Production Centre and Regional Sericulture Research Station in the state.[11] This livelihood option needs to be relooked with more species beyond mulberry silkworm and oak tasar silkworm. If the possibility is explored in areas other than Bhimtal, Nainital, Gopeswar where it is produced in commercial scale in other parts of the state especially in the hills, it might reduce distress migration.

Some Policy Asks

From the facts and figures presented above it is understood that there is a huge need of intensifying and creating new opportunities in the field of animal husbandry for increasing employment generation and enterprise development in the state.

Doorstep Animal Breeding Facilities and Production Support Activities to the Livestock Farmers Through its Vast Institutional Network to Improve Animal Productivity and Employment is the need of the hour. Providing Prophylactic and Therapeutic Veterinary Services in the hills can help in encouraging animal husbandry as a livelihood option as the agriculture in the hilly part of the state is continuously being threatened by human animal conflict and hence resulting in forced migration.

Endeavours like E Pashuhaat[12] by the Union Ministry are highly welcome, and such activities are of great need at the district level in the state of Uttarakhand.

Migratory livestock farming is a very common process in the hills of Uttarakhand, where sheep, goat etc are seasonally migrated from one place to another due to adverse climatic condition. Owners of migratory livestock farming to be consulted from time to time by animal husbandry department, for making their livelihood economically sustainable and also taking care of their animals.

Scientific animal management and smooth credit facilities for animal owners through regular awareness programmes in the villages through time based targets has a huge possibility for major changes.

Animal holding by households and providing animals by the government has to be subject to certain criteria and hence licensing for animal keeping needs to be introduced. Otherwise in many cases those animals are not properly reared and are left in merciless conditions.

By means of overgrazing, climate change, natural disasters like floods, forest fires, earthquakes etc, natural pastures have been lost in many parts of the hills of the state. Rejuvination and microirrigation with solar energy can give a boost to such natural resources of the state.

Animal ration card for procuring animal feed from government agency to maintain certain nutritional standards, animal health card to streamline the reporting process regarding animal health and to facilitate easy access to data regarding the animals past health condition can no doubt help in improving health status of the animals.

Non-productive (occasionally disowned by the owner later) animals and aged animals to be given space through separate arrangements in the state.

Poultry industry in the hills by developing block poultry farms with strong market linkages can enhance livelihood options in the hills.

The agro based activity of bee keeping can supplement income generation in rural areas and also improve nutritional intake of rural population. It can be a major self employment programme in the hills especially for forest based population. The huge potential of this agro based activity should be leveraged in the state to help in enhancing self employment options. An estimate[13] shows 3,00,000 mandays are generated for maintaining 10,000 bee colonies. It is also estimated that around 75,000 mandays are created for manufacturing enough appliances for 10,000 bee colonies.The net income from 100 bee colonies varies between ₹ 2,50,000 to ₹ 3.00.000 annually. Hence this huge scope and potential in the state for bee keeping should be boosted at commercial level.

Sericulture in the state needs to expand its base with not only geographical expansion but also species diversification for production of tasar and silk. Uttarakhand can create its own brand of silk and restore livelihood opportunities in the hills.

Realising the potential of the animal husbandry sector to strengthen the rural hill economy of the state where there are lesser options of livelihood, the budgetary allocation in this sector needs to be relooked.

Concluding Remarks

The paper was an effort to know the potential of animal husbandry in the state of Uttarakhand since its inception and to explore the possibilities of economic activity linked to it. It can be concluded on the basis of analysis that animal husbandry is one of the potential areas of economic activities for people in the state especially in the hills. All the districts of the state both hilly and plains has huge potential of animal husbandry with different capacities.The policy should take into consideration the comparative advantage of each district to explore the potential further. Predominantly in the hilly regions of the state marginal and small farmers have sheep and goats as subsidiary activity which can reduce distress migration to a large extent.

Villages in Uttarakhand hills are left mostly in the hands of women with men migrated for employment in other regions. Livestock production activities are therefore are largely in the hands of women. The rapidly increasing demand for livestock products can create opportunities for their empowerment. However, it would require addressing constraints that women face in the hills. Appropriate policy and institutional arrangements such as establishment of "Associations like Mahila Mangal Dal" would facilitate availing credit, insurance and other inputs and marketing services. Training women by government in partnership with NGOs would reduce drudgery to women and improve animal productivity and enhance their economic returns. The constitution of sheep and wool development board by the government is an appreciative action in this direction. Therefore the fact cannot be ignored that the state has already taken some initiatives in this direction but yet a huge possibility lies to explore the sector for employment generation.

References

Gaur, R D et al. Madhu utapadan mein Garhwal ke makrandpadpon ka mahatwa, Vaigyanik, (2000) 80-85 and Determination of floral origin of some Himalayan honeys, J. Ind. Bot. Soc., 80 (2001) 19-23.

Government of India (GOI). 2015. Basic Animal Husbandry Statistics. Ministry of Agriculture. Department of Animal Husbandry, Dairying and Fisheries. New Delhi.

Government of India (GOI). 2014. Basic Animal Husbandry Statistics. Ministry of Agriculture. Department of Animal Husbandry, Dairying and Fisheries. New Delhi.

Islam, M. M et al Scenario of Livestock and Poultry in India And Their Contribution to National Economy, International Journal of Science, Environment and Technology, Vol. 5, No 3, 2016, 956-965.

Sarswat, B.L Beekeeping for Youths: Perspectives and Opportunities, Kurukshetra, Vol. 65, No. 3, 2017.

Samal, P. K., Palni, L. M. S. and Agrawal, D. K., Ecology, ecological poverty and sustainable development in Central Himalaya region of India. International Journal of Sustainable Development and World Ecology, 2003, 10, 157-168.

Tiwari et al. Traditional beekeeping with the Indian honey bee (Apiscerana F.) in District Chamoli, Uttarakhand, India, International Journal of Rural Studies (IJRS) Vol. 20 no. 1 April 2013.

Tuteja, U; Agriculture Profile of Uttrarakhand, Agricultural Economics Research Centre, University of Delhi, Delhi, January 2013.

http://ahd.uk.gov.in/pages/display/125—statistics-and-census

http://www.uldb.org/

http://ahd.uk.gov.in/pages/display/121-projects-and-schemes

http://ahd.uk.gov.in/pages/display/108-institutional-setup

http://www.ilocis.org/documents/chpt70e.htm

Notes

1. BAHS 2015, Government of India.
2. Islam, M. M et al Scenario of Livestock and Poultry in India and Their Contribution To National Economy, International Journal of Science, Environment and Technology, Vol. 5, No. 3, 2016, 956-965.
3. Samal, P. K., Palni, L. M. S. and Agrawal, D. K., Ecology, ecological poverty and sustainable development in Central Himalaya region of India. International Journal of Sustainable Development and World Ecology, 2003, 10, 157-168.
4. BAHS 2014.
5. USWDB.
6. The Exotic and Crossbred Category is one of the high yielding categories of animals in cattle.
7. Animals which belongs to Descript (identified)/Non-descript (non-identified) breeds of indigenous origin are considered as indigenous animals.
8. Gaur, R D et al. *Madhuutapadanmein Garhwalkemakrandpadponk-amahatwa*, Vaigyanik, (2000) 80-85 and Determination of floral origin of some Himalayan honeys, J. Ind. Bot. Soc., 80 (2001) 19-23.
9. Tiwari et al. Traditional beekeeping with the Indian honey bee (Apiscerana F.) in District Chamoli, Uttarakhand, India, International Journal of Rural Studies (IJRS) Vol. 20, No. 1 April 2013.
10. *Ibid.*
11. Tuteja U; Agriculture Profile of Uttarakhand, Agricultural Economics Research Centre, University of Delhi, Delhi, January 2013.
12. www.epashuhaat.gov.in
13. Sarswat, B.L Beekeeping for Youths: Perspectives and Opportunities, Kurukshetra, Vol. 65, No. 3, 2017.

Section VI: Human Development

18

Labour Force Participation, Composition, Skill Requirement and Future Challenges: An Investigation for the Mountain State Uttarakhand

Dhanya M B and Rajlakshmi Datta

Introduction

The agitations for a separate state of Uttarakhand was demanded on the ground that the mountain part of Uttar Pradesh was neglected and was not getting the benefit of policies and programmes implemented in the undivided state. The neglect of the mountain character in development jeopardised its mountain communities- their education and skill development, livelihood etc. With the formation of the new state, livelihood security crisis of the people in the state, especially in the hills was expected to scale down. However, after fifteen years of state formation, governments have changed a number of times with new developmental perspectives as their agenda, yet there is apprehension about how far the people of the mountains of this state have received their share of the pie. Research studies (Kar, 2007, Mamgain, 2007, Mittal *et al.* 2008, Chopra, 2014) show that the concentration of development has been focussed, on the plain districts of the state with a pro-plain approach rather than a pro mountain approach in development though significant area of the state is in the mountains. It is argued that this approach in development has a direct consequence in the labour force participation, composition, skill requirement in the hilly districts and plain districts of the state. If such a pro-plain approach of development continues, the ground on which Uttarakhand was formed as a separate political entity may get diluted.

Labour is the source of all wealth as the political economists assert and it really is the source – next to nature, which supplies it with the material that it converts into wealth. But it is even infinitely more than this (Engels, 1876). India's labour force is growing at a brisk rate despite the fact that more young people are increasingly opting to prolong their years of education. By 2030, India's workforce will be larger than that of China. Most of the new entrants will be in the urban areas. Providing education and skills to the growing young population and meeting their job aspirations pose enormous challenge. As the pace of migration and urbanisation is likely to accelerate in the future, there will be the huge task of planning urban growth and formulating effective labour market policies. Failure to do so can be disastrous (IHD, 2014). In the context of the hill state of Uttarakhand too, this remains a very critical area of concern as migration from the hills are predominant in recent years and the reasons are largely job aspirations and education.

As mountain migration is a highly engendered process, with mostly men leaving and women staying behind, it is of particular importance to better understand the effects of this mostly male outmigration in order to develop (gender) sensitive solutions to improve the development relevance of remittances.[1] Moreover, the changing pattern of growth of the three major sectors over the years after state formation has a direct bearing on the composition, participation and way ahead for the labour force in the state.

The main objective of this paper is to prepare a comprehensive document of composition of the labour force participation after the state was formed till recent years and to understand the nature of skill requirement for the state with some policy initiatives so far. The level parameters of the labour force vary with industry, occupational category, region, demography, gender and standard of living; this is mainly because the activity participation of the people is dynamic and multidimensional. Therefore this paper has considered different aspects of the labour force participation and analyses the parameters like labour force participation rate, worker - non-worker population, percentage change in farmers population among total main workers in the districts of the state, percentage change in agricultural labours in total main workers districtwise, percentage change of population in family business among total workers, structure of rural employment, overall structural shift in employment, growth of employment, proportion of usually working male and female by broad industry division in rural areas of the state. Data from different rounds of NSS, Census, Economic Census, Ministry of Labour and Employment, Government of India have been used for the study along with data from Directorate of Economics and Statistics, Uttarakhand. In order to understand the skill development in the state and future challenges in this area, incremental manpower demand, incremental manpower supply, skill gap, minimally skilled, semi-skilled and skilled labour available district-wise, initiatives by Uttarakhand Skill Development Mission [UKSDM] etc are analysed. The data for skill assessment are mostly taken from National Skill Development Council [NSDC] and Uttarakhand Skill Development Mission (UKSDM). Challenges ahead with some policy asks have been covered in the last section.

Composition of Labour Force Participation

Changes in the composition of district-wise labour force participation by workers and non-workers; farm and nonfarm workers will illustrate how the composition of labour force participation has been changed over a period. In order to analyse the employment and unemployment growth in Uttarakhand over time, the census data have been used as shown in Table 18.1.

Among the total 13 districts, seven districts show continuous fall in the percentage points of main workers except three plain districts Dehradun (2.52 per cent points), US Nagar (3.05 per cent points), and Haridwar (1.76 per cent points) and only two hill districts Pithoragarh (3.25 per cent points) and Chamoli (3.3 per cent points). Nainital (2.08 per cent points) too shows increase in main workers as it is understood that a part of the district lies in the plains. In the case of marginal workers, a marginal fall is observed only in four districts namely, Chamoli, Pithoragarh, Champawat and Haridwar. As far as total workers category is concerned most districts have shown an increase but the increase is not very significant. However, the hill district of Champawat, has shown a downward trend while Bageshwar has shown a sharp increase in total workers. On examining the non-working population it is observed that except Pauri and Almora all the other districts show an increase in the percentage of non-working population over the span of time. All those who had not worked at all during the year before the census year, are recorded as non-workers. Persons engaged in household duties, students, dependents, retired persons,

Table 18.1: District-wise composition of percentage of workers and non-workers

	Percentage of Workers						Percentage of Non-Workers	
	Main workers		Marginal Workers		Total workers			
	2001	2011	2001	2011	2001	2011	2001	2011
Uttarkashi	38.93	35.86	7.14	8.76	46.07	47.65	48.2	58.58
Chamoli	26.16	29.4	18.31	16.81	44.48	46.2	52.51	56.88
Tehri Garhwal	29.96	26.81	13.81	18.5	43.77	45.31	54.94	55.97
Pauri Garhwal	24.62	23.93	14.09	15.96	38.71	39.89	62.16	59.26
Rudraprayag	33.44	32.59	11.42	14.07	44.86	46.65	51.76	56.83
Pithoragarh	26.84	30.09	16.15	14.69	42.98	44.78	54.52	57.75
Almora	32.34	32.3	13.83	15.6	46.17	47.9	54.36	51.24
Bageshwar	34.64	30.04	13.44	17.53	48.08	82.2	50.26	55.13
Champawat	25.01	24.15	15.16	14.2	40.17	38.35	51.74	71.29
Nainital	28.97	31.05	7.6	8.35	36.56	39.41	50.7	75.82
Average Hill districts	30.09	29.62	13.09	14.44	43.18	47.83	53.11	59.87
Dehradun	26.25	28.77	4.99	5.58	31.23	34.34	51.96	86.88
US Nagar	24.29	27.34	7.45	8.53	31.74	35.87	51.15	85.58
Haridwar	24.43	26.19	4.95	4.39	29.39	30.58	54.06	90.68
Average Plain Districts	24.99	27.43	5.79	6.16	30.78	33.59	52.39	87.71

Source: Census 2001 and Census 2011.

rentiers, beggars are some of the categories grouped into non-workers. It is interesting to note that while the change in non-workers category from 2001 to 2011 for average of all hill districts have not been very remarkable, the change is very significant in average of three plain districts (52.39 to 87.71).

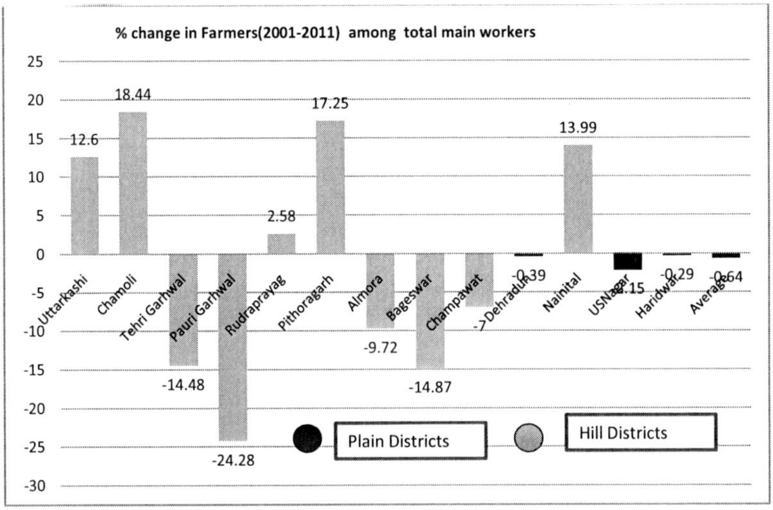

Data Source: Census 2001 and Census 2011 and authors' calculation.

Figure 18.1: Percentage Change in Farmers (2001-2011) population (main workers).

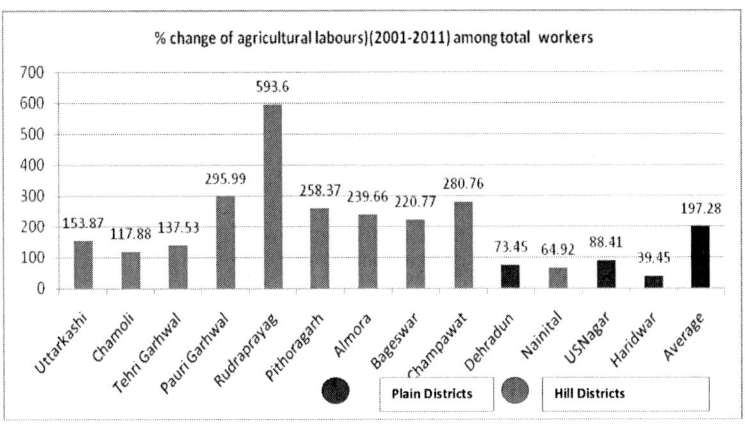

Data Source: Census 2001 and Census 2011 and authors' calculation.

Figure 18.2: Percentage Change in Agricultural Labours (2001-2011) population (main workers).

Figure 18.1 clearly indicates that percentage change in farmers in a decade increased in the districts of Uttarkashi, Chamoli, Rudraprayag, Pithoragarh and Nainital while it has decreased in Tehri Garhwal, Pauri Garhwal, Almora, Bageshwar, Champawat, Dehradun, US Nagar and Haridwar. While a sharp fall is observed in Pauri followed by Bageswar and Tehri and Almora, the rise is significant in Chamoli and Pithoragarh districts. The average change is in the form of a decrease is by 0.64 percentage points. However, no significant dichotomy is observed in hill and plains as far as the percentage change in farmer's population among main workers are concerned.

Figure 18.2 shows the decadal change of agricultural labours among total main workers. While the average decadal percentage change is 197.28, districts of Haridwar, US Nagar, Nainital, Dehradun, Tehri, Chamoli and Uttarkashi show a change below average while rest of the districts show a more than average decadal change. The percentage change in agricultural labours among total main workers is less than average for all the plain districts of the state.

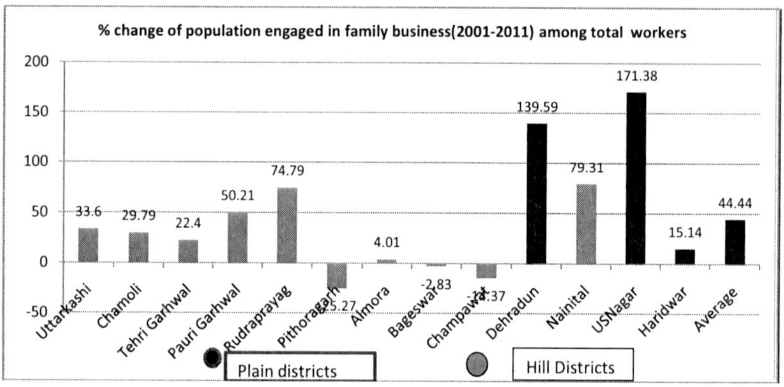

Data Source: Census 2001 and Census 2011 and authors' calculation.

Figure 18.3: Percentage Change in population engaged in family business (2001-2011) population among total main workers.

Decadal change of percentage of population engaged in family business have decreased in Pithoragarh, Bageswar, Champawat while in all other districts it has increased as evident from Figure 18.3. Average change being 44.44, a higher rate of change is observed in the districts of Pauri, Rudraprayag, Dehradun, Nainital and US Nagar. A significant change is observed in two of the three plain districts. Dehradun and US Nagar show more than average change of population engaged in family business among total main workers. However, only the plain district of

Haridwar shows a below average change. A probable explanation for this may be that huge level of in-migration have taken place in Dehradun and US Nagar while Haridwar being a hub of Hindu pilgrimage for a long time have already reached a saturation level and hence the scope of expansion of family business is relatively less.

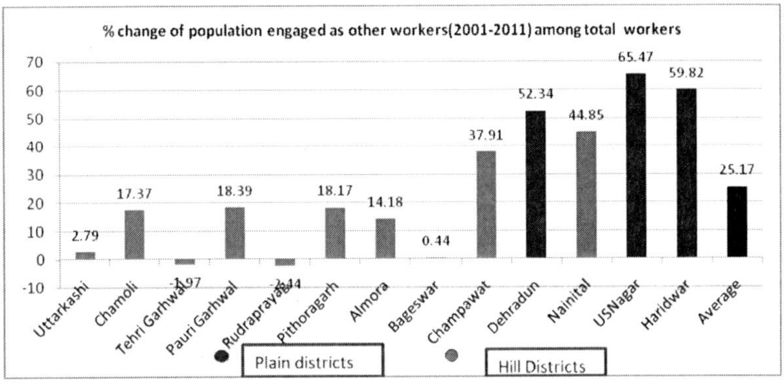

Data Source: Census 2001 and Census 2011 and authors' calculation.

Figure 18.4: Percentage change (2001-2011) in population district-wise engaged as other worker among main workers.

Figure 18.4 shows that the decadal change of percentage of the population engaged as other workers among main workers have decreased only in Tehri and Rudraprayag districts. While the increase has been very insignificant in Uttarkashi and Bageswar, the districts which show more than average change are Haridwar, US Nagar, Nainital, Dehradun and Champawat. It is very interesting to observe that the entire plain districts show more than average change of population engaged as other workers among total workers and is a clear indication of the skewed change pattern of the workforce in hills and plains of the state.

Labour force participation by Sectors

In order to understand the labour force participation by sectors, the percentage contribution of the three sectors in GSDP is considered. It is evident (Figure 18.5a and 18.5b) that primary sector has shown a sharp downfall from 2001-02 to 2013-14 while both secondary and tertiary sectors have shown an increase. Hence, it is apparent that this has a direct bearing on present labour force composition of the state.

Here, an attempt has been made to portray the structural changes in the employment of Uttarakhand as shown in Table 18.2. There has been

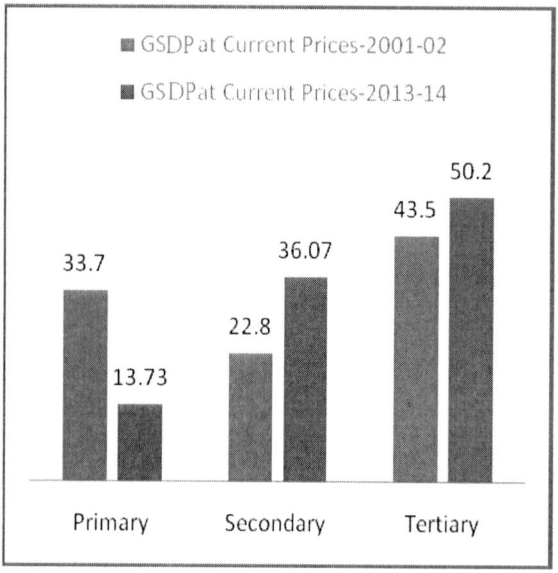

Figure 18.5(a): Percentage contribution of major sectors in GSDP at current price [2001-02 and 2013-14] of Uttarakhand.

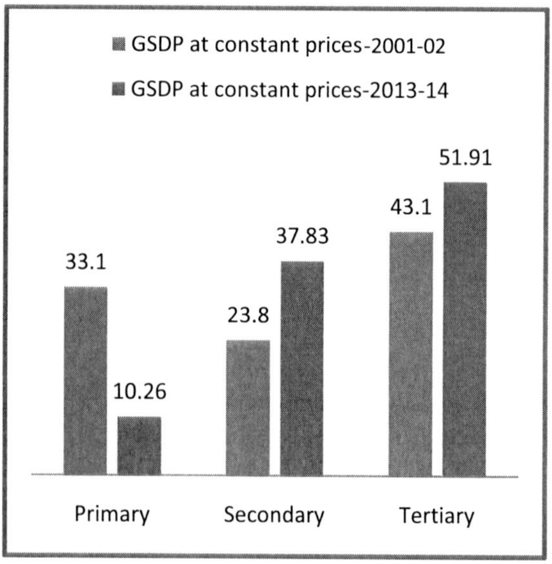

Data Source: DES, Uttarakhand.

Figure 18.5(b): Percentage contribution of major sectors in GSDP at constant price [2001-02 and 2013-14] of Uttarakhand.

a considerable structural shift in employment in Uttarakhand particularly over a period of eight years. The share of agriculture has declined by about three percentage points, from 64.46 per cent in 1999-2000 to 61.69 per cent in 2004-05 which dropped sharply to 42.11 in 2008. The relative share of the secondary sector has increased over time. The share of the construction sector is seen to rise constantly over time. Public administration, education and community services show a persistent increase. The structural shift in employment in the sectors clearly justifies the changes in the contribution of the sectors in GSDP.

Table 18.2: Sector-wise Structural Shifts in Employment in Uttaranchal / Uttarakhand (Per cent)

Industry	*1993-94*	*1999-00*	*2004-05*	*2008**
Agriculture and allied activities	58.56	64.46	61.69	42.11
Mining and quarrying	0.25	0.00	0.00	1.14
Manufacturing	2.12	5.50	5.54	15.90
Electricity, water etc.	0.18	1.06	0.48	0.69
Construction	3.29	8.23	7.16	12.93
Trade, hotel and restaurant	2.83	6.75	10.06	3.32
Transport and Communication	1.26	2.43	3.33	7.44
Finance, insurance and business etc.	0.73	1.70	1.05	0.80
Public administration, education and community services	8.09	9.87	10.66	15.68
Total	**100.00**	**100.00**	**100.00**	**100.00**

Source: Various Round of NSSO and authors' estimates based on Labour Ministry Report

*Industry Section based on NIC 2008 according to Usual Principal Status Approach (ps) for each State.

Labour force participation rate by activity status

Table 18.3 shows that while 46.87 per cent of the urban male were self employed in 2001(NSS 56th round), it rose to 51.1 per cent in 2011(NSS 68th round). However, for the urban female the figure decreased from 55.14 to 53.4 and for total persons, it rose from 48.22 per cent to 51.45 per cent. In regular wage salaried category, the urban male did not show much significant change while the urban female showed an increase from 39.25 per cent to 42.5 per cent. Casual labour percentage for both urban male and urban female dropped.

Table 18.3: Labour force participation Rate by usual activity (Principal Status plus Subsidiary Status)

	Working		
56th round NSS	***Self-employed***	***Regular wage/ Salaried***	***Casual Labour***
Urban Male	46.87	38.18	14.95
Urban Female	55.14	39.25	5.61
Urban Person	48.22	38.51	13.27
68th round NSS	***Self-employed***	***Regular wage/ Salaried***	***Casual Labour***
Urban Male	51.1	39.4	9.5
Urban Female	53.4	42.5	4.1
Urban Person	51.45	39.83	8.71

Source: NSSO rounds 56th and 68th.

The comparison of the structure of rural employment in the state of Uttarakhand and all-India for 2001 and 2011 is shown (Ref Table 18.4) for analysing the composition of labour in the rural Uttarakhand. In comparison to all-India, cultivators share is more in the state compared to all-India average for both 2001 and 2011.

As far as agricultural labours are concerned, the state is far below all-India average in both 2001 and 2011. Household industry workers in Uttarakhand are less compared to all-India average in both 2001 and 2011 but the difference is not much significant. In the case of other workers, Uttarakhand has a higher share compared to all-India average. Moreover, figures show that while cultivators in rural Uttarakhand have decreased from 2011 to 2001, agricultural labours have increased by 4.7 percentage points. This clearly indicates that there has been an increase of people working in others land in this Himalayan State over a decade.

Table 18.4: Structure of Rural Employment in Uttarakhand (Per cent)

	Cultivators		***Agricultural[2] Labours***		***Household Industry Workers***		***Other Workers***	
	2001	*2011*	*2001*	*2011*	*2001*	*2011*	*2001*	*2011*
Uttarakhand	62.3	54.0	9.8	12.9	2.3	2.7	25.7	30.4
India	40.2	33.0	33.0	39.3	3.9	3.4	22.8	24.3

Source: Census 2001 and 2011.

Table 18.5 shows the gender differences in the industries in rural Uttarakhand. While rural male and female participation decreased in agriculture, construction has shown a remarkable climb for male. The male participation in trade, hotel and restaurant has shown some increase but for female participation it is very insignificant. Participation of rural males in manufacturing have increased while that of women have decreased.

Table 18.5: Proportion of usually working male and female (Principal Status (PS) and Subsidiary Status (SS) taken together by Broad Industry Division)

Sectors	*Rural*			
	2004-05		*2009-10*	
	Male	*Female*	*Male*	*Female*
Agriculture	63.3	96.0	50.5	92.9
Manufacturing	5.2	1.3	6.1	0.7
Construction	10.9	0.5	21.9	2.5
Trade, Hotel and Restaurant	8.1	0.0	8.7	0.2
Transport etc	3.7	0.1	3.0	0.0
Other Services	8.4	2.0	8.8	3.7
Mining and Quarring	0.0	0.0	0.4	0.0
Electricity, Water etc	0.4	0.0	0.4	0.0
Total	**100**	**100**	**100**	**100**

Source: NSSO various rounds of employment unemployment survey.

The transportation sector has shown a persistent fall for both male and female. Mining and quarrying, electricity, water etc do not show much significant changes. The percentage of female participation in agriculture in both the years is very high. The most probable reason for this is that the basic socio-cultural framework of Uttarakhand insists women folk to work in the agricultural fields. In rural areas of the state even if the male partner is unemployed, the society would expect the women in the house to work in agriculture, do the household chores and bring fodder from the forests. And this is true for larger part of Himalayan states.

Growth in Employment and Employment situation index

The growth in employment in the districts of Uttarakhand from 2005 to 2015 clearly shows more than average change in all rural, urban and combined areas for the districts of Haridwar, US Nagar and Dehradun which are largely the plain districts. Some districts like Tehri, Rudraprayag,

Pauri have shown more than average growth in the urban category. However, the urban areas in those hill districts are basically of semi-urban nature with a few urban characteristics. The districts which have shown more than average increase in combined category are not very significant except the plain districts. The remarkable growth in plain districts clearly defend the argument of biased development in favour of plain districts.

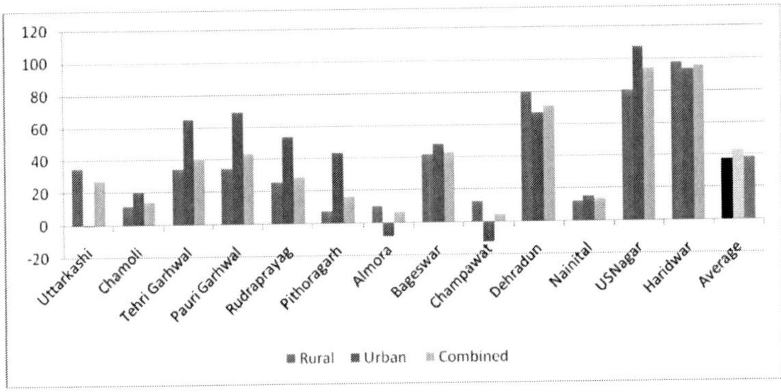

Source: Economic Census.

Figure 18.6: Growth in employment in the districts of Uttarakhand [From 5th to 6th Economic Census, 2005-2015].

Employment situation index is an attempt to prepare a composite index of different indicators of employment by scholars of Institute of Human Development. The indicators used in the construction of the index are percentage employed in regular formal work, work participation rate, percentage employed as casual labour, percentage of self-employed workers below poverty line, average wage of casual labourers, unemployment rate for secondary educated and above, percentage of unionised informal workers (IHD, 2014).

Table 18.6: Employment Situation Index (ESI) - 2011-12

State	ESI
Uttarakhand	12
Himachal Pradesh	1
Jammu and Kashmir	9
Jharkhand	16
Chhattisgarh	17

Source: India Labour and Employment Report 2014.

The figures in Table 18.6 show ranking of some of the states in ESI. If the three neighbouring hill states are compared in their performance, Himachal Pradesh has a rank of one in all-India level, while Jammu and

Kashmir ninth and Uttarakhand ranks twelfth. However, if the peer groups of the three new states formed during 2000 are compared, Uttarakhand has comparatively the best rank among them followed by Jharkhand at 16 and Chattisgarh at 17. This area needs a special attention from the Government in the context of Uttarakhand as a Himalayan State.

Skill Development in the State

Skill development is an important driver to address poverty reduction by improving employability, productivity and helping sustainable enterprise development and inclusive growth. It facilitates a cycle of high productivity, increased employment opportunities, income growth and development.[3] The National Policy on Skill Development aims to train about 104.62 million people afresh and additional 460 million are to be re-skilled, up-skilled and skilled by 2022 (GoI, 2015). In the context of mountain economies like Uttarakhand, the challenge is to meet the skilled manpower requirement of the high growing sectors like the tertiary sector on the one hand through better synergy between employers in the sector and the training providers, increased investment in the training infrastructure and also to ensure that the large informal economy also have skilled manpower wherein the informally trained skills are recognised and helps in a movement towards formal sector.

Improved productivity through skill development must be complemented by economic growth and employment opportunities. Skill development is, collectively, a prerequisite to the Government's pursuit of holistic development of the nation. Only two per cent of the country's work force are skilled labour. This is very low when compared to the other developed nations like Germany and Japan, where more then 80 per cent of the labour are skilled as per a report in the pioneer on June 2016. On the supply side, India is failing to create enough job opportunities and on the demand side, professionals entering the job market are lacking in skill sets. At the national level, to bridge our demographic dividend more substantially and meaningfully, the government launched the "Skill India" campaign along with "Make in India". Hussain (2005) in his paper claims that there is no long-term or short-term advantage for any business with low cost labour. For economic and social development, skill excellence and human resource development is necessary. Skill development is an independent variable and growth and productivity are dependent variables.

Studies (Okada 2012, Hajela 2012, Sinha 2013) show that the predominant reasons for the lack of skills in India are high rate of poverty, nature of dropout rates in school education, ignorance of skill development in school education which focuses primarily on academic training, lack of institutes which imparts skill training, gender discrimination in industries. However, given the nature of topography with the larger portion in the hills, Uttarakhand's skill development is largely constrained by lack of opportunities in the hills. The State of Uttarakhand is a developing State and for its development it requires trained employees in all the sectors. The State has constituted Uttarakhand Skill Development Society to look into this matter and to plan and facilitate skill development in Uttarakhand. With a plan of training 6.5 lakh youth and generating employment opportunities, the society is supposed to look after organised and unorganised sector, public and private sector and the urban and rural sector for providing trainings and finding beneficiaries from these sectors.

The move by the government of Uttarakhand to increase the number of ITIs was aimed at training unemployed youth in the skills of their choice thereby checking the unabated migration of families from rural areas to cities in Uttarakhand. After the skill training from the ITIs, the youth would have to decide on what sort of business they would like to set up on their own, thereby assisting and encouragement in self-employment. Self employment and creating employment opportunities for others as the 'core mantra' has huge scope to bring difference in the state especially the hilly areas.

The government has taken steps in different sectors to develop the skills and to provide training to the people, like the ministry of agriculture has launched schemes like Rastriya Krishi Vikas Yojna, big dairy scheme for dairy entrepreneur, Swaranjayanti Gram Swarojgar Yojana with the main focus on training farmers, encourage dairy entrepreneur and provide them with initial financial assistance at concessional interest rates.

Demand, supply and skill gap in Uttarakhand

The incremental manpower demand by sectors between 2017 and 2022 in Uttarakhand is shown in Figure 18.7. It is obvious that the sector that will have highest demand for labour force is manufacturing followed by tourism, hospitality and trade. The demand for manpower in agriculture will have the third priority followed by education and then building construction and real estate. Very insignificant manpower requirement will be in metal and mining sector, unorganised sector, electricity, water and gas, public administration, postal and communication and banking and financial services.

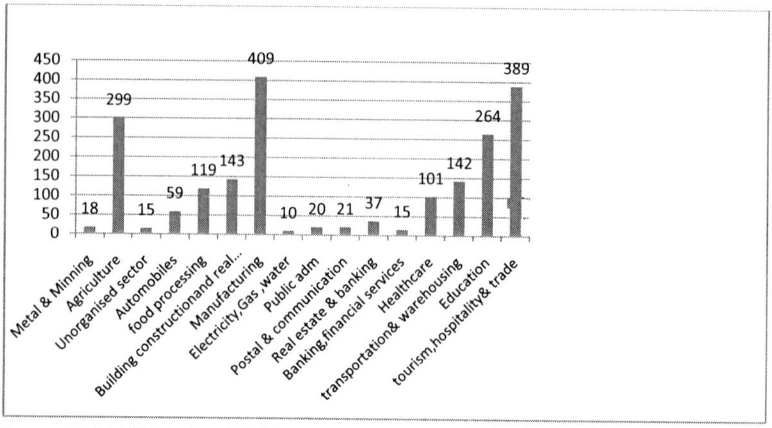

Source: N.S.D.C (National Skill Development Council).

Figure 18.7: Incremental Manpower Demand by sectors (2017-22).

To cater to the incremental demand for manpower, the nature of the supply of manpower that Uttarakhand can offer is shown in Figure 18.8 by depicting both available and projected labour force for the state. It is very clear from the figure that working age population will be higher in the state compared to projected labour force that will be available. Obviously, there will be a scarcity in labour force.

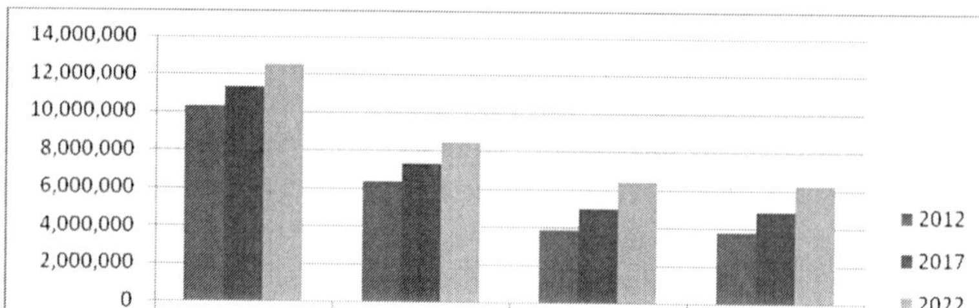

	total population	Working age population	Available labour force	Projected labour force
2012	10,304,421	6,365,110	3,874,703	3,788,457
2017	11,321,334	7,323,918	4,984,229	4,870,409
2022	12,483,222	8,455,056	6,413,144	6,269,986

Source: N.S.D.C (National skill development council).

Figure 18.8: Incremental Manpower Supply (2012-2017-2022).

The following Figure 18.9 shows the gap of human resource requirement and its availability in Uttarakhand. The gap between availability and requirement in the category of skilled and semi-skilled labour, clearly shows that the demand or requirement for skilled or semi-skilled labour is more than the availability. However, the gap is wider in case of minimally skilled labour followed by skilled labour and then semi-skilled labour. In the category of minimally skilled labour, human resource availability will be more than requirement.

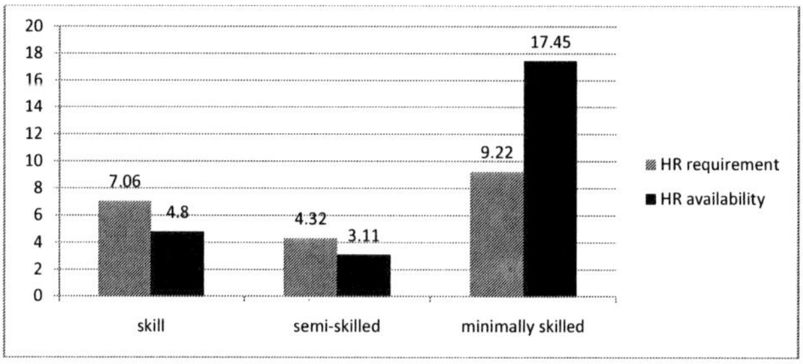

Source: N.S.D.C (National Skill Development Council).

Figure 18.9: Summary of Skill Gap in Uttarakhand (in lakhs).

Composition of skilled/semi/minimally skilled labour in Uttarakhand

Size and the composition of skilled, semi-skilled and minimally skilled labour in Uttarakhand is shown in the following figures in the different districts.

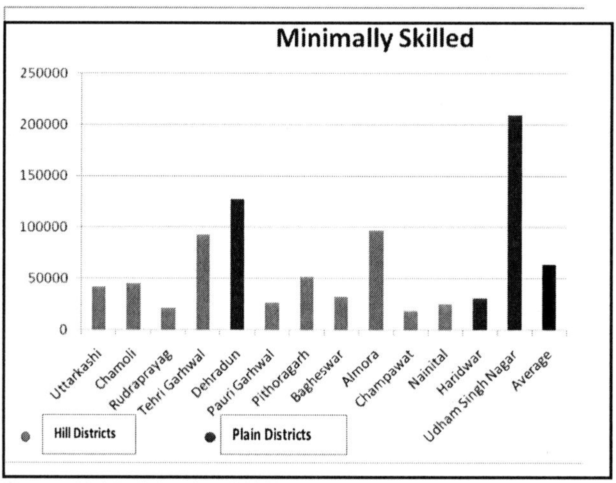

Source: N.S.D.C (National Skill Development Council).

Figure 18.10: District-wise Number of Minimally Skilled labour Available in Uttarakhand 2012.

Figure 18.10 shows the minimally skilled labour available in the districts as on 2012. While the two plain districts Dehradun and US Nagar have high level of minimally skilled labour, the plain district of Haridwar shows less than average availability of minimally skilled labour. Tehri and

Almora are among the hill districts which have more than average minimally skilled labour. The hill districts of Uttarkashi, Chamoli, Rudraprayag, Pauri Garhwal, Pithoragarh, Bageshwar, Champawat and Nainital shows below average minimally skilled labour.

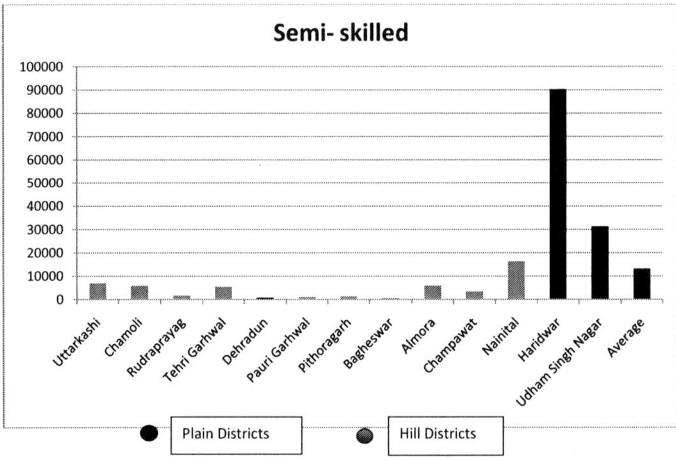

Data Source: N.S.D.C (National Skill Development Council).

Figure 18.11: District-wise Number of Semi-Skilled Labour Available in Uttarakhand.

Figure 18.11 shows the status of semi-skilled labours in the districts of the state. The two plain districts Haridwar and US Nagar show not only more than average semi-skilled labour but also very high level of semi-skilled labour. Among the plain districts, Dehradun shows a very low level of semi-skilled labour. However, except Nainital, among the hill districts all other districts show below average level of semi-skilled labour. It is seen that Dehradun is having high level of minimally skilled labour and comparatively high skilled labour but semi-skilled labour is very negligible. One of the reasons for such a trend may be that being the district with the capital of the state, a good amount of in migration of minimally skilled labour force in search of informal work is there and the figures of skilled labour force represents the labour force in most of the government offices located in Dehradun along with a number of educational institutes both at school level and higher education.

Figure 18.12 shows that the number of skilled labour in the plain district of Haridwar is much higher compared to all other districts while among plain districts, Dehradun shows above average numbers of skilled labour available, US Nagar has very less number of skilled labour, even less than many of the hill districts. Among the hill districts, Nainital shows more than the average number of skilled labour. A probable reason for this may be the growing level of tourism in the district and presence of many government offices including the high court in the district.

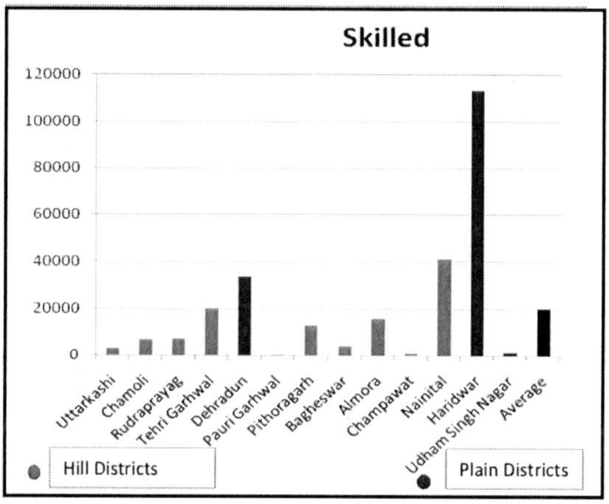

Data Source: N.S.D.C (National Skill Development Council).

Figure 18.12: District-wise Number of Skilled labour Available in Uttarakhand.

It is very interesting to note from Figure 18.10, Figure 18.11 and Figure 18.12 that Haridwar has very low minimally skilled labour compared to its peer group of plain districts but have the highest number of skilled and semi skilled labours in the state. Followed by Haridwar, are Dehradun and Nainital in skilled labour force as evident from Figure 18.12. All other districts of the state have skilled labour either very near to average of the state or below the average level. The figures of Udham Singh Nagar also draws attention because while in skilled category it is far below average, in minimally skilled category it leads among the districts and in semi-skilled category, it is just after Haridwar (the district with the maximum semi-skilled human resource).

To bridge the skill gap and to address the challenges of unemployment and ensuring gainful and sustainable employment to the youth of the state, Uttarakhand Skill Development Mission (UKSDM) was formed in February 2013. Uttarakhand Skill Development Mission (UKSDM) has been providing free skill development training to youth over all 13 districts urban and rural sectors of the state. The main objectives of UKSDM are

- To skill the unskilled youth and upgrade the skills of skilled workers.
- To promote skill development activities to help and monitor skilling programmes implemented by different government agencies.

- To formulate appropriate and innovative strategies to facilitate large scale employment for vulnerable people of the state.
- To improve livelihoods by enhancing earning capacities through skills development.

UKSDM provide operational training to youth in association with 120 partner agencies and contributing in total 39 sectors.[4] In order to understand district-wise performance of UKSDM, District-wise Registered Active Training Providers and Sector-wise training batches etc, the analysis in subsequent section is done.

Skill development training/schemes

District-wise Registered Active Training Providers of UKSDM in Figure 18.13 and Sector-wise Training batches of UKSDM in Figure 18.14 gives an idea of running training centres by sector and also by districts. By considering the registered active training providers, the two plain districts of Dehradun and Haridwar has the maximum share followed by the three hill districts namely, Nainital, Uttarkashi and Pauri Garhwal as shown in Figure 18.13. The plain district of Udham Singh Nagar has low value in registered active training providers while Almora, Bageshwar, Chamoli, Champawat and Rudrapryag are far behind. It is observed in Figure 18.14 that training in information and technology, beauty and wellness, garment, fashion designing, food processing has been prioritised. Some areas that needs to be focussed especially given the nature of livelihood options in the hills are agriculture, floriculture, horticulture and of course tourism and allied sectors. Wellness has to be leveraged as it has a huge potential given the natural resource that the state owns.

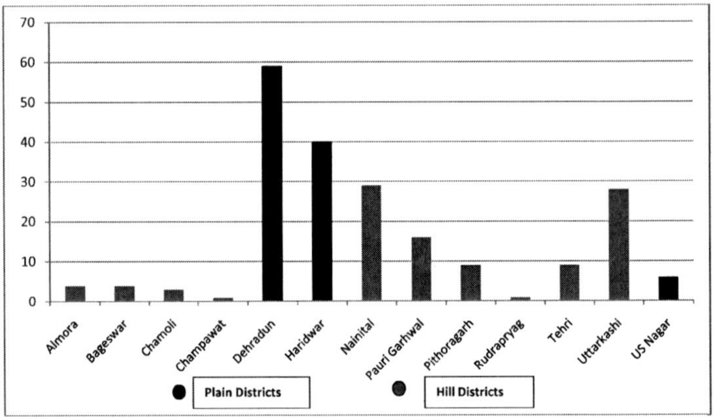

Data Source: http://www.uksdm.org.

Figure 18.13: District-wise Registered Active Training Providers of UKSDM.

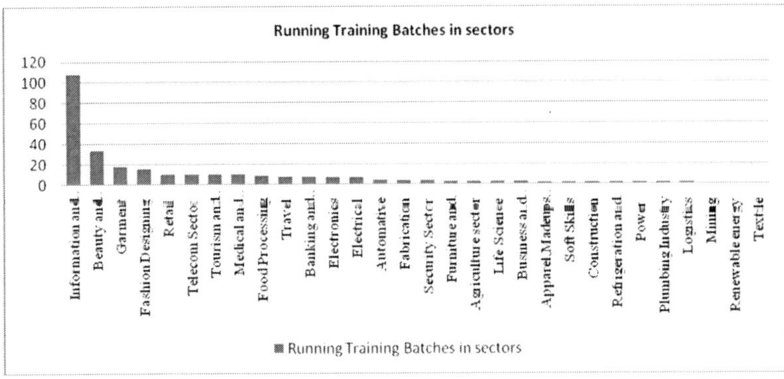

Data Source: http://www.uksdm.org.

Figure 18.14: Sector-wise Training batches of UKSDM.

The Figure 18.15 shows the strength of students in Polytechnic Institutes, Industrial Training Institutes and Teacher Training Institutes for each district of the state indicating the nature of district-wise differences in the level of institutional skill development in the state. While Dehradun, Pauri, Almora, Nainital and Udham Singh Nagar show an increasing trend, it can be mainly attributed to the fact that most of the institutes are concentrated in those districts.

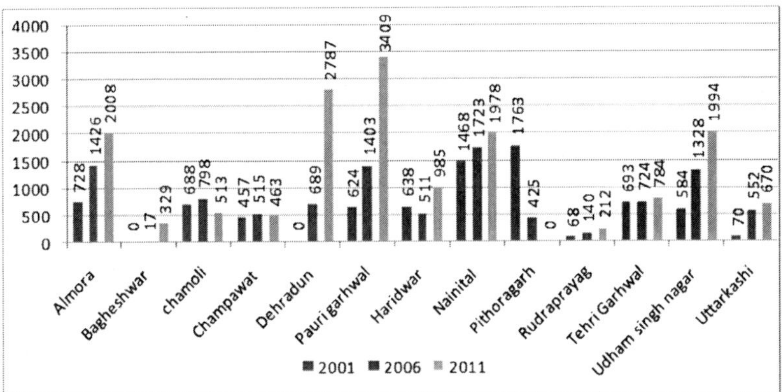

Source: Uttarakhand Statistical Diary 2001, 2006 and 2011.

Figure 18.15: District-wise Comparison of Strength in Polytechnic, ITI and TTI in Uttarakhand (2001-2006-2011)

Figure 18.16 clearly indicates a huge gap in total trainees trained and the trainees who have set up units. Except the figures of 2005-06 and 2006-07, there is a continuous trend in the increasing number of total

Table 18.7: Government Promoted Skill Development Schemes

Ministry/Department	*Schemes/programmes/ institutions*	*Key points*
Ministry of Agriculture	Rastriya Krishi Vikas Yozna, Big dairy scheme for dairy entrepreneur, Swaranjayanti Gram Swarojgar Yojana [SGSY]	Focuses on training farmers, encourages dairy entrepreneur and provides them with initial financial assistance at concessional interest rates.
Ministry of Labour and Employment	Rural employment generation programme Sampoorna Gramin Rojgar Yojana, Training of rural youth for self-employment	Skills are made bankable and individuals are enabled to convert their knowledge and skills, through Testing and Certification, into higher diplomas and degrees and learner can pay the skill provider directly.
Ministry of Textiles	Integrated skill development schemes implemented by Lakshmi cotsyn limited	Caters to skilled manpower needs of Textile and related segments through skill development training programmes. Envisages participation of training institutes associated with the Ministry and the private sector as implementing agencies.
MSME-Development Institute, Haldwani	Skill development initiatives DC-MSME implemented through MSME development institute	Engaged in promotion and development of Micro, Small and Medium Enterprises in the State of Uttarakhand, about 2321 persons were trained in 2011-12.
Ministry of Rural Development	Swaranjaynti Gram Swarojgar yojana [SGSY]	Focus is on SC/ST, women and disabled poor.
Ministry of Tourism Development	Uttarakhand Tourism Development master plan	Provision of a strategic spatial planning framework for improved tourism.

Source: National Skill Development Corporation.

trained trainees. However, the actual effect of such training may be assessed by the number of trainees who have set up units. It is evident that while the number of trainees increased over time, the gap between the numbers trained and number of trainees who have set up units have increased.

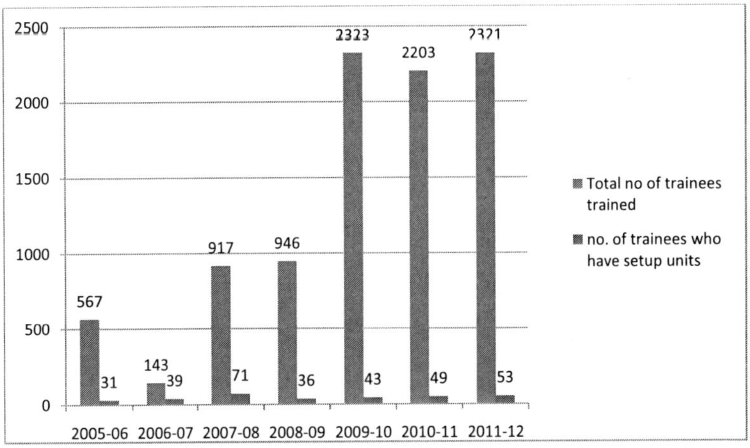

Source: Annual report 2011-12 MSME, Haldwani.

Figure 18.16: Total number of trainees and the number of trainees who have setup units till 2011-12.

There are various government programmes/schemes implemented under the various departments/ ministries for skill development. Tourism being a niche area for Uttarakhand, the core focus is in improved tourism in terms of infrastructure, services etc. MSME Development Institute is focussing and promoting micro, small and medium enterprises given the lesser possibility of large scale or heavy industries due to terrain constraints in larger part of the state. Schemes like SGSY, SGRY in the state is focussing on livelihood enrichment in the state.

Challenges Ahead for Uttarakhand and some Policy asks

The state of Uttarakhand faces multi facet challenges as far as labour force participation, employability, skill availability etc are concerned. The inequalities and disparities that exist in access to employment across regions especially given the nature of hill plain dichotomy remains a huge challenge for the state. This is particularly evident in the distribution of employment in some sectors, which is skewed in favour of plain regions of the state. The unequal access of women to employment, and discrimination in the labour market acts as a major challenge. An important reason for the declining participation of women in work is the lack of appropriate employment opportunities and accessibility and the decline in urban female self employment portrays that simplification for start up is the need of the hour.

Although, overall, open unemployment is low, the problem of youth unemployment, particularly that of educated youth, is gradually becoming a major concern for the state. There has been significant growth in sectors of the economy especially tourism in the tertiary sector. The spillover effect of this sector needs to be properly utilised to face the challenges of unemployment and underemployment in the state. Uttarakhand being a landlocked state faces challenges of high logistic costs which discourages entrepreneurs for a new venture in hilly areas which can enhance some livelihood opportunities. However, with the laying of the foundation stone of all weather road connecting the 'chardham', and some work in progress there is an expectation of some spillover effect in the years to come once such infrastructures are developed.

Since the Himalayan State has huge scope for developing tourism and tourism related skills, a tourism training and development institute is in huge need which will impart training separately for high valued tourists and other category tourists as largely the needs are different. The percentage of high valued tourists especially foreign tourists visiting this state being poor needs special focus from the Government which can generate a huge amount of revenue for the state. Moreover tourism related services like tourist website development for each and every tourist spot with updated information and 24×7 services are in need. Other tourism related skill development endeavours like spa management, tourist guide training, *unani* and herbal treatment training, adventure tourism guide, country cuisine training, foreign language training, Uttarakhand heritage and cultural tourism training, spiritual tourism guide etc has huge scope to generate employment in the state and in return attract more tourists to the state for a better and comfortable stay. The youth of the region needs rigorous formal training to compete the other tourist destinations of the country. Skill development should not be theoretical learning inside the four walls only but rather field based learning to cater the world market. Internship with foreign tourists and domestic tourists can make difference before they enter the market. The state which has one of the country's best ski resorts is still unable to attract large number of tourists and hence there is a huge need to be streamlined in this direction. The world market needs to know 'what the state has and what are its comparative advantages' and that needs huge focus on Information Technology development and skill development in the area.

As far as agriculture and horticulture are concerned training for diversification of crops, multiple cropping, soil testing, biological farming, food processing, food preservation, organic farming, aromatic plants farming etc needs to be focused. However these endeavours can become successful only when small scale enterprises are developed in difficult accessible terrains of the state for value addition and storage of such products so that they can be marketed later as per the weather conditions which is largely a natural phenomenon. For middle hills and plains, marketing linkages needs to be leveraged.

In skill development, Pradhan Mantri Kaushal Yojna and the state government's own policy Din Dayal Upadhay Gram Vikas Yojna are on move but there is a great need to enhance accountability and transparency in such schemes as far as the progress in the state is concerned. The skewed livelihood option, employment, skill availability in favour of the plain districts is very clear. The road ahead is to explore the potential areas of livelihood in each district and within the different areas of the district through 'skill mapping' and move accordingly. If such a strategy is not taken with a clear vision, the very purpose of curving out the state from Uttar Pradesh will get diluted and the hallucination of double digit growth for the state will just be a jugglery of numbers. A medium- to long-term employment strategy should be envisaged for the state to deal with the challenges in this area.

References

Bhattacharya, B B and S Sakthivel (2004), 'Regional Growth and Disparity in India: Comparison of Pre- and Post-Reform Decades', Economic and Political Weekly, March 6, pp. 1071-77.

Census of India (1991), Social and Cultural Tables, Series 1-India, Part IVA- C Series, Registrar General and Census Commissioner, India, New Delhi.

Census of India (2001), Office of the Registrar General, Government of India, New Delhi.

Census of India (2011), Office of the Registrar General, Government of India, New Delhi.

Chopra, R. (2014), Uttarakhand: Development and Ecological Sustainability, OXFAM, India.

Engels Frederick (1876), "Ape to Man (The Part played by Labour in the Transition from Ape to Man)", Progress Publishers, Moscow, can be accessed at https://www.marxists.org/archive/marx/works/1876/part-played-labour

Gaur, Achal Kumar, (2010), "Regional Disparities in Economic Growth: A Case Study of Indian States", The International Association for Research in Income and Wealth, St. Gallen, Switzerland.

GoI (2013), "Annual Report 2012-13", Ministry of Micro, Small and Medium Enterprises, Accessed on 31 Mar. 2016, http://dcmsme.gov.in/

GoI (2015), National Policy for Skill Development and Entrepreneurship- 2015, Ministry of Skill Development and Entrepreneurship, Government of India, New Delhi.

Hamid, Abdul, and J. Hanns PIchler (2009), "Human Capital Spillovers, Productivity and Growth," The Pakistan Development Review, Pakistan Institute of Development Economics, Islamabad, pp. 125-140.

Hussain, Mian Tajammal (2005), The Pakistan Development Review, Vol. 44, No. 4, Papers and Proceedings part ii, Twenty-first Annual General Meeting and Conference of the Pakistan Society of Development Economists Islamabad, December 19-21, pp. 1153-1155, Pakistan Institute of Development Economics, Islamabad.

Hajela, R (2012) Shortage of Skilled workers: A Paradox of the Indian Economy SKOPE Research Paper No. 111, November, University of Oxford.

IHD (2014), India Labour and Employment Report 2014- Workers in the era of Globalisation, Institute of Human Development, New Delhi.

Kar, Sabyasachi (2007), Inclusive Growth in Hilly Regions: Priorities for the Uttarakhand Economy, E/281/2007, IEG Working Paper, New Delhi.

Mamgain, R. P (2007), "Growth, Poverty and Employment in Uttarakhand" Institute For Human Development, New Delhi.

Mathur, Ashok (1983), "Regional Development and Income Disparities in India: A Sectorial Analysis", Economic Development and Cultural Charge.

Mathur, Ashok (1992), "Regional Economic Change and Development Policy in India", Indian Journal of Applied Economics.

Mittal *et al.* (2008), Development Strategy for the Hill Districts of Uttarakhand, ICRIER.

NSSO (2001), Unorganised Manufacturing sector in India 2000-2001: Key results, NSS 56th Round, Ministry of Statistics and Programme Implementation, Government of India, New Delhi.

NSSO (2012), Employment Unemployment Situation in India 2011-12, NSS 68th Round, Ministry of Statistics and Programme Implementation, Government of India, New Delhi.

National Skill Development Corporation, Accessed at http://www.nsdcindia.org/

OKada A (2012) Skills Development for Youth in India: Challenges and Opportunities, CICE Hiroshima University, Journal of International Cooperation in Education, Vol. 15, No. 2 (2012) pp. 169-193.

Report of the Task Force on Improving Employment Data available at http://niti.gov.in/

Sinha P (2013) EFQM, Friedrich - Ebert - Stiftung Department for Global Policy and Development Hirashimastr ISBN 978-3-86498-481-5

Notes and References

1. Labour Migration and Remittances in the Mountains of Pakistan Kiran Hunzai, ICIMOD http://lib.icimod.org/record/26942/files/attachment_748.pdf
2. Note: A person is classified as cultivator if he or she is engaged in cultivation of land owned or held from government or held from private persons or institutions for payment in money, kind or share. Agricultural labour is a person who works on another person's land for wages in money or kind or share is regarded as an agricultural labour. Household industry worker is defined as an industry conducted by one or more members of the household at home or within the village in rural areas and only within the precincts of the house where the household lives in urban areas. The larger proportion of workers in the household industry consists of members of the household. Other Worker- are all workers i.e. those who have been engaged in some economic activity during the last one year, but are not cultivators or agricultural labours or in household industry, are other workers. The type of workers that come under this category include all government servants, municipal employees, teachers, factory workers, plantation workers, those engaged in trade, commerce, business, transport, banking, mining, construction, political or social work, priests, entertainment artists etc.
3. Sanghi et al available at http://niti.gov.in/
4. http://www.uksdm.org

19

Child Health and Maternal Health in Uttarakhand: Where does this Hill State Stand after 15 Years?

Rita Ray

Introduction

Health plays a significant role in the growth of a country (Barro, 1996). Childhood malnutrition and poor health are connected and have an adverse impact on intellectual development (Brown and Pollitt, 1996), educational attainment (Moock and Leslie, 1986), educational performance (Jamison, 1986), productivity and earning (Wolfe and Behrman, 1982; Horton and Steckel, 2013). Child and maternal health are closely related (Filippi, *et al.*, 2006), and both have a direct impact on educational outcomes, productivity and future earnings (Figure 19.1). The future growth of Uttarakhand depends on its current status of child and maternal health. Therefore, to evaluate this state's current economic status and to develop effective future policies to maintain sustainable growth, it is important to examine Uttarakhand's successes and failures with respect to child and maternal health.

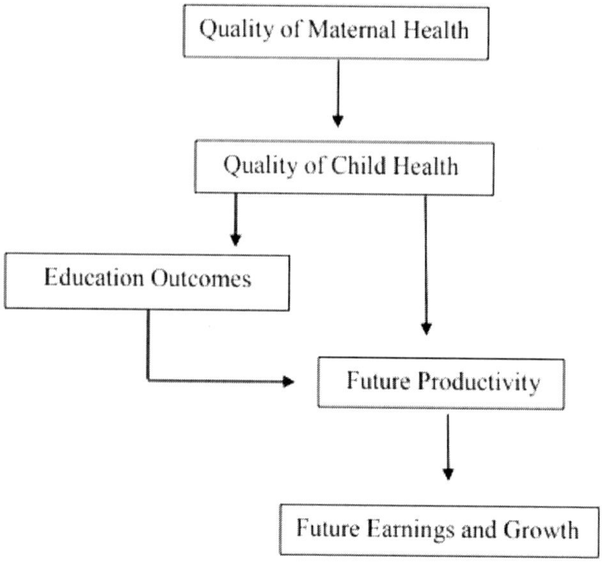

Figure 19.1: Connection between Maternal Health and Child Health and Future Earnings and Growth

Reducing infant mortality from 43 per 1000 live births in 2011 to 30 in 2012 and achieving full immunisation in 2012 were two main child health goals[1] of Uttarakhand's government. Unfortunately, Uttarakhand had not achieved either of these goals by 2014-15. According to the National Family Health Survey, in 2014-15, the infant mortality remained at forty, and only 57.7 per cent of children between ages 12 and 23 months had been fully immunised. Despite the fact that Uttarakhand's per capita income is two-and-a-half times that of Bangladesh, its child health outcomes with respect to infant mortality and immunisation are lower. Additionally, the nutritional status of its children is not very promising. Only 8.5 per cent of children between ages 12 and 23 months had an adequate diet in 2014-15. Although this state is doing slightly better than Bangladesh in terms of the percentage of children who are underweight and the percentage who have stunted growth, the percentage of its children who experience wasting is higher.

Uttarakhand's achievements in child health outcomes is mixed. This state is steadily progressing in terms of infant and child mortality, but in terms of immunisation and nutritional status, it is progressing on some indicators but deteriorating on others. Infant mortality and mortality under age five have decreased by almost five per cent and sixteen per cent, respectively, between 2005-06 and 2014-15. Immunisation of children for BCG and measles has increased by nine percentage points and for DPT to almost 13 percentage points between 2005-06 and 2014-15. However, the incidence of full vaccination and three doses of polio vaccine has decreased by 2.3 percentage points and 12.3 percentage points, respectively, in the same period. The prevalence of stunting and being underweight has decreased approximately 11 percentage points, but wasting and severe wasting in children under age five have increased almost 1 and 4 percentage points, respectively.

The government of Uttarakhand is trying to reduce the geographical variation in child health outcomes. However, the dispersion of child health outcomes across districts and among the rural and total populations within a district ranges from 4 per cent to 70 per cent. The highest and lowest dispersions on child immunisation are observed for full immunisation of children in the rural population and BCG vaccination for both the total and rural population, respectively. For full immunisation, the variation is 14 per cent, with the highest being 71 per cent in Rudraprayag and the lowest being 44 per cent in Udham Singh Nagar. For BCG vaccination, both the highest and the lowest percentages of children are much higher than those for full vaccination: Champawat has the highest percentage, at almost 99, whereas Haridwar has the lowest, at 88 per cent. Among thirteen districts, only two (Bageswar and Haridwar) have less than 90 per cent of their children with BCG vaccination, and the dispersion is also the lowest. The percentage of children with severe wasting increased between the third and fourth NFHS surveys. Additionally, the dispersion is also the highest - 69 per cent for the children who with severe wasting. Udham Singh Nagar has the lowest percentage of children who are severely wasted - three-and-a-half per cent - while Tehri Garwal has the highest - 28 per cent.

With respect to maternal health, Uttarakhand wants to improve prenatal and postnatal visits for pregnant women. The outcomes are mixed: the state is improving some aspects but failing to improve others. The percentage of antenatal checkups in the first trimester and consumption of iron folic acid increased from 43.3 per cent to 53.5 per cent and from 23.8 per cent to 24.9 per cent respectively, between NFHS surveys 3 and 4. However, the state's record has deteriorated with respect to the percentage of pregnant women who have at least four antenatal visits. This percentage decreased from 34.9 to 30.9 between NFHS surveys 3 and 4.

The state is showing progress by increasing the percentage of institutional births, births assisted by healthcare professionals and postnatal checkups by health professionals. Institutional births more than doubled, and births assisted by healthcare professionals and postnatal checkups by health professionals almost doubled between 2005-06 and 2014-15.

Like child health, outcomes of maternal health are widely dispersed among the districts of Uttarakhand. The highest and the lowest dispersions are observed for full antenatal care and neonatal tetanus. Dehradun has the best outcomes with respect to antenatal checkups in the first trimester, at least four antenatal checkups, neonatal tetanus, institutional births, births assisted by health professionals, and mothers receiving postnatal care by health professionals for its total and rural populations. Nainital has the highest percentage of pregnant women who take iron folic acid for both the total and rural populations. Even though Nainital and Dehradun have the best outcomes with respect to full antenatal care for the total and rural populations, respectively, more than 75 per cent of women donot receive full antenatal care in these districts. Antenatal checkups in the first trimester are lowest in Bageswar for the total population and in Haridwar for the rural population. Rudraprayag has the lowest per cent of the women who have at least four antenatal checkups for both the total and rural populations. Udham Singh Nagar and Haridwar have the poorest outcomes with respect to neonatal tetanus and consumption of iron folic acid for the total and rural populations, respectively. Rudraprayag has the lowest per cent of the women who receive full antenatal care for both the total and rural populations; almost 90 per cent of women do not receive full antenatal care in Rudraprayag. Chamoli has the lowest percentage of institutional births for the rural and total populations. Chamoli and Haridwar have the lowest percentage of births assisted by healthcare professionals for the total and rural populations, respectively. Bageswar's performance is the worst with respect to postnatal checkups by a health professional for both the total and rural populations.

To assess the current status of child health in Uttarakhand, this paper uses infant and child mortality rates; immunisation; and childhood diseases, treatments and nutritional status. For maternal health, the paper uses visits for antenatal care, use of iron folic acid by pregnant women, protection by neonatal tetanus, institutional delivery, delivery by health professionals, and postnatal checkups by health professionals. Additionally, this paper investigates the variation in child and maternal health conditions and outcomes among the 13 districts of Uttarakhand. To explain child and maternal health status and outcomes in Uttarakhand and its districts, this paper uses data from the National Family Health Surveys 3 and 4. Additionally, the paper uses data from the Census of India, the World Bank and the Bangladesh Demographic and Health Survey.

The paper is organised as follows: Sections 2 and 4 describe the current status and the change in the status of child and maternal health in Uttarakhand between 2005-06 and 2014-15. Sections 3 and 5 discuss the dispersion of child and maternal health statuses among the 13 districts of Uttarakhand in 2014-15. Section 6 describes the association between education and child and maternal health outcomes. That section also discusses the link between water and sanitation infrastructure and child health outcomes. Section 7 provides future policy suggestions.

2. Current Status and Change in Status of Child Health in Uttarakhand

This paper utilises three main variables to explain the current status and change in status of child health in Uttarakhand: (1) infant and child mortality rate; (2) immunisation outcomes; and (3) childhood diseases, treatment and nutritional status. Data from the National Family Health Survey 3 and 4, the World Bank and the Bangladesh Demographic and Health Survey are used to explain the achievements and failures of Uttarakhand in child health.

Infant and Under-five Mortality Rate

Table 19.1: Infant and Under-five Mortality Rate in Uttarakhand, India and Bangladesh

	Infant mortality rate	*Under-five mortality rate*
Uttarakhand: NFHS – 3, 2005 – 2006	42	56
Uttarakhand: NFHS – 4, 2014 – 2015	40	47
India: World Bank, 2005	56	75
India: World Bank, 2014	39	50
Bangladesh: BDHS, 2007	52	65
Bangladesh: BDHS, 2014	38	46

Data Sources: National Family Health Survey: India, World Bank Databank and Demographic Health Survey: Bangladesh.

The infant mortality rate decreased from 42 to 40 per 1000 live births between 2005-06 and 2014-15 in Uttarakhand, a decrease of almost five per cent. While this is, indeed, progress, it is much lower[2] than in India as a whole. In the same period, India reduced its infant mortality by

29 per cent. Infant mortality in Bangladesh is not only five-per cent lower than in Uttarakhand, but it also decreased by 27 per cent within seven years. The under-five mortality rate in Uttarakhand is higher than the world average of 44 deaths per 1000 live births. Although the progress in this area has been much higher than that for infant mortality, the under-five mortality rate is still much worse (47) than the infant mortality rate (40). Uttarakhand's status on the under-five mortality rate is slightly better than India's, but slightly worse than Bangladesh's.

In summary, Uttarakhand is making progress with respect to infant mortality and under-five mortality. However, the progress on the infant mortality rate is not on par with that of Bangladesh and India as a whole. For under-five mortality, this progress is lower than in Bangladesh.

Child Immunisation

In India, immunisation is free and publicly provided, but, still, not every child is immunised. The most alarming fact for Uttarakhand is that the percentage of children who are fully immunised and who have received three doses of polio vaccine has decreased by 2.3 and 12.3 percentage points, respectively, between 2005-06 and 2014-15. Only 57.7 per cent and 68 per cent of children between ages 12 and 23 months received full vaccination and three doses of polio vaccine, respectively, in 2014-15. Uttarakhand has made improvements regarding BCG, DPT, the measles vaccination and providing Vitamin A doses. The largest improvement has occurred in providing Vitamin A - an increase of 24.1 percentage points. Data for India as a whole are not available from NFHS 4. Therefore, the paper uses World Bank data. Unlike Uttarakhand, India is showing improvement in every category of immunisation. In India, the greatest progress is observed in Hepatitis B vaccinations, and the least progress is observed in BCG vaccinations. Whereas the percentage of children who have received the polio vaccine has decreased in Uttarakhand, it has increased by 16.5 percentage points in India. In summary, Uttarakhand's achievement in terms of immunisation outcomes is somewhat mixed. This state is progressing in terms of BCG, DPT, measles and Hepatitis B vaccinations and in providing Vitamin A, but in terms of the three doses of polio vaccine and full immunisation, Uttarakhand is failing.

2.3 Childhood Diseases, Treatments and Nutritional Status

The prevalence of diarrhea and receipt of oral rehydration solutions (ORS) have been used as proxies for childhood diseases and treatments,

Table 19.2: Child Immunisation in Uttarakhand, India and Bangladesh

Indicators	***Children age 12-23 months fully immunised (BCG, measles, and 3 doses each of polio and DPT) (per cent)***	***Children age 12-23 months who have received BCG (per cent)***	***Children age 12-23 months who have received 3 doses of polio vaccine (per cent)***	***Children age 12-23 months who have received 3 doses of DPT vaccine (per cent)***	***Children age 12-23 months who have received measles vaccine (per cent)***	***Children age 12-23 months who have received 3 doses of Hepatitis B vaccine (per cent)***	***Children age 9-59 months who received a vitamin A dose in last 6 months (per cent)***
Uttarakhand: NFHS – 3, 2005 – 2006	60	83.5	80.3	67.1	71.6	–	12.8
Uttarakhand: NFHS – 4, 2014 – 2015	57.7	92.9	68	80	80.6	59.4	36.9
India: World Bank, 2005	–	86	65.5	65	68.5	7	–
India: World Bank, 2014	–	91	82	83	83	70	–
Bangladesh: BDHS, 2007	81.9	96.8	90.8	91.1	83.1	82.7	88.3
Bangladesh: BDHS, 2014	83.8	97.9	91.4	–	86.1	–	62.1

Data Sources: National Family Health Survey: India, World Bank Databank and Demographic Health Survey: Bangladesh.

respectively. Nutritional status has been measured by five variables: adequate diet, stunting, wasting, severe wasting and underweight. The reported prevalence of diarrhea in children and the percentage of children receiving ORS packets increased by 4.2 percentage points and 23 percentage points, respectively, between 2005-06 and 2014-15. It is impossible to conclude whether this increase is due to the increase in the percentage of children with diarrhea or to the increase in reported cases of diarrhea. However, it is certain that Uttarakhand is making progress by providing ORS packets to children suffering from diarrhea and that this state's achievement is better than that of Bangladesh. Although Uttarakhand is doing better regarding childhood treatment, its achievement is disappointing on several measures of child nutrition status over the years. Only 8.5 per cent of children receive an adequate diet in Uttarakhand, whereas in Bangladesh, the number is 23 per cent, even though Bangladesh's per capita income is two-and-a-half times lower than Uttarakhand's.

One major concern about childhood nutrition in Uttarakhand is that the percentages of children who are wasted and severely wasted have increased by 0.7 percentage point and 3.7 percentage points, respectively. Additionally, the percentage of children who suffered wasting in this state was three percentage points higher than in Bangladesh in 2014. Uttarakhand is improving with respect to the percentage of children whose growth is stunted and who are underweight. These percentages decreased by 10.9 and 11.4 percentage points, respectively, between NFHS 3 and 4, and they are both lower compared to those in Bangladesh in 2014.

In summary, Uttarakhand is making progress with children who are underweight and have stunted growth, and providing ORS packets has improved the health of children with diarrhea, but the state has failed to improve the percentage of children who are wasted and severely wasted.

3. Child Health Status in the Districts of Uttarakhand

Child health status varies widely across the districts of Uttarakhand. This section uses NFHS 4 data to examine the current status and dispersion of child health outcomes among the districts. Child immunisation, childhood diseases and treatments, and nutritional status have been used to describe the status of and variation in child health.

Table 19.3: Childhood Diseases, Treatments and Nutritional Status in Uttarakhand and Bangladesh

Indicators	*Children under 5 with prevalence of diarrhea (reported) in the last 2 weeks preceding the survey (per cent)*	*Children under 5 with diarrhea in the last 2 weeks who received oral rehydration salts (ORS) (per cent)*	*Total children age 6-23 months receiving an adequate diet (per cent)*	*Children under 5 years who are stunted (height-for-age) (per cent)*	*Children under 5 years who are wasted (weight-for-height) (per cent)*	*Children under 5 years who are severely wasted (weight-for-height) (per cent)*	*Children under 5 years who are underweight (weight-for-age) (per cent)*	*Children age 6-59 months who are anemic (<11.0 g/dl) (per cent)*
Uttarakhand: NFHS – 3, 2005 – 2006	12.8	33.1	–	44.4	18.8	5.3	38	60.7
Uttarakhand: NFHS – 4, 2014 – 2015	17	56.1	8.5	33.5	19.5	9	26.6	59.8
Bangladesh: BDHS, 2014	9.8	62.4	42	43	17	–	41	
Bangladesh: BDHS, 2014	5.7	45.8	23	36	14	–	33	

Data Sources: National Family Health Survey: India, and Demographic Health Survey: Bangladesh.

Child Immunisation

To understand the immunisation outcomes, data on full immunisation, BCG, DPT, measles, Hepatitis B, three doses of polio vaccine and Vitamin A doses have been used for the total number of children and rural children.

The highest and the lowest dispersions of child immunisation outcomes are observed for receiving Vitamin A and BCG vaccination, respectively. The second-highest dispersion is observed for full immunisation. On average, almost two-fifths of the children are not fully immunised, and the coefficient of variation equals 13 per cent. Only half of the districts have a higher percentage of children who are fully immunised compared to the district average. Pithoragrah has the highest percentage and Udham Singh Nagar has the lowest percentage of fully immunised children. The outcomes of BCG vaccination is the best, and eleven districts have more than 90 per cent of children who have received this vaccination. Almost 30 per cent of the children have not received three doses of polio vaccine, and only eight districts are doing better compared to the district average. The variation among districts with respect to the percentage of children receiving Vitamin A doses is not only the highest; the average is also the lowest. Almost 60 per cent of children do not receive Vitamin A. Almora is the only district in which slightly more than 50 per cent of children receive Vitamin A doses. Pithoragrah is the only district that has a higher percentage than the district average for all measures of immunisation outcomes.

As in the total population, the highest and the lowest dispersions have been observed for Vitamin A doses and BCG vaccination, respectively, for the rural population. For full immunisation, the dispersion is the second-highest and slightly higher than for the total child population. Full immunisation is 0.8 percentage point lower for the rural population. The outcomes of BCG vaccination is the best and the same for the total and rural child populations. Almost 30 per cent of children do not receive the three doses. The outcomes for the Vitamin A dose is the worst, and only in Almora do half of the children between ages nine and 59 months receive Vitamin A.

In summary, we observe four outcomes: (1) the highest dispersion is observed for Vitamin A and the lowest for BCG vaccination, for both the total and rural populations of children; (2) two-fifths of the total and rural children do not receive full immunisation; (3) almost 30 per cent of the total and rural children do not receive three doses of polio vaccine; and

Table 19.3: Child Immunisation in the Districts of Uttarakhand, Total

Districts	Children age 12-23 months fully immunized (BCG, measles, and 3 doses each of polio and DPT) (%)	Children age 12-23 months who have received BCG (%)	Children age 12-23 months who have received 3 doses of polio vaccine (%)	Children age 12-23 months who have received 3 doses of DPT vaccine (%)	Children age 12-23 months who have received measles vaccine (%)	Children age 12-23 months who have received 3 doses of Hepatitis B vaccine (%)	Children age 9-59 months who received a vitamin A dose in last 6 months (%)
Almora	60.6	97.8	71.7	83.7	85.5	52.3	**53.4**
Bageswar	60.2	89.6	70.9	89.6	80.5	60.0	34.1
Chamoli	62.2	93.2	74.3	76.4	81.6	54.3	38.6
Champawat	68.4	**98.9**	**80.2**	**92.0**	86.3	52.0	35.7
Dehradun	60.7	94.0	68.5	85.8	87.5	61.7	34.6
Garhwal	61.2	96.4	79.4	78.2	80.1	65.4	40.3
Haridwar	55.3	**88.2**	63.6	**75.0**	**71.9**	60.6	**28.3**
Nainital	59.0	91.6	72.6	76.2	78.5	61.1	49.5
Pithoragarh	**74.2**	96.8	77.8	89.9	90.3	**71.5**	46.1
Rudraprayag	70.3	95.5	76.8	85.7	87.2	58.3	49.1

(Contd...)

Districts	**Children age 12-23 months fully immunized (BCG, measles, and 3 doses each of polio and DPT) (%)**	**Children age 12-23 months who have received BCG (%)**	**Children age 12-23 months who have received 3 doses of polio vaccine (%)**	**Children age 12-23 months who have received 3 doses of DPT vaccine (%)**	**Children age 12-23 months who have received measles vaccine (%)**	**Children age 12-23 months who have received 3 doses of Hepatitis B vaccine (%)**	**Children age 9-59 months who received a vitamin A dose in last 6 months (%)**
Tehri Garhwal	51.1	98.5	**59.0**	85.4	85.6	**51.2**	29.0
Udham Singh Nagar	**47.4**	93.1	62.2	75.8	78.7	56.1	39.5
Uttarkashi	72.0	95.1	73.6	86.1	**95.1**	65.0	28.4
Average	61.7	94.5	71.6	83.1	83.8	59.2	39.0
Maximum	74.2	98.9	80.2	92.0	95.1	71.5	53.4
Minimum	47.4	88.2	59.0	75.0	71.9	51.2	28.3
Coefficient of Variation	0.13	0.04	0.09	0.07	0.07	0.10	0.22

Data Source: National Family Health Survey 4: India.

Table 19.4: Child Immunisation in the Districts of Uttarakhand, Rural

Districts	Children age 12-23 months fully immunized (BCG, measles, and 3 doses each of polio and DPT) (%)	Children age 12-23 months who have received BCG (%)	Children age 12-23 months who have received 3 doses of polio vaccine (%)	Children age 12-23 months who have received 3 doses of DPT vaccine (%)	Children age 12-23 months who have received measles vaccine (%)	Children age 12-23 months who have received 3 doses of Hepatitis B vaccine (%)	Children age 9-59 months who received a vitamin A dose in last 6 months (%)
Almora	58.6	97.6	70.8	82.2	84.1	**49.5**	**53.7**
Bageswar	61.1	89.3	72.2	89.3	79.8	60.9	33
Chamoli	58.7	92.2	70.3	72.8	81.1	49.6	39.5
Champawat	68.4	**98.6**	**81.1**	**91.9**	85	52.1	33.6
Dehradun	69.6	96.2	73.5	88.1	93.1	67.1	36.2
Garhwal	60.8	96	79	79.7	81.9	67.4	42.4
Haridwar	55.2	89.2	65.8	74	**71.2**	61.4	**26.2**
Nainital	53.7	**87.5**	67.3	**69.4**	74.2	56.7	45.6
Pithoragarh	69.2	96.1	73.5	88	88.5	**70.8**	46
Rudraprayag	**71.4**	95.3	75.5	85	89.2	58.8	46.7

(Contd...)

Districts	Children age 12-23 months fully immunized (BCG, measles, and 3 doses each of polio and DPT) (%)	Children age 12-23 months who have received BCG (%)	Children age 12-23 months who have received 3 doses of polio vaccine (%)	Children age 12-23 months who have received 3 doses of DPT vaccine (%)	Children age 12-23 months who have received measles vaccine (%)	Children age 12-23 months who have received 3 doses of Hepatitis B vaccine (%)	Children age 9-59 months who received a vitamin A dose in last 6 months (%)
Tehri Garhwal	50.3	98.4	58.3	85.1	85.3	50.3	27.1
Udham Singh Nagar	**44.1**	97.1	**58.1**	73.5	81.7	58.1	40.8
Uttarkashi	71.2	95.1	73.6	86.1	**95.1**	65.0	28.4
Average	60.9	94.5	70.7	81.9	83.9	59.1	38.4
Maximum	71.4	98.6	81.1	91.9	95.1	70.8	53.7
Minimum	44.1	87.5	58.1	69.4	71.2	49.5	26.2
Coefficient of Variation	0.14	0.04	0.10	0.09	0.08	0.12	0.22

Data Source: National Family Health Survey 4: India.

(4) in Almora, the highest percentage of children - slightly more than 50 per cent receives Vitamin A.

Childhood Diseases and Treatments and Nutritional Status in the Districts of Uttarakhand

The prevalence of diarrhea and children receiving ORS have been used to explain childhood diseases and treatments. The percentage of children who have an adequate diet, those whose growth is stunted, and those who are wasted, severely wasted and underweight have been used to describe childhood nutritional status.

Reported cases of diarrhea vary from a low of 14.4 per cent in Rudraprayag to a high of 21.9 per cent Uttarkashi. Although Rudraprayag has the lowest reported percentage of diarrhea, this district has the highest percentage of children who receive ORS packets. Uttarakhand, as a state, is doing very poorly with respect to the percentage of children who receive an adequate diet. In nine districts, the percentage of children who receive an adequate diet is higher than the district average. Almost 90 per cent of children have an inadequate diet; 31.4 per cent have stunted growth; one-fifth are wasted; one-tenth are severely wasted; and one-fourth are underweight. The highest dispersion is observed for children who are severely wasted, and the lowest dispersion is observed for children whose growth is stunted.

The reported cases of diarrhea are slightly higher for rural children, who may suffer from diarrhea due to the lack of a sanitation and water infrastructure. Although the percentage of reported cases is higher in rural areas, a smaller percentage of these children receive ORS packets. The nutritional status of rural children is slightly worse for all measures of nutritional status, except for the percentage of children who are wasted, where it is equal. As with the total number of children, among rural children, the coefficient of variation is the highest for those who are severely wasted. The coefficient of variation is the lowest for children whose growth is stunted. Champawat is the only district in which the nutritional status is better with respect to all measures.

Five observations emerged from the above data: (1) reported cases of diarrhea are less than 20 per cent, and only 55 per cent of the children with diarrhea receive ORS packets; (2) less than ten per cent of children receive an adequate diet; (3) slightly more than 30 per cent of children have stunted growth; (4) one-fifth and one-tenth of the children are wasted and severely wasted, respectively; and (5) one-fourth of the children are underweight.

Table 19.5: Childhood Diseases, Treatments and Nutritional Status in the Districts of Uttarakhand, Total

Districts	Prevalence of diarrhea (reported) in the last 2 weeks preceding the survey (%)	Children with diarrhea in the last 2 weeks who received oral rehydration salts (ORS) (%)	Total children age 6-23 months receiving an adequate diet (%),	Children under 5 years who are stunted (height-for-age) (%)	Children under 5 years who are wasted (weight-for-height) (%)	Children under 5 years who are severely wasted (weight-for-height) (%)	Children under 5 years who are underweight (weight-for-age) (%)
Almora	15.1	64.1	10.6	32.9	14.4	7.7	22.5
Bageswar	21.1	46.5	11.1	25.1	26.3	13.5	27.2
Chamoli	20.1	60.8	10.7	33.7	18	7.2	22.3
Champawat	15.2	43.1	9.8	30.5	17.4	6.1	21.2
Dehradun	17.9	56.4	11.5	28.5	30.1	12	30.7
Garhwal	14.7	64	3.7	**22.9**	27.4	18.1	27.9
Haridwar	18	63.8	**3.5**	**39.1**	12.3	5.3	24.7
Nainital	16.2	52.8	12	32.1	**9**	3.7	17
Pithoragarh	21.1	**31.9**	**13.7**	30.6	20.6	9.2	**16.6**
Rudraprayag	**14.4**	**69.9**	9.6	29.9	18.4	7.5	25.9
Tehri Garhwal	14.5	53.9	5.7	30.1	**46.9**	**28.1**	**44.2**

(Contd...)

Districts	Prevalence of diarrhea (reported) in the last 2 weeks preceding the survey (%)	Children with diarrhea in the last 2 weeks who received oral rehydration salts (ORS) (%)	Total children age 6-23 months receiving an adequate diet (%),	Children under 5 years who are stunted (height-for-age) (%)	Children under 5 years who are wasted (weight-for-height) (%)	Children under 5 years who are severely wasted (weight-for-height) (%)	Children under 5 years who are underweight (weight-for-age) (%)
Udham Singh Nagar	15	48.4	11.3	37.8	12	**3.5**	27.1
Uttarkashi	**21.9**	60.9	5.3	35.2	39.4	23.6	40.3
Average	17.3	55.1	9.1	31.4	22.5	11.2	26.7
Maximum	21.9	69.9	13.7	39.1	46.9	28.1	44.2
Minimum	14.4	31.9	3.5	22.9	9	3.5	16.6
Coefficient of Variation	0.16	0.19	0.37	0.14	0.50	0.69	0.30

Data Source: National Family Health Survey 4: India.

Table 19.6: Childhood Diseases, Treatments and Nutritional Status in the Districts of Uttarakhand, Rural

Districts	Prevalence of diarrhea (reported) in the last 2 weeks preceding the survey (%)	Children with diarrhea in the last 2 weeks who received oral rehydration salts (ORS) (%)	Total children age 6-23 months receiving an adequate diet (%)	Children under 5 years who are stunted (height-for-age) (%)	Children under 5 years who are wasted (weight-for-height) (%)	Children under 5 years who are severely wasted (weight-for-height) (%)	Children under 5 years who are underweight (weight-for-age) (%)
Almora	15.8	63.5	9.1	34.3	13.7	6.8	23
Bageswar	21.2	46	11.3	25.2	26.4	13.3	27.3
Chamoli	21.4	60.5	10.9	37.5	19	8.2	23.5
Champawat	14.9	42.6	9.8	31.4	17.1	5.9	20.4
Dehradun	20.5	53.9	**13.2**	32.9	30.4	15	34.5
Garhwal	**13**	61.7	2.8	**22.9**	25.1	16.9	27.1
Haridwar	15.2	53.3	**2.6**	**38.5**	10.7	4.3	26
Nainital	14.5	51.2	6.9	33.7	**8.9**	4.1	18.8
Pithoragarh	**23.2**	**28.5**	13.1	31.6	23.4	10.2	**18.2**
Rudraprayag	15.2	**69**	10.4	29	19.5	8.2	26.9
Tehri Garhwal	14.9	50.9	6.6	32.2	**45.6**	**26.1**	**41.9**

(Contd...)

Districts	Prevalence of diarrhea (reported) in the last 2 weeks preceding the survey (%)	Children with diarrhea in the last 2 weeks who received oral rehydration salts (ORS) (%)	Total children age 6-23 months receiving an adequate diet (%)	Children under 5 years who are stunted (height-for-age) (%)	Children under 5 years who are wasted (weight-for-height) (%)	Children under 5 years who are severely wasted (weight-for-height) (%)	Children under 5 years who are underweight (weight-for-age) (%)
Udham Singh Nagar	16.2	47.8	6.6	36.8	13.1	4.1	24.2
Uttarkashi	21.2	62.2	5.5	36.2	40.1	24	41.4
Average	17.5	53.2	8.4	32.5	22.5	11.3	27.2
Maximum	23.2	69	13.2	38.5	45.6	26.1	41.9
Minimum	13	28.5	2.6	22.9	8.9	4.1	13.2
Coefficient of Variation	0.20	0.20	0.42	0.14	0.49	0.65	0.28

Data Source: National Family Health Survey 4, India.

Table 19.6: Antenatal Care in Uttarakhand

	Mothers who had antenatal check-up in the first trimester (%)	Mothers who had at least 4 antenatal care visits (%)	Mothers who had full antenatal care (%)	Mothers whose last birth was protected against neonatal tetanus (%)	Mothers who consumed iron folic acid for 100 days or more when they were pregnant (%)
Uttarakhand: NFHS – 3, 2005 – 2006	43.3	34.9	12.7	68.5	23.8
Uttarakhand: NFHS – 4, 2014 – 2015	53.5	30.9	11.5	91.4	24.9

Data Sources: National Family Health Survey 3 and 4: India.

Table 19.7: Postnatal Care in Uttarakhand

	Institutional births (%)	Births assisted by a doctor/nurse/LHV/ANM/ other health personnel (%)	Mothers who received postnatal care from a doctor/nurse/LHV/ANM/ midwife/other health personnel within 2 days of delivery (%)
Uttarakhand: NFHS – 3 2005 – 2006	32.6	38.5	27.7
Uttarakhand: NFHS – 4 2014 – 2015	68.6	71.2	54.8

Data Source: National Family Health Survey 4, India.

Current Status and Change of Status of Maternal Health in Uttarakhand

Antenatal and Postnatal Care in Uttarakhand

Child health depends to a great extent on parental knowledge and measures to protect their children's health. Parents' knowledge and behaviour are reflected in mothers' pre (ante) and postnatal care. Uttarakhand is improving with respect to mothers' initial (first trimester) antenatal checkup, which increased from 43.3 per cent to 53.5 per cent between NFHS 3 and 4. However, the state is failing with respect to the completion of antenatal care. Mothers who receive full antenatal care have fallen by 1.2 percentage points. In India, more than fifty per cent[3] of women suffer from anemia during pregnancy, and it is believed that at least half of them are suffering from iron deficiency (WHO, 2012). Therefore, iron supplements are very important during pregnancy for improving both maternal and child health (WHO, 2012). Between NFHS 3 and 4, the consumption of iron folic acid increased by 1.1 percentage points. Despite these challenges regarding antenatal care, the state is improving in institutional births, births assisted by healthcare professionals and postnatal care. The number of mothers receiving postnatal care from professional health personnel almost doubled in this period. Institutional births more than doubled; births assisted by healthcare professionals and the percentage of mothers who receive postnatal care almost doubled between 2005-06 and 2014-15.

Maternal Health Status in the Districts of Uttarakhand

Like child health, maternal health outcomes vary widely across the districts of Uttarakhand. This section uses NFHS 4 data to examine the current status and dispersion of maternal health outcomes among the districts. Prenatal and postnatal outcomes have been used to describe the status of and the variation in maternal health.

Prenatal Care in the Districts of Uttarakhand

Several factors regarding the total and rural populations have been used to describe the outcomes of prenatal care in the districts of Uttarakhand: antenatal check-up in first trimester; four additional antenatal visits; full antenatal care; births protected by neonatal tetanus and consumption of iron folic acid.

The outcomes of neonatal care in the total population is dispersed among the districts of Uttarakhand. The highest dispersion is observed for the percentage of mothers who receive full antenatal care, and the

Table 19.8: Prenatal care in the Districts of Uttarakhand, Total

District	Mothers who had antenatal check-up in the first trimester (%)	Mothers who had at least 4 antenatal care visits (%)	Mothers who had full antenatal care (%)	Mothers whose last birth was protected against neonatal tetanus (%)	Mothers who consumed iron folic acid for 100 days or more when they were pregnant (%)
Almora	57.7	31.7	18.7	91.4	35.7
Bageswar	**42**	23.4	10.7	92.1	23.6
Chamoli	49.2	20.3	5.9	90.7	18.8
Champawat	43.7	29	11.1	95.2	27.3
Dehradun	**71.9**	**47.1**	18.9	**97.5**	29.2
Garhwal	61.4	36.4	11.9	95.6	26.3
Haridwar	42.6	24.2	7.6	87.9	19.1
Nainital	65.7	40.4	**20.5**	91.6	**40.9**
Pithoragarh	49.9	30.8	14.7	92.7	28.7

(Contd...)

District	Mothers who had antenatal check-up in the first trimester (%)	Mothers who had at least 4 antenatal care visits (%)	Mothers who had full antenatal care (%)	Mothers whose last birth was protected against neonatal tetanus (%)	Mothers who consumed iron folic acid for 100 days or more when they were pregnant (%)
Rudraprayag	55.5	**17.2**	**5.7**	95.4	24.4
Tehri Garhwal	53.8	23.8	7.2	92.6	24.4
Udham Singh Nagar	46.4	26.6	5.8	**86.9**	**16.6**
Uttarkashi	42.5	20.3	9.4	92.8	27.7
Average	52.5	28.6	11.4	92.5	26.4
Maximum	71.9	47.1	20.5	97.5	40.9
Minimum	42	17.2	5.7	86.9	16.6
Coefficient of Variation	0.18	0.30	0.46	0.03	0.25

Data Source: National Family Health Survey 4: India.

lowest is observed for the percentage of mothers who receive neonatal tetanus protection. With respect to the antenatal checkup in the first trimester, at least four additional antenatal checkups, and neonatal tetanus, Dehradun district has the best outcomes compare to all other districts. Nainital has the highest percentage of pregnant women who take iron folic acid and receive full antenatal care. Antenatal checkups in first trimester are lowest in Bageswar, where 58 per cent of women receive no antenatal checkups. Less than 18 per cent of the women have at least four antenatal checkups in Rudraprayag. While the outcomes are promising for neonatal tetanus in every district, the performance is the worst in Udham Singh Nagar. Udham Singh Nagar also shows the poorest outcomes with respect to pregnant women consuming iron folic acid, with less than 17 per cent of women taking the supplement during pregnancy. Rudraprayag has the lowest percentage of mothers - less than six per cent - who receive full antenatal care.

The differences in outcomes of neonatal care are not very significant between the rural and total population. Like the total population, the highest and the lowest dispersions for the rural population are observed for full antenatal care and neonatal tetanus, respectively. Also as in the total population, among the rural population, Dehradun has the best outcomes with respect to antenatal checkups in the first trimester, at least four antenatal checkups, and neonatal tetanus. However, 51.2 of rural mothers receive at least four antenatal checkups, whereas 47.1 of mothers in the total population receive such care. As in the total population, Nainital has the highest percentage of rural mothers who receive iron folic acid. With regard to full antenatal care, the highest outcomes differ between the total and rural populations. In Dehradun, the highest percentage (23.2) of rural mothers receives full antenatal care, compared to the percentage of the total population (20.5). Haridwar's rural population has the worst outcomes with respect to antenatal checkups in first trimester, neonatal tetanus and consumption of iron folic acid. Rudraprayag has the lowest percentage of mothers who have at least four antenatal checkups, and full antenatal care for the rural population also.

The findings from these data include: (1) almost 90 per cent of pregnant women do not receive full antenatal care; (2) almost 50 per cent of pregnant women do not receive antenatal checkups for the first trimester; (3) more than 70 per cent of pregnant women do not have at least four antenatal checkups; and (4) almost three-fourths of pregnant women do not take iron folic acid supplements.

Table 19.9: Prenatal care in the Districts of Uttarakhand, Rural

District	Mothers who had antenatal check-up in the first trimester (%)	Mothers who had at least 4 antenatal care visits (%)	Mothers who had full antenatal care (%)	Mothers whose last birth was protected against neonatal tetanus (%)	Mothers who consumed iron folic acid for 100 days or more when they were pregnant (%)
Almora	56.3	28.4	16.9	90.7	34.1
Bageswar	41.1	22.7	10.9	91.9	24.2
Chamoli	47	17.8	3.8	91.8	17.2
Champawat	41.9	26.1	7.8	94.3	24.3
Dehradun	**68.1**	**51.2**	**23.2**	**97**	32.9
Garhwal	59.5	33.1	10.3	96.4	25.8
Haridwar	**33.8**	16.3	3.6	**83.7**	**14.9**
Nainital	55.8	31.8	14.7	90.4	**35.4**
Pithoragarh	48.9	23.1	11.4	91.7	26.7

(Contd...)

District	Mothers who had antenatal check-up in the first trimester (%)	Mothers who had at least 4 antenatal care visits (%)	Mothers who had full antenatal care (%)	Mothers whose last birth was protected against neonatal tetanus (%)	Mothers who consumed iron folic acid for 100 days or more when they were pregnant (%)
Rudraprayag	51.8	**11.5**	**2.3**	95	21.9
Tehri Garhwal	48.2	17.3	3.9	91.4	20.6
Udham Singh Nagar	44.5	22.1	4.5	86.3	17.5
Uttarkashi	42.5	20.3	9.4	92.8	27.7
Average	49.2	24.7	9.4	91.8	24.9
Maximum	68.1	51.2	23.2	97	35.4
Minimum	33.8	11.5	2.3	83.7	14.9
Coefficient of Variation	0.18	0.41	0.65	0.04	0.26

Data Source: National Family Health Survey 4: India.

Postnatal Care in the Districts of Uttarakhand

The percentage of institutional births, births assisted by healthcare professionals, and postnatal check-ups by healthcare professionals for the total and rural populations have been used to describe the status of postnatal care in the districts of Uttarakhand.

Dehradun has the highest percentage of institutional births, births assisted by health professionals and mothers receiving postnatal care by health professionals for both populations. Chamoli and Bageswar have the lowest percentage of institutional births and mothers receiving postnatal care by health professionals for both population. For births assisted by health professionals, Chamoli and Haridwar have the lowest achievement for the total and the rural population, respectively.

Two main observations emerge: (1) approximately 30 per cent of the mothers have home deliveries without the assistance of healthcare professionals; and (2) almost half of the mothers do not receive any postnatal care help from health professionals within two days of delivery.

Discussion

Uttarakhand is making progress on some measures of child health, such as infant and child mortality; BCG, DPT, measles vaccination and providing Vitamin A doses; treatment of diarrhea, stunting and underweight. However, the progress is very slow, and in several cases, this state has been unable to reach its goals. Despite its progress on several measures, this state is failing on other measures of child health, such as full immunisation, three doses of polio vaccine, wasting and severe wasting.

With regard to maternal health, this state is progressing in antenatal care in the first trimester, neonatal tetanus, institutional births, births assisted by healthcare professionals and postnatal care by healthcare professionals. However, an alarming fact is that the outcomes in this state are deteriorating with respect to full antenatal care, at least four antenatal visits and consumption of iron folic acid by pregnant women.

To understand the mixed achievements regarding child and maternal health outcomes, this paper investigates the influence of education on child and maternal health and the effect of sanitary infrastructure on child health.

The percentage of literate men and women increased in Uttarakhand between the third and fourth rounds of the National Family Heath Survey. More importantly, women with ten or more years of schooling increased by 11.1 percentage points in this time period. However, slightly more than

Table 19.10: Postnatal care in the Districts of Uttarakhand, Total

District	**Institutional births (%)**	**Births assisted by a doctor/nurse/LHV/ANM/other health personnel (%)**	**Mothers who receivedpostnatal care from a doctor/nurse/LHV/ANM/midwife/other health personnel within 2 days of delivery (%)**
Almora	66.3	69.6	58
Bageswar	55.9	62.3	**42.1**
Chamoli	**53.3**	**61.8**	47.9
Champawat	73.3	74	50.7
Dehradun	**83.7**	**85.2**	**68.6**
Garhwal	74.5	74.9	56.3
Haridwar	62.8	63.6	52.7
Nainital	64.7	70.4	59.5
Pithoragarh	73	75.6	56.4

(Contd...)

District	Institutional births (%)	Births assisted by a doctor/nurse/LHV/ANM/other health personnel (%)	Mothers who receivedpostnatal care from a doctor/nurse/LHV/ANM/midwife/other health personnel within 2 days of delivery (%)
Rudraprayag	66.5	67.6	57.5
Tehri Garhwal	71.1	71.9	52.7
Udham Singh Nagar	67.5	72.1	46.4
Uttarkashi	65.1	65.5	45.6
Average	67.5	70.3	53.4
Maximum	83.7	85.2	68.6
Minimum	53.3	61.8	42.1
Coefficient of Variation	0.12	0.09	0.13

Data Source: National Family Health Survey 4: India.

Table 19.11: Postnatal care in the Districts of Uttarakhand, Rural

District	Institutional births (%)	Births assisted by a doctor/nurse/LHV/ ANM/other health personnel (%)	Mothers who received postnatal care from a doctor/nurse/LHV/ANM/ midwife/other health personnel within 2 days of delivery (%)
Almora	64	67.6	55.9
Bageswar	56	62.3	**41.3**
Chamoli	**50.1**	57.2	48.3
Champawat	71.9	71.5	49.2
Dehradun	**81.7**	**84.4**	**57.4**
Garhwal	72.3	72.2	54.7
Haridwar	54.7	**55.3**	43.8
Nainital	54.3	61.1	50.8
Pithoragarh	68.9	72	51.2

(Contd...)

District	Institutional births (%)	Births assisted by a doctor/nurse/LHV/ ANM/other health personnel (%)	Mothers who received postnatal care from a doctor/nurse/LHV/ANM/ midwife/other health personnel within 2 days of delivery (%)
Rudraprayag	63.6	64.8	53.9
Tehri Garhwal	66.9	67.7	51.4
Udham Singh Nagar	64.5	68.5	43
Uttarkashi	64.4	64.8	45.3
Average	64.1	66.9	49.7
Maximum	81.7	84.4	57.4
Minimum	50.1	55.3	41.3
Coefficient of Variation	0.14	0.11	0.10

Data Source: National Family Health Survey 4: India.

Table 19.12: Education; Water and Sanitation Infrastructure in Uttarakhand

	Uttarakhand: NFHS - 3, 2005 - 2006	*Uttarakhand: NFHS - 4, 2014 - 2015*
Education		
Women with 10 or more years of schooling (%)	33.5	44.6
Women who are literate (%)	64.7	76.5
Men who are literate (%)	86.3	90.7
Water and Sanitation Infrastructure		
Households with an improved drinking water source (%)	87.4	92.9
Households using improved sanitation facility (%)	44.4	64.5

Data Sources: National Family Health Survey 3 and 4: India.

55 per cent of women still have fewer than ten years of schooling. Access of households to improved water and sanitation has increased. Use of improved sanitation facilities has also increased by 20.1 percentage points, but more than one-third of the population still does not use these facilities.

To understand the immunisation and nutritional status in the districts, this paper examines the association of female education with full immunisation and nutritional status (Figure 19.2) and water and sanitation infrastructure with nutritional status (Figure 19.3). The existing literature finds that the higher education of the mother and/or the parents affects child health outcomes through higher socioeconomic status, better information about the outside world, greater exposure to the media and better utilisation of healthcare services. However, the results are somewhat mixed. Whereas some studies (Parashar, 2005; Abuya, *et al.*, 2011; Aslam and Kingdon, 2012; Vikram, et al., 2012) find that the mother's or the father's education has a positive impact on child immunisation, others (Desai and Alva, 1998) find that this effect is not statistically significant.

NFHS 4 does not provide data on mothers' education. Therefore, this paper uses women with ten or more years of schooling as a proxy for the mother's education. Years of schooling may not be the best measure of education, and the quality of education varies widely across the districts of Uttarakhand and depends on the socioeconomic background of the area.

Figure 19.2: Connection between Female Education and Child Immunisation and Nutritional Status in the Districts of Uttarakhand

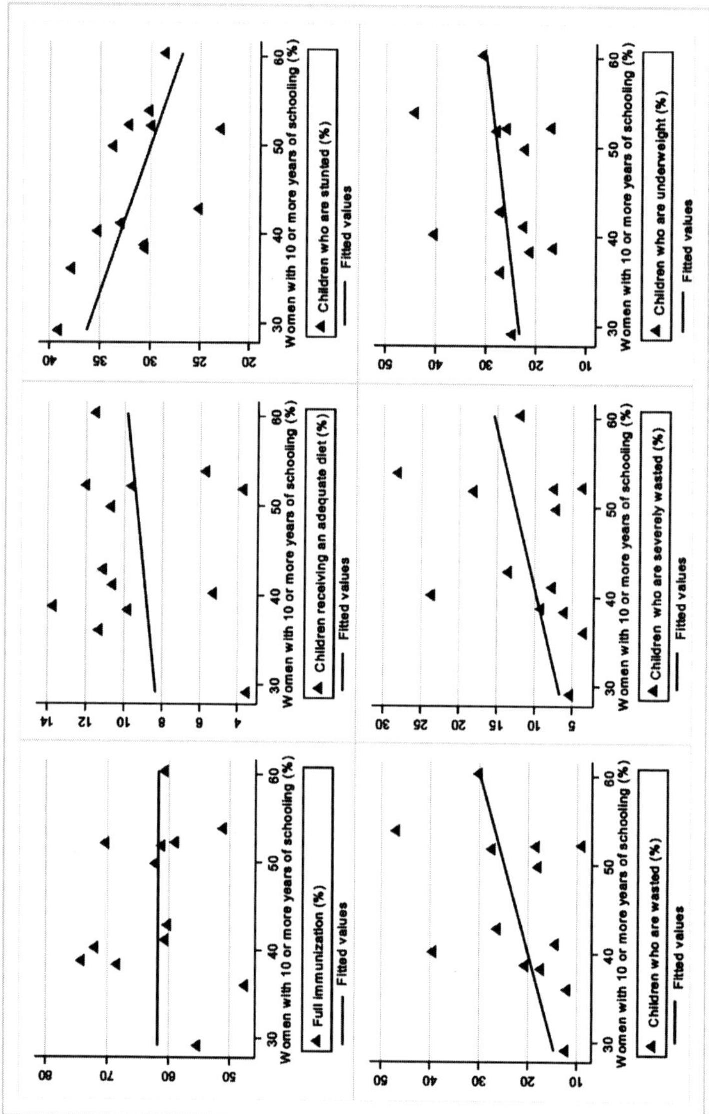

Figure 19.3: Connection between Water and Sanitation Infrastructure and Child Nutritional Status in the Districts of Uttarakhand

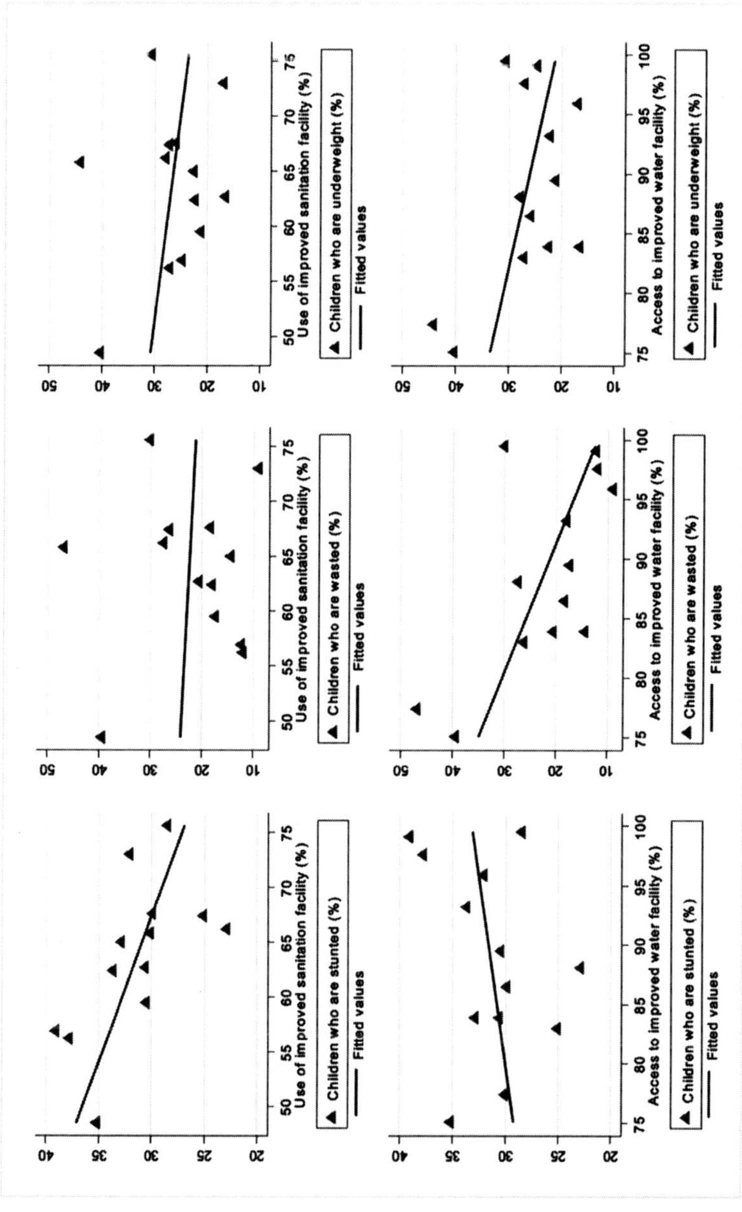

However, an increase in years of schooling provides women better exposure, better knowledge about nutrition, better communication skills, and a better understanding of how to utilise the medical facilities. However, the data do not support the literature and show that a higher percentage of children are fully immunised in those districts of Uttarakhand in which the percentage of educated women is lower.

The results on the effect of the mother's and/or the parents' education on child nutritional status also are mixed. Studies show that education can have positive impact on child nutritional status (Cochrane, *et al.,* 1982; Khan and Raza, 2014; Novignon *et al.,* 2015) and diet (Guldan *et al.,* 1993; Frost *et al.,* 2005) and on child height (Handa, 2002; Semba *et al.,* 2008; Abuya *et al.,* 2011; Aslam and Kingdon, 2012) and weight (Aslam and Kingdon, 2012). However, some studies find that the mother's education has little or no impact and even an adverse impact on child nutrition (Bicego and Boerma, 1993) and child stunting (Desai and Alva, 1998; Amugsi *et al.,* 2013). Female education appears to be favourably associated with adequate diet and child stunting; districts with a higher percentage of women with ten or more years of schooling have a higher percentage of children with an adequate diet and a lower percentage of children whose growth is stunted. Two alarming facts are that the percentage of children who are wasted and severely wasted increased between the third and fourth round of NFHS in the state; and that the districts with a higher percentage of educated women have a higher percentage of children who are wasted, severely wasted and underweight.

Access to improved water and sanitation facilities have had a negative effect on child mortality (Lee *et al.,* 1997; Ezeh *et al.,* 2014; Spears, 2012), diarrhea (Esrey *et al.,* 1991; Jalan and Ravallion, 2003), a positive impact on child growth (Merchant *et al.,* 2003; Patil *et al.,* 2014) and child nutritional status (Buttenheim, 2008; Spears, 2012; Spears, 2013). In Uttarakhand, the association between the use of water and sanitation facilities and child nutritional status is somewhat mixed. The districts in which a higher percentage of people use improved sanitation facility have a lower percentage of children with stunted growth and children who are wasted and underweight. The association between the use of water and child nutritional status is the opposite. Higher percentages of children are stunted in the districts in which a higher percentage of people use improved water. The associations are favourable between the use of improved water and wasting and underweight.

Figure 19.4: Connection between Female Education and Outcomes of Pre-and Post-Natal Care in the Districts of Uttarakhand

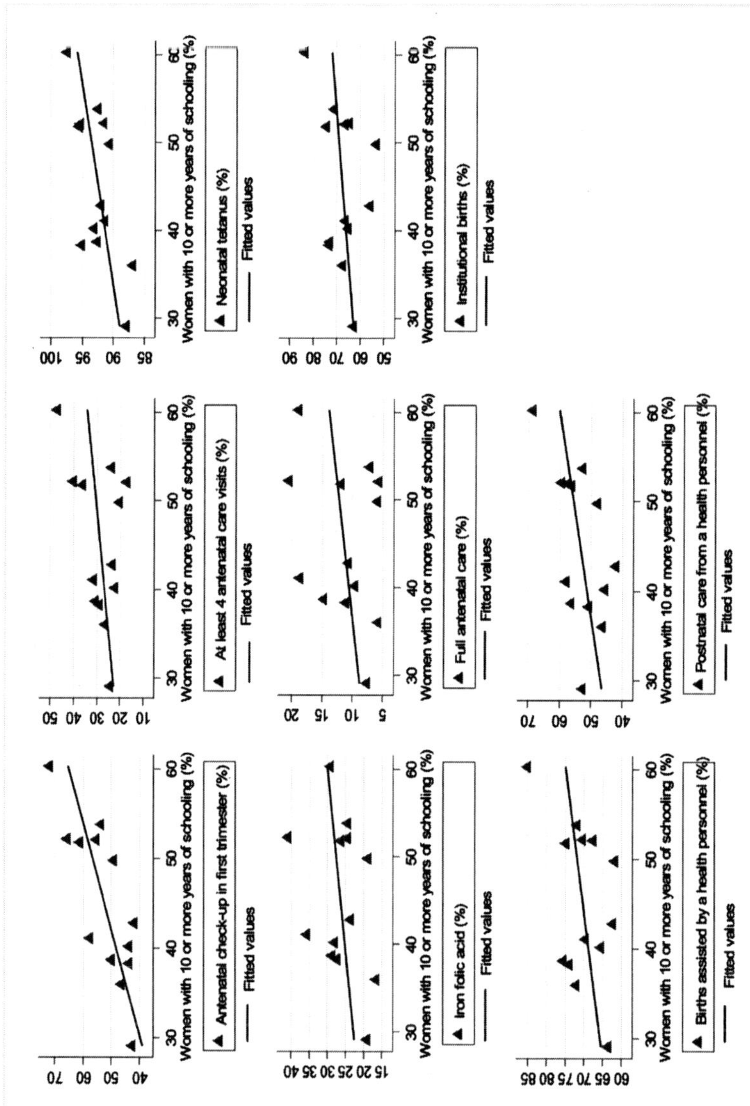

Women's education has a positive impact on the use of prenatal care (Bhatia and Cleland, 1995; Pallikadavath *et al.,* 2004; Vecino–Ortiz, 2008). The districts of Uttarakhand are no exception. Districts with a higher percentage of women with ten or more years of schooling have a higher use of prenatal care, including the percentage of pregnant women who have antenatal checkups in the first trimester; those who have at least four antenatal checkups; mothers whose last birth was protected against neonatal tetanus (per cent); pregnant women who use iron folic acid supplements; and pregnant women who receive full antenatal care. As with prenatal care, women's education helps to increase the use of institutional delivery (Agha and Carton, 2011; Amano *et al.,* 2012). Districts with a higher percentage of women with ten and more years of schooling have higher percentages of institutional deliveries, institutional delivery by health professionals and postnatal care by a health professional within two days of delivery.

Future Policy Recommendations

In spite of a huge effort to increase vaccination coverage and provide prenatal care, the percentage of children with full immunisation and the percentage of women with full antenatal care decreased from 60 to 57.7 and from 12.7 to 11.5, respectively, between 2005-06 and 2014-15. This implies that more than two-fifths of children under age five are not fully immunised, and almost 90 per cent of pregnant women do not receive full antenatal care. Improved access to healthcare facilities, lower absenteeism of healthcare professionals and better communication between healthcare workers and parents and/or prospective parents can increase both the immunisation rate (Rainey, *et al.,* 2011) and full antenatal care. However, these factors are not enough to ensure the completion of a full course of vaccinations and the complete set of antenatal check-ups. In a randomised control experiment in rural Rajasthan, the treatment group received the small incentive of raw lentils and metal plates to complete the full immunisation process. This incentive resulted in an increase in the full immunisation rate from six per cent to 38 per cent (Banerjee *et al.,* 2010). Although 38 per cent is far below the 90 per cent goal set by the World Health Organisation, the experiment was conducted in villages in which the initial rate of full immunisation was far below ten per cent, and, therefore, the increase of 32 percentage points can be seen as a great achievement. The randomised experiment method can be retested on a small scale in the remote villages of Uttarakhand, where the rate of full immunisation and recipients of full antenatal care are far lower than the state average. If it is a success, this incentive programme may be extended.

A belief system plays a major role in the success of increased immunisations and antenatal checkups. The lack of proper information and the fear of adverse effects are often a huge barrier to the success of immunisation programmes and antenatal checkups. The government of Uttarakhand planned to utilise the mass media for communication (Immunisation Week 2012-2013, Draft, Directorate Medical Health and Family Welfare, Uttarakhand). However, no specific strategies have been adopted to utilise the media. Soap operas, serials or dramas on the radio and television can have a positive impact on family planning decisions when they are used as a tool to provide information (Valente *et al.,* 1994; Rogers *et al.,* 1999) or to change people's belief in favour of the small families that these Programmes depict (La Ferrara *et al.,* 2012). It is a common strategy in India to enlist the help of popular film stars to disseminate information about immunisations, regular antenatal checkups, the consumption of iron folic acid, and neonatal tetanus. The government of Uttarakhand could also use this strategy for providing information on child and maternal care. In addition, the government could use popular radio and television programmes (soap operas) by inserting information relevant to these important healthcare issues into their storylines. The placement of large billboards containing basic information, pros and cons, and helpline numbers in villages and towns might help Uttarakhand's government to achieve its goals.

Another area in which Uttarakhand struggles is the provision of satisfactory nutrition for children. Less than ten per cent of the children in the state receive an adequate diet, despite the fact that the average income and literacy rate are higher in Uttarakhand than in India as a whole. The percentage of children with wasting and severe wasting has increased, and almost one-fourth of all children are underweight, and one-third have stunted growth. Poor households face the challenges of food security and nutrition education simultaneously. Additionally, this situation is worsened when an older sibling (also a child) is responsible for taking care of the younger sibling(s) when both parents and other elder members in the family are absent due to work. For middle class and upper middle class households, food security may not be a problem, but the lack of nutrition education may still have an adverse impact on children's diet, height and weight. The government of Uttarakhand could start a programme by engaging community healthcare workers into four ways: (1) educate the community about nutrition and sanitation; (2) provide free micronutrient supplements; (3) assess regularly whether the community is using this nutrition education; and (4) keep regular records for comparison and future strategy change. Additionally, the government can use religious leaders and community leaders to teach the community.

The present status of child and maternal health is important to sustaining future growth. Uttarakhand needs to improve its achievement in child and maternal health to maintain future growth.

Acknowledgements

The author sincerely thanks Dr Rajlakshmi Datta for her comments that helps to improve the manuscript. The author thanks Rena Henderson for her editing service. The financial support for the editing service of the final version of the paper was given by the Department of Economics, Augsburg College.

Bibliography

Abuya, B. A., Onsomu, E. O., Kimani, J. K. and Moore, D., 2011. Influence of maternal education on child immunisation and stunting in Kenya. *Maternal and Child Health Journal,* 15(8), pp. 1389-1399.

Agha, S. and Carton, T. W., 2011. Determinants of institutional delivery in rural Jhang, Pakistan. *International Journal for Equity in Health,* 10 (1), pp. 1-12.

Amano, A., Gebeyehu, A. and Birhanu, Z., 2012. Institutional delivery service utilisation in Munisa Woreda, South East Ethiopia: a community based cross-sectional study. *BMC Pregnancy and Childbirth,* 12(1), pp. 1-6.

Amugsi, D., Mittelmark, M. and Lartey, A., 2013. An analysis of socio-demographic patterns in child malnutrition trends using Ghana demographic and health survey data in the period 1993-2008. *BMC Public Health,* Volume 13:960, pp. 1-16.

Aslam, M. and Kingdon, G. G., 2012. Parental education and child health – understanding the pathways of impact in Pakistan. *World Development,* 40(10), pp. 2014-2032.

Banerjee, A. V., Duflo, E., Glennerster, R. and Kothari, D., 2010. Improving immunisation coverage in rural India: clustered randomised controlled evaluation of immunisation campaigns with and without incentives. *BMJ,* Volume 340:c2220, pp. 1-9.

Barro, R., 1996. *Health and economic growth,* s.l.: World Health Organisation.

Bhatia, J. C. and Cleland, J., 1995. Determinants of maternal care in a region of South India. *Health Transition Review,* 5(2), pp. 127-142.

Bicego, G. T. and Boerma, J. T., 1993. Maternal education and child survival: a comparative study of survey data from 17 countries. *Social Science and Medicine,* 36(9), pp. 1207-1227.

Brown, J. L. and Pollitt, E., 1996. Malnutrition, poverty and intellectual development. *Scientific American,* 274(2), pp. 38-43.

Buttenheim, A. M., 2008. The sanitation environment in urban slums: implications for child health. *Population and Environment,* 30(1–2), pp. 26-47.

Cochrane, S. H., Leslie, J. and O'Hara, D. J., 1982. Parental education and child health: intracountry evidence. *Health Policy and Education,* 2(3), pp. 213-250.

Desai, S. and Alva, S., 1998. Maternal education and child health: Is there a strong causal relationship?. *Demography,* 35(1), pp. 71-81.

Esrey, S. A., Potash, J. B., Roberts, L. and Shiff, C., 1991. Effects of improved water supply and sanitation on ascariasis, diarrhoea, dracunculiasis, hookworm infection, schistosomiasis, and trachoma. *Bulletin of the World Health Organisation,* 69(5), pp. 609-621.

Ezeh, O. K. et al., 2014. The impact of water and sanitation on childhood mortality in Nigeria: evidence from demographic and health surveys, 2003–2013. *International Journal of Environmental Research and Public Health,* 11(9), pp. 9256-9272.

Filippi, V. et al., 2006. Maternal health in poor countries: the broader context and a call for action. *The Lancet,* 368(9546), pp. 1535-1541.

Frost, M. B., Forste, R. and Haas, D. W., 2005. Maternal education and child nutritional status in Bolivia: finding the links. *Social Science and Medicine,* 60(2), pp. 395-407.

Guldan, G. S. et al., 1993. Maternal education and child feeding practices in rural Bangladesh. *Social Science and Medicine,* 36(7), pp. 925-935.

Handa, S., 2002. Raising Primary School Enrolment in Developing Countries: The Relative Importance of Supply and Demand. *Journal of Development Economics,* 69(1), pp. 103-128.

Horton, S. and Steckel, R. H., 2013. Malnutrition: global economic losses attributable to malnutrition 1900–2000 and projections to 2050. In: *How Much Have Global Problems Cost the World? A Scorecard from 1900 to 2050.* s.l.:Cambridge University Press, pp. 247-272.

Jalan, J. and Ravallion, M., 2003. Does piped water reduce diarrhea for children in rural India?. *Journal of Econometrics,* 112(1), pp. 153-173.

Jamison, D. T., 1986. Child malnutrition and school performance in China. *Journal of Development Economics,* 20(2), pp. 299-309.

Khan, R. E. A. and Raza, M. A., 2014. Nutritional status of children in Bangladesh: measuring composite index of anthropometric failure (CIAF) and its determinants. *Pakistan Journal of Commerce and Social Sciences,* 8(1), pp. 11-23.

La Ferrara, E., Chong, A. and Duryea, S., 2012. Soap operas and fertility: Evidence from Brazil. *American Economic Journal: Applied Economics,* 4(4), pp. 1-31.

Lee, L. F., Rosenzweig, M. R. and Pitt, M. M., 1997. The effects of improved nutrition, sanitation, and water quality on child health in high–mortality populations. *Journal of Econometrics,* 77(1), pp. 209-235.

Merchant, A. T. *et al.,* 2003. Water and sanitation associated with improved child growth. *European Journal of Clinical Nutrition,* 57(12), pp. 1562-1568.

Moock, P. R. and Leslie, J., 1986. Childhood malnutrition and schooling in the Terai region of Nepal. *Journal of Development Economics,* 20(1), pp. 33-52.

Novignon, J., Aboagye, E., Agyemang, O. S. and Aryeetey, G., 2015. Socioeconomic related inequalities in child malnutrition: evidence from the Ghana multiple indicator cluster survey. *Health Economics Review,* 5(1), pp. 1-11.

Pallikadavath, S., Foss, M. and Stones, R. W., 2004. Antenatal care: provision and inequality in rural north India. *Social Science and Medicine,* 59(6), pp. 1147-1158.

Parashar, S., 2005. Moving beyond the mother-child dyad: women's education, child immunisation, and the importance of context in rural India. *Social Science and Medicine,* 61(5), pp. 989-1000.

Patil, S. R. et al., 2014. The effect of India's total sanitation campaign on defecation behaviours and child health in rural Madhya Pradesh: a cluster randomised controlled trial. *Plos Med,* 11(8), pp. e1001709, 1-17.

Rainey, J. J. et al., 2011. Reasons related to non-vaccination and under-vaccination of children in low and middle income countries: findings from a systematic review of the published literature, 1999-2009. *Vaccine,* 29(46), pp. 8215-8221.

Rogers, E. et al., 1999. Effect of an entertainment–education radio soap opera on family planning behavior in Tanzania. *Studies in Family Planning,* 30(3), pp. 193-211.

Semba, R. D. et al., 2008. Effect of parental formal education on risk of child stunting in Indonesia and Bangladesh: a cross-sectional study. *The Lancet,* 371(9609), pp. 322-328.

Spears, D., 2012. Effects of Rural Sanitation on Infant Mortality and Human Capital: Evidence from a Local Governance Incentive in India. *Princeton University, Princeton.*

Spears, D., 2013. How much international variation in child height can sanitation explain?. *World Bank Policy Research Working Paper* No. 6351, pp. 1-55.

Valente, T. W. et al., 1994. Radio promotion of family planning in the Gambia. *International Family Planning Perspectives,* 20(3), pp. 96-100.

Vecino–Ortiz, A. I., 2008. Determinants of demand for antenatal care in Colombia. *Health Policy,* 86(2), pp. 363-372.

Vikram, K., Vanneman, R. and Desai, S., 2012. Linkages between maternal education and childhood immunisation in India. *Social Science and Medicine,* 75(2), pp. 331-339.

WHO, 2012. *Daily iron and folic acid supplementation in pregnant women Guideline,* Geneva: World Health Organisation.

Wolfe, B. L. and Behrman, J. R., 1982. Determinants of child mortality, health, and nutrition in a developing country. *Journal of Development Economics,* 11(2), pp. 163-193.

Notes

1. Health Indicator, Uttarakhand Health and Family Welfare Society.
2. NFHS 4 data are not available for India during the study.
3. World Bank Databank 2011.

20

Elementary Education in the Himalayan State of Uttarakhand: Examining the Past and the Present with a Future Agenda

Rajlakshmi Datta and Amrita Jaiswal

Introduction:

The 27th state of Indian Union, Uttarakhand (earlier Uttaranchal) born on November 2000 shares a bond by default with Article 21A of Indian Constitution introduced in 2002 because of the vicinity of the time period they share. Incidentally, nearly at the same time, during April 2000, the international community assembled in Dakar, Senegal, with India as a participant, to set an agenda for making progress in education by 2015. At this World Education Forum, governments from 164 countries, met together with the representatives of regional groups, international organisations, donor agencies, non-government organisations (NGOs) and civil society to adopt a Framework for Action (later known as 'the Dakar Framework') to deliver education for all. And again the Millenium Development Goal on 2000 with Goal 2 as achieving Universal primary education, set a required background for the state of Uttarakhand to start with a fresh beginning ; a beginning of a political entity in the direction of better education for all.

The Constitution (Eighty-sixth Amendment) Act, 2002 inserted Article 21-A in the Constitution of India to provide free and compulsory education of all children in the age group of six to fourteen years as a Fundamental Right in such a manner as the State may, by law, determine. The Right of Children to Free and Compulsory Education (RTE) Act, 2009, which represents the consequential legislation envisaged under Article 21-A, means that every child has a right to full time elementary education of satisfactory and equitable quality in a formal school which satisfies certain essential norms and standards. Article 21-A and the RTE Act came into effect on 1 April 2010.[1]

As an intervention of educational flagship programme Sarva Siksha Abhiyan (SSA) was operational from 2002-2003 in Uttarakhand though the programme was launched in India on 1st January 2001. The responsibility for implementation of the programme in Uttarakhand was vested with *'Uttarakhand Sabhi Ke Liye Shiksha Parishad'*, an autonomous Parishad. The Parishad was registered on 16th February 2001 to implement all types of educational projects in the State. The '*Parishad*' was headed by the Hon'ble Chief Minister as President with the Education Minister as Vice President and Chief Secretary and other officers, teachers and community representative as members.[2] Equity in elementary education opportunity was the core *mantra* of the endeavour.

Till 2004-05, District Primary Education Programme (DPEP) was operative in the Six Districts of the Himalayan state of Uttarakhand namely–Bageshwar district, Champawat district, Pithoragarh district, Haridwar district, Tehri district and Uttarkashi district. *Sarva Shiksha Abhiyan* (SSA) was initially launched in seven districts of the state, Almora, Chamoli, Dehradun, Nainital, Pauri Garhwal, Rudraprayag and US Nagar. The DPEP was over in 2004-05 and SSA which started to operate in the state from 2002-03 became functioning in all the 13 districts of the state.

The state completed its fifteenth birthday on November 2015. One and a half decade is quite a reasonable period to assess the achievements and failures of the state. Hence a need to uncover the journey of education, especially elementary education before a new beginning unfolds was felt. The basic objective of this paper is to prepare a comprehensive document of key indicators on the journey of elementary education in the state since the state was born with a brief sketch of the past, to identify the challenges that the state is facing in elementary education after completing more than one and a half decade of voyage and suggest on way ahead for the journey in the years to come. Though the state was born on November 2000, most of the data have been taken from the year 2002 from District Information System for Education (DISE) as prior to that in many categories data could not be accessed. In case of performance indicators only the present and recent scenario have been presented as the agencies like Annual Status of Education Report (ASER) or The National Council of Educational Research and Training (NCERT) carried such survey for the first time after a few years of state formation. For sketching the past, rare collections of literature have been consulted.

The paper has been divided into VIII sections. Following the introduction, the role of education in development has been discussed briefly in Section II. In Section III, exclusive nature of mountain education has been argued with a brief sketch of elementary education in the past in the region in Section IV. Section V discusses the achievement of the state in fifteen years based on data from DISE. Section VI portrays where the state really stands in elementary education today based on performance indicators from ASER and NCERT, MHRD, Government of India. Section VII summarises the main findings with conclusions through discussion and the last section suggests a way forward in elementary education for the state.

The role of education in development

In this framework of development, education helps in five distinct ways to help to broaden the sphere of human choices. ***First,*** education has intrinsic value i.e. being educated is important in itself, ***second,*** education has instrumental personal value i.e. education is important for getting a job and more generally for making use of economic opportunities. The resulting increase in incomes and economic means, in turn adds to the personal freedom to achieve functioning that he or she values. ***Third,*** instrumental social value, whereby education facilitates public discussion of social needs and encourage informed collective demands ***fourth,*** instrumental process role i.e. the benefit, besides the explicitly educational functions. For example, the incidence of child labour is intimately connected with non-schooling of children, and the expansion of schooling can reduce the distressing phenomena of child labour. Schooling also brings young people in touch with one another and thereby broaden their horizon. ***Fifth,*** role that education plays is of empowerment and distributive justice: Greater literacy and educational achievements of disadvantage groups can increase their ability to resist oppression to organise politically and to get a fair deal. The redistributive effects can be important not only between different social groups or households, but also *within* the family since there is evidence that better education (particularly female education) contribute to reduction of gender based inequalities.[3] This shows that eminent social scholars have visualised education as an instrument of promoting equity and empowerment with justice.

Education in every sense is one of the fundamental factors of development. No country can achieve sustainable economic development without substantial investment in human capital. Education enriches people's understanding of themselves and world. It improves the quality of their lives and leads to broad social benefits to individuals and society. Education raises people's productivity and creativity and promotes entrepreneurship and technological advances. In addition, it plays a very crucial role in securing economic and social progress and improving income distribution.[4] Hence education has a clear external economies and a spillover effect as it not only affects the individual who is educated but also the society around him/her.

The role of education in development has been recognised ever since the days of Plato. Education, Plato believed, is indispensable to the economic health of a good society, for education makes citizens 'reasonable men'. Since education has high economic value, Plato argued that a considerable part of the community's wealth must be invested in education. Major contribution to the discussion on the relationship between education and economic growth was made first by Adam Smith, followed by a long honourable tradition of classical and neo-classical economists until Alfred Marshall who emphasised in 1980 that "the most valuable of all capital is that invested in human beings". However, "in line with the biased post-war approach it was largely forgotten", and no systematic study on the contribution of education to economic growth could be found in the literature, until Schultz's presidential address to the American Economic Association in 1960, which created what is later aptly described as "human investment revolution in economic thought" as documented by Bowman in 1966. Schultz's pioneering research followed by a mammoth growth of research in the area of Economics of Education, and the untiring research has clearly established that education is not merely a consumption activity, but for the most part an investment. It leads to the formation of human capital, comparable to physical capital, making a significant contribution to economic growth.[5] Thus, it reveals that starting from Plato to Marshal, from Smith to Schultz the visionaries have recognised that education has a crucial role in economic growth and development.

Elementary education is the only stage of education whose completion is compulsory for the whole population of pupils.[6] In India, the 93rd

Constitutional amendment making the right to elementary education a fundamental right was a historic decision by policy-makers in the direction of equal opportunity for accessibility of elementary education. This stage of education is the plinth of the human resource of the nation and hence undoubtedly has a massive role to play in the country's growth story and developmental journey

Exclusive nature of education in mountains

Mountains and hilly terrains have their own unique characteristics like accessibility constrained by slope, altitude, landscape and topography, seasonal hazards, cost of development like transportation, building roads etc, fragility in terms of slope or altitude, low carrying capacity, land degradation, productivity, etc. Besides, there are issues like marginality due to the nature of concentration of habitations[7]. Hence the mountain or hill regions cannot be expected to get the same uniform policy treatment as that of other geographical regions. Though another school of thought may argue that difference in policy action may lead to 'asymmetrical federalism'.

The stress on 'sustainability' and 'inclusion' in the vision and aspirations of the medium term growth trajectory of India, as finalised for the Twelfth Five Year Plan period, for the first time creates some conceptual space for fresh planning and mid-course correction for the mountain regions of India. However, in a vision of a 'Faster, Sustainable and More Inclusive Growth' simultaneous achievement of each of these three elements will continue to remain critical for the success of the Plan.[8] In the context of school education, the first and last elements are more crucial as 'time' and 'target group' plays an intrinsic role in educational development.

Mountain education are highly affected by natural disasters like earthquake, cloud bursts, flash floods, landslides etc which often is not only a threat to the continuity of study but a threat to infrastructure like roads, school buildings, water sources etc and acts as a constraint for the teacher and the student to have a routine teaching learning activity. Often the scale of destruction of infrastructure is so large that it consumes a number of months or even a year or more to restore back to normal life and education is affected. There are often instances of school students reaching their 'temple of learning' in very fragile and risky mode, post-natural disaster period, in the mountains as the roads are not restored back into normal situation in time.

Distance of school from residence, forests, attack of wild animals, disruption due to rivers and streams, road conditions, limited transportation facilities etc are the limits that almost all the mountain regions have to face. Hence education or rather the elementary education which has been given the status of a right is not as convenient for a student in the hills as compared to the plains. A very common scene in the hills are of students walking in groups for miles to reach their school and back home and often asking for a lift from the vehicle driver on their way back when they are really tired and are walking on a motorable road. Since this is a daily practice, their plea is rejected in most cases! And hence the struggle to obtain school education especially elementary level education for the larger section of students in the mountains remains a challenge for them.

Uttarakhand Elementary Education in the past: A brief sketch

Literatures of the past reveal that region specific disadvantages affected the elementary education even on those days. In hill areas problems of elementary education, was not only economic including opportunity cost, but also rooted in social cultural setting. The physiographic settings like sparse and scattered distribution of population in tiny settlement over large area as well and scarcity of teachers, had heavy toll on education development especially of girls in the past. These two causes were the greatest obstacles in expansion of schools in mountains. A perusal of notes of district officers reveal that in Terai and Babahr region of the present day US Nagar district, the southern part of Nainital and Garhwal districts, that the migratory habits of people and general poverty were the formidable problems in educational development. The tenants were in the habit of shifting from one village to another as per the availability of land and terms and condition of cultivation. This situation very often rendered school non-functional. During bad weather and busy agricultural season, when all boys joined family in fields or in tendering cattle, attendance in schools were reduced to negligible. In the Tharu and Boksa[9] villages in the *tarai* it was next to impossible to attract children to school, unless the teachers were from their own community, and keeping the very low level of literacy in these villages, to find an educated person in these communities was almost not possible. The quality of education, as per the standards of that time was also a matter of great concern. The motivation level of teachers were low and attrition rate was high, the infrastructure were impoverished and above all, as the top bureaucrats felt, that because of vast expanse of the district, monitoring and supervision was also difficult. Consequently, the learning levels of children were low to the extent that in the year 1903, in Nainital District, out of the total 15 candidates sent for public examination only one could pass the vernacular middle school and rest failed badly.[10]

It was British who introduced modern education and made it available to all those who could afford it. The first modern school in Uttarakhand was established in 1839 at Srinagar[11] (District Pauri Garhwal) by Captain Huddleston and its expenses were borne from the proceeds of the unclaimed assets of the pilgrims. In this school only Sanskrit and Hindi were taught. However, one section of people of the region were worried about the decline of the learning of *Shastra,* in their opinion *that too in a region which was supposed to protect it.* The residents of Almora town petitioned to Lord Bishop and requested him to establish a *Pathsala* to impart the teaching of *Shastra.* Lushighton, then Commissioner of Kumaon, yielding to this demand, opened a *Pathsala* in Almora which could function only for eight years. Every district was to have six teachers, three tehsil visitors (similar to present Deputy Inspector of School) and one district visitor. In this way every district was to incur around rupees 4000 to rupees 4500 annually. By 1853, with the endeavour of H. Ried, the Visitor of School of North West Province, the first elementary school text book in Hindi *Vidhyarrathi Ke Partham Pushtak,* was developed and introduced in school. This textbook was supplied at concessional price and was designed to impart instruction in spelling, letter writing, arithmetic and mensuration, which was usually deemed sufficient for ordinary purpose of villagers.[12] This clearly reveals the disorientation of past Uttarakhand towards Western model of education either because of its remoteness or because the habitants who were mostly *Pundits* and *Rajputs* did not feel the need of western model of education. During the past since livelihood in hills revolved around agriculture, work as priests/ pundits etc. education was not meant for all. Imparting and receiving of education was as sacred as anything can be, for example, education started and ended with certain prescribed religious rituals. Hence Sanskrit, *Shastra* etc were the priorities for the region.

In 1896, a primary school for girls and boys was started in Gudoli near Chopra. Later this institution was raised to a Middle School in 1903 and in 1905 for the first time, girls from this centre appeared in the Middle School Examination.[13] English Education was introduced in the state by Pratap Shah when he established the Pratap High School in Tehri in 1875.[14] On 31st March 1908, the total number of students in Pratap High School were 233.[15] Thus, the coverage of school education and especially English medium education was not very noticeable in the region in the past.

Except a few pockets like Almora, Nainital, Srinagar, Tehri etc, the larger part of the hilly region didnot show any remarkable progress in school education in the past.

What has Uttarakhand achieved in those 15 years?

Uttarakhand has traversed some way since its inception in 2000. Policy documents have been framed since then for the Himalayan state bifurcated from Uttar Pradesh with a focus on development for this newly formed Himalayan state. To what extent the policy commitments have been realised in elementary education is a pertinent question before the state. Some state level and district level key indicators are identified in this section to analyse the journey of the fifteen years period for the state.

A. State level indicators

Some key indicators for the Elementary Education in the state of Uttarakhand (earlier Uttaranchal).

Table 20.1: Number of Schools in different categories and growth rate

Indicators	*2002-03*	*2009-2010*	*Growth from 2002-2010*	*2014-15*	*Growth from 2002-03 to 2014-15*	*Growth from 2009-10 to 2014-15*
Total Government Primary Schools	10,864	12689	16.80	12606	16.035	-0.654
Total Private Primary Schools	1294	2657	105.33	2829	118.62	6.4735
Total Rural Govt. Primary Schools	10275	12282	19.53	12217	18.90	0.529
Total Rural Private Primary Schools	933	2074	122.29	2171	132.69	4.6769
Primary with Upper Primary, Govt. Schools	148	35	-76.35	18	-87.84	-48.57
Primary with Upper Primay, Private Schools	325	802	146.77	1292	297.54	61.097
Only UPS, Govt. Schools	2256	3034	34.49	2829	25.398	-6.757
Only UPS, Pvt. Schools	306	702	129.41	678	121.57	-3.41

Source: State Report Cards, DISE of different years and authors' calculation.

Table 20.1 clearly shows that there is an increase by 16.80 per cent in total government primary schools from 2002-2010. This growth rate was sustained in the later years i.e. till 2014-15 where the growth accounted to 16.03 per cent from 2002-03 to 2014-15. However, this growth rate was negative in the period 2009-10 to 2014-15 at -0.654 per cent.

The total private primary schools showed an increase with almost doubling their numbers, this growth rate stood at 105.33 per cent from 2002-2010. The growth rate was at 118.62 per cent from 2002-03 to 2014-15 and positive growth rate of 6.47 per cent during the period 2009-10 to 2014-15. The growth rate of private schools were seven times more than that of government schools in the period 2002-03 to 2014-15.

The total rural government primary schools increased in numbers with the overall increase of 19.53 per cent from 2002-2010, the growth rate was 18.90 per cent from 2002-03 to 2014-15 with a declining growth of 0.529 per cent between 2009-10 to 2014-15.

The total rural private primary schools more than doubled itself during the period 2002-2010 with an increase of 122.29 per cent. This increase in percentage was 132.69 per cent during the period 2002-03 to 2014-15. The period between 2009-10 to 2014-15 witnessed an increase in total rural private primary schools at the rate of 4.6 per cent.

The number of primary with upper primary government schools declined during the period 2002-2010. The overall decline was 76.35 per cent during this period. The decline continued further too and was at the rate of -87.84 per cent from 2002 to 2014-15. However, the decline was at the rate of -48.57 per cent from 2009-10 to 2014-15.

On the other hand the primary with upper primary private schools witnessed an increase of 146.77 per cent with the growth per cent of 297.54 during the period 2002-03 to 2014-15. This growth rate was 61.97 per cent from 2009-10 to 2014-15.

The only upper primary (UP) government schools demonstrated an increasing trend from 2002 to 2010 with an increase of 34.49 per cent from 2002-03 to 2009-10. This growth rate was 25.39 per cent from 2002-03 to 2014-15. However, a decline of 6.75 per cent was observed during 2009-10 to 2014-15.

The only UPS private schools also increased during the period 2002-03 to 2009-10 with an increasing percentage of 129.41 per cent during 2002-03 to 2009-10. This increasing percentage was 121.57 during 2002-03 to 2014-15. However, a declining growth rate of -3.41 per cent during 2009-10 to 2014-15 was witnessed. Thus, a shift in growth rate is visible in the later part of the one and a half decade journey in both government and private schools.

Table 20.2: Some State level key performance indicators in Elementary Education

Indicators	*2002-03*	*2009-2010*	*Growth from 2002-2010*	*2014-15*	*Growth from 2002-03 to 2014-15*	*Growth from 2009-10 to 2014-15*
Per cent Single classroom school, Primary	2.9	1.8	-1.1	2.8	-0.1	1
Per cent Single classroom school, Primary with Upper Primary	0.8	0.4	-0.4	00	-0.8	-0.4
Per cent Single Classroom School, Upper Primary Only		0.6	----	00	00	-0.6
Per cent Single Teacher School, Primary	21.5	16.3	-5.2	14.3	-7.2	-2
Per cent Single Teacher School, Primary with UP	3.4	2.0	-1.4	00	-3.4	-2
Per cent Single Teacher School, Only Upper Primary	2.3	5.7	3.4	11.9	9.6	6.2
Per cent Girls enrolment, Primary	49.7	49.1	-0.6	51.3	1.6	2.2
Per cent Girls enrolment, Primary with Upper Primary	42.8	41.0	-1.8	39.0	-3.8	-2
Per cent Girls enrolment, Only Upper Primary	48.6	50.7	2.1	54.6	6	3.9
Pupil Teacher Ratio, Primary	30	23	-7	18	-12	-5
Pupil Teacher Ratio, Primary with Upper Primary	21	26	5	25	4	-1
Pupil Teacher Ratio, Only Upper Primary	18	17	-1	14	-4	-3

Source: State Report Cards, DISE of different years and authors' calculation.

Table 20.2 illustrates state level key performance indicators in elementary education. The percentage of single classroom school at primary level declined from 2.9 per cent in 2002-03 to 1.8 per cent in 2009-2010, a decline of 1.1 per cent during the period. It stood at 2.8 per cent in 2014-15 which again shows a drop of 0.1 per cent from 2002-03 to 2014-15. However, an increase of one per cent is observed from 2009-10 to 2014-15.

The percentage of single classroom schools, primary with upper primary level show a decline of 0.4 per cent from 2002-03 to 2009-10. It was at zero per cent during 2014-15 which is a complete drop of 0.8 per cent from 2002-03 to 2014-15. Similar decline of 0.4 per cent was observed from 2009 to 2014-15. Percentage of single classroom schools, upper primary was at 0.6 per cent in 2009-10.

The percentage of single teachers at primary level witnessed a decline of 5.2 per cent from 2002-03 to 2009-10. It stood at 21.5 per cent in 2002-03 and 16.3 per cent in 2009-10. Further it was at 14.3 per cent in 2014-15 which clearly indicates a decline of 7.2 per cent from 2002-03 to 2014-15 and a decline of 2 per cent from 2009-10 to 2014-15.

The percentage of single teachers in primary with upper primary schools dropped by 1.4 per cent from 3.4 per cent in 2002-03 to 2 per cent in 2009-10. It was at zero per cent in 2014-15 and witnessed a total decline of 3.4 per cent from 2002-03 to 2014-15 and 2 per cent decline from 2009-10 to 2014-15.

The percentage of single teacher in only upper primary schools increased by 3.4 per cent from 2002-03 to 2009-2010. It was at 2.3 per cent in 2002-03 and 5.7 per cent in 2009-2010. It was 11.9 per cent in 2014-15 which clearly shows an increase of 9.6 per cent from 2002-03 to 2014-15 and increase of 6.2 per cent from 2009-10 to 2014-15.

The percentage of girls enrollment in primary school decreased by 0.6 per cent from 2002-03 to 2009-10. It was at 49.7 per cent in 2002-03 and 49.1 per cent in 2009-2010. It was 51.3 per cent in 2014-15 which clearly shows an increase of 1.6 per cent from 2002-03 to 2014-15 and an increase of 2.2 per cent from 2009-10 to 2014-15.

The percentage of girls enrolment in primary with upper primary schools show a decline of 1.8 per cent from 2002-03 to 2009-10. It was at 42.8 per cent in 2002-03 and 41.0 per cent in 2009-10. It was at 39.0 per cent in 2014-15 which shows a clear decline of 3.8 per cent from 2002-03 to 2014-15 and a decline of 2 per cent from 2009 to 2014-15.

The percentage of girls enrolment in only upper primary schools show an increase of 2.1 per cent from 2002-03 to 2009-10. It was at 48.6 per cent in 2002-03 and 50.7 per cent in 2009-10. It was at

54.6 per cent in 2014-15 which shows a clear increase of 6 per cent from 2002-03 to 2014-15 and an increase of 3.9 per cent from 2009-10 to 2014-15.

The pupil teacher ratio in primary schools declined by 7 per cent from 2002-03 to 2009-10. It was at 30 per cent in 2002-03 and 23 per cent in 2014-15. It was 18 per cent in 2014-15 which again shows a decline of 12 per cent from 2002-03 to 2014-15 and a decline of 5 per cent from 2009-10 to 2014-15.

The pupil teachers ratio in primary with upper primary increased by 5 per cent from 2002-03. It was at 21 per cent in 2002-03 and 26 per cent in 2009-10. It was 25 per cent in 2014-15 which again shows an increase of 4 per cent from 2002-03 to 2014-15 and a decrease of 1 per cent from 2009-10 to 2014-15.

The pupil teacher ratio in only upper primary schools decreased by 1 per cent from 2002-03 to 2009-10. It was at 18 per cent in 2002-03 and 17 per cent in 2009-10. It was at 14 per cent in 2014-15 which clearly show a decrease of 4 per cent from 2002-03 to 2014-15 and a decrease of 3 per cent from 2009-10 to 2014-15.

Table 20.3: Enrolment in Schools by major medium of instruction in Uttarakhand

Indicators	*2002-03*		*2014-15*	
	Hindi Medium	*English Medium*	*Hindi Medium*	*English Medium*
Per cent of Enrolment by medium of Instruction, Primary only	99	0.24	93.57	4.36
Per cent of Enrolment by medium of Instruction, Primary with UP	96.59	3.06	65.22	29.06
Per cent of Enrolment by medium of Instruction, Upper Primary Only	99.54	0.03	96.92	1.90

Source: Authors' calculation from DISE statistics.

The year 2002-03 shows an inclination towards Hindi as a medium of instruction in Uttarakahnd. Table 20.3 shows that the percentage of enrolment by medium of instruction for primary schools only was at 99 per cent in Hindi as a medium of instruction in 2002-03 whereas enrollment in English as medium of instruction was at only 0.24 per cent in the same period. However, this percentage declined in 2014-15 with percentage of enrolment in Hindi as medium of instruction at primary only schools at 93.57 per cent and increasing percentage in enrolment in English as a medium of instruction at 4.36 per cent.

Similar trends were observed in percentage enrolment by medium of instruction for primary with upper primary where percentage of enrolment in Hindi as a medium of instruction was at 96.59 per cent and percentage of enrolment in English as a medium of instruction was at 3.06 per cent. However significant changes were observed in 2014-15 where a sharp fall in this percentage was observed in Hindi as a medium of instruction. The percentage enrolment in Hindi as medium of instruction came down to 65.22 per cent in 2014-15 and percentage enrolment in English as a medium of instruction increased significantly to 29.06 per cent.

In case of only upper primary schools the percentage enrolment in Hindi as a medium of instruction was 99.54 per cent in 2002-03 and in case of English it was at 0.03 per cent. In 2014-15, the percentage enrolment in Hindi as medium of instruction came down to 96.92 per cent where a slight increase in case of English was observed where it rose to 1.90 per cent in 2014-15.

Table 20.4: GER, NER, Caste distribution, Gender distribution, Rural Urban distribution for the state in Elementary Education

Indicators	*2002-03*	*2014-15*
GER Primary[16] School	89.5#	100.54
GER Upper Primary School	51.3#	85.53
NER[17] Primary School	76.3#	85.40
NER Upper Primary School	39.2#	64.07
Per cent of Rural enrolment to total enrolment, only primary government School	74.80	61.57
Per cent of Rural enrolment to total enrolment, primary with Upper Primary government School	1.32	0.14
Per cent of Rural enrolment to total enrolment, only Upper Primary government School	16.43	16.02
Per cent of Rural enrolment to total enrolment, only primary private School	57.29	32.10
Per cent of Rural enrolment to total enrolment, Primary with Upper primary private School	16.69	29.64
Per cent of Rural enrolment to total enrolment, Only Upper primary private School	13.08	6.99
Per cent of SC enrolment, Primary School	26.7	23.9
Per cent of SC enrolment, Upper Primary School	21.2	24.6
Per cent of SC girls to SC enrolment, Primary School	49.4	48.3
Per cent of SC girls to SC enrolment, Upper Primary School	44.3	49.4
Per cent of ST enrolment, Primary School	4.1	2.8
Per cent of ST enrolment, Upper Primary School	4.4	3.1
Per cent of ST girls to ST enrolment, Primary School	49.4	48.1
Per cent of ST girls to ST enrolment, Upper Primary School	47.1	48.5

Source: Authors' calculation based on state report cards, DISE. # Data for 2004 has been used from DISE as data for 2002-03 was NA during the study.

From Table 20.4, it is observed that in 2002-03 the GER Primary was at 89.5 per cent which increased to 100.54 per cent in 2014-15. A total increase of 11.04 per cent was observed during the period. In 2002-03, the GER in Upper Primary was at 51.3 per cent which increased to 85.53 per cent in 2014-15. A total increase of 34.23 per cent was observed during the period. In 2002-03, the NER primary level was at 76.3 which increased to 85.40 in 2014-15. A total increase of 9.1 was observed during the period. In 2002-03, the NER upper primary was at 39.2 which increased to 64.07 in 2014-15. A total increase of 24.87 points was observed during the period.

In 2002-03, in the category of percentage of rural enrolment to total enrolment, only primary government schools were at 74.80 per cent which decreased to 61.57 per cent in 2014-15. A decrease of 13.23 per cent was witnessed during the period. In 2002-03, the percentage of rural enrolment to total enrolment, primary with upper primary government schools stood at 1.32 per cent which decreased to 0.14 per cent in 2014-15. A decrease of 1.18 per cent was observed during the period. In 2002-03, the percentage of rural enrolment to total enrolment, government upper primary only schools was at 16.43 per cent which decreased by 16.02 per cent in 2014-15. A decrease of 0.41 per cent was observed during the period. In 2002-03, the percentage of rural enrolment to total enrolment private primary only schools were at 57.29 per cent which came down to 32.10 per cent in 2014-15, a decrease of 25.19 per cent was observed during the period. In 2002-03, the percentage of rural enrolment to total enrolment, primary with upper primary private was at 16.69 per cent which increased to 29.64 per cent in 2014-15. An increase of 12.95 per cent was observed during the period. In 2002-03, the percentage of rural enrolment to total enrolment, only upper primary private was at 13.08 per cent which decreased to 6.99 per cent in 2014 -15. A decrease of 6.09 per cent was observed during the period. In 2002-03, the percentage of SC enrolment, primary schools stood at 26.7 per cent which reduced to 23.9 in 2014-15. A decrease of 2.8 per cent was observed during the period. In 2002-03, the percentage of SC enrolment, upper primary was at 21.2 per cent which increased to 24.6 per cent in 2014-15. An increase of 3.4 per cent was observed during the period. In 2002-03, the percentage of SC girls to SC enrolment primary was at 49.4 per cent which decreased to 48.3 per cent in 2014-15. A decrease of 1.1 per cent was thus observed during the period.

In 2002-03, the percentage of SC girls to SC enrolment, upper primary schools was at 44.3 per cent which increased to 49.4 per cent in 2014-15. An increase of 5.1 per cent was observed during the period. Compared to primary level, the increase in upper primary is a welcome sign for the state which portrays the encouragement of SC girl students for not only primary education but upper primary education as well.

In 2002-03, the percentage of ST enrolment in primary school was at 4.1 per cent which decreased to 2.8 per cent in 2014-15. Again, in 2002-03 the percentage of ST enrolment upper primary was at 4.4 per cent which decreased to 3.1 per cent in 2014-15. In 2002-03, the percentage of ST girls to ST enrolment primary stood at 49.4 per cent which decreased to 48.1 per cent in 2014-15, a decrease of 1.3 per cent during the period. In 2002-03, the percentage of ST girls to ST enrolment, upper primary school was at 47.1 per cent which increased to 48.5 per cent in 2014-15, an increase of 1.4 per cent during the period. Thus, in case of both SC and ST girls though enrolment in primary decreased but the increase in enrolment in Upper Primary is observed in both the categories.

Table 20.5: Key indicators related to teachers in Elementary Education in the State

Indicators	*2002-03*	*2014-15*	*Growth per cent*
Number of Government Primary School Teachers	23178	27913	20.428
Number of Government Primary with Upper Primary School Teachers	651	96	-85.253
Number of Government only Upper Primary School Teachers	9016	9550	5.923
Number of Private Primary School Teachers	5610	13876	147.34
Number of Private Primary with Upper Primary School Teachers	2508	9924	295.69
Number of Private only Upper Primary School Teachers	1354	3136	131.61
Percentage of teachers trained in service, primary	38.0	35.8	-5.79
Percentage of teachers trained in service, primary with upper primary schools	1.3	0.6	-53.85
Percentage of teachers trained in service, only upper primary schools	4.2	42.3	907.143

Source: Authors' calculation based on state report cards, DISE.

As far as some key indicators related to teachers are concerned, Table 20.5 reveals that the number of teachers increased during the period 2002-03 to 2014-15.The number of Government primary school teachers, the number of Government only upper primary school teachers, number of private primary school teachers, number of private primary with upper primary school teachers, number of private only upper primary school teachers increased during the period. However, the number of Government primary with upper primary school teachers saw a decline during the reference period since government schools with primary and upper primary level together have been closed in last few years in the state. The percentage of teachers trained in service at primary and primary with upper primary schools decreased in the reference period while it increased tremendously at only upper primary level.

(B) Key district level indicators over time

Table 20.6: Number of Government and Private only Primary Schools

	Govt. only Primary		*Private Only Primary*		*Growth per cent in Govt. Primary only*	*Rank Govt. Primary Schools only*	*Growth per cent in Private Primary only*	*Rank Private Primary Schools only*
Districts	2002-03	2014-15	2002-03	2014-15	2002-2015		2002-15	
Almora	1238*	1412	70*	190	14.05	9	171.43	4
Bageshwar	380	604	22	97	58.95	1	340.91	3
Chamoli	904	973	83	112	7.63	13	34.94	13
Champawat	449	512	38	100	14.03	10	163.16	5
Dehradun	824	963	162	420	16.87	7	159.26	6
Haridwar	602	692	250	410	14.95	8	64	12
Nainital	898	986	149	262	9.799	11	75.84	11
Pauri Garhwal	1510	1647	3	181	9.073	12	5933.3	1
Pithoragarh	975	1190	52	134	22.05	3	157.69	7
Rudraprayag	482	568	9	105	17.84	5	1066.67	2
Tehri	1230	1479	130	229	20.24	4	76.154	10
Udham Singh Nagar	690	809	246	443	17.25	6	80.08	8
Uttarkashi	629	771	82	146	22.58	2	78.05	9

Source: DISE and Authors' calculation; *Since data for Almora only was not available for 2002-03, it has been substituted by figures of 2003-04.

Figures in Table 20.6 reveal that all the 13 districts of the state witnessed an increase in government only primary schools. The highest growth rate was observed in Bageshwar district with 58.95 per cent increase from 2002-03 to 2014-15. All the 13 districts also witnessed an increase in only private primary schools, with a tremendous increase in Pauri Garhwal district and Rudraprayag district both hill districts of the state. The lowest growth in both government primary and private primary school was found in Chamoli district.

Table 20.7: Number of Government and Private only Primary with Upper Primary Schools

Districts	*Govt. only Primary with Upper Primary*		*Private Only Primary with Upper Primary*		*Change in Govt. Primary with Upper Primary schools 2002-3 to 2014-15*	*Change in Private Primary with Upper Primary schools 2002-03 to 2014-15*
	2002-03	*2014-15*	*2002-03*	*2014-15*		
Almora	7*	1	9*	72	-6	63
Bageshwar	0	0	5	17	0	12
Chamoli	12	1	43	69	-11	26
Champawat	1	0	4	9	-1	5
Dehradun	35	1	115	285	-34	170
Haridwar	6		70		----	----
Nainital	14	3	20	117	-11	97
Pauri Garhwal	2	1	2	108	-1	106
Pithoragarh	19	6	12	89	-13	77
Rudraprayag	4	0	1	29	-4	28
Tehri	12	3	15	70	-9	55
Udham Singh Nagar	11	0	13	148	-11	135
Uttarkashi	25	1	15	52	-24	37

Source: DISE and Authors' calculation; *Since data for Almora only was not available for 2002-03, it has been substituted by figures of 2003-04.

As per figures of Table 20.7, all the districts show a drop in the number of government only primary with upper primary schools. This drop was highest in the district of Dehradun followed by Uttarkhasi and Pithoragarh. On the other hand all the districts show an increase in the number of private only primary with upper primary schools. The increase was highest in the district of Dehradun followed by Udham Singh Nagar and Pauri Garhwal. Almora district witnessed an increase in this respect with a increase in number of schools by 63. The drop in primary with upper primary schools government were primarily because of the state government's policy to close such combined level of schools a few years back.

Table 20.8: Number of Government and Private only Upper Primary Schools

	Govt. only Upper Primary		Private Only Upper Primary		Growth in Govt. Upper Primary Only %	Rank in growth of Govt. Upper Primary schools only	Growth in Private Upper Primary only %	Rank in growth of Private Upper Primary Only
Districts	2002-03	2014-15	2002-03	2014-15	2002-03 to 2014-15	2002-03 to 2014-15	2002-03 to 2014-15	2002-03 to 2014-15
Almora	149*	192	22*	34	28.86	6	54.55	9
Bageshwar	53	119	11	23	124.53	1	109.09	7
Chamoli	170	216	11	30	27.06	7	172.73	5
Champawat	96	101	6	33	5.208	10	450	2
Dehradun	187	277	21	86	48.128	3	309.52	3
Haridwar	66		40		----	---	----	---
Nainital	250	231	49	63	-7.6	11	28.57	10
Pauri Garhwal	361	291	1	57	-19.39	12	5600	1
Pithoragarh	171	238	9	33	39.18	4	266.67	4
Rudraprayag	100	136	10	22	36	5	120	6
Tehri	305	377	35	45	23.61	8	28.57	10
Udham Singh Nagar	183	204	79	132	11.48	9	67.089	8
Uttarkashi	149	275	9	11	84.56	2	22.22	11

Source: DISE and Authors' calculation;

*Since data for Almora only was not available for 2002-03, it has been substituted by figures of 2003-04.

Districtwise figures of government and private UPS, as given in Table 20.8 shows that all the districts except Nainital and Pauri Garhwal show an increase in the number of government only upper primary schools. This increase was highest in district Bageshwar where the increase was more than 124 per cent. However, in the district of Pauri Garhwal and Nainital a declining trend was observed. The government only upper primary schools declined at the rate of 19.39 per cent in Pauri Garhwal district and at the rate of 7.6 per cent in Nainital district during the period 2002-03 to 2014-15.

All the districts show an increase in the number of private only upper primary schools. This growth was highest in the district of Pauri Garhwal where it grew from mere one private only upper primary school in 2002-03 to 57 in 2014-15. This was followed by district Champawat where the increase in percentage was 450 per cent i.e. grew from six private only upper primary schools in 2002-03 to 33 private only upper primary schools in 2014-15.

Table 20.9: Total Enrolment in Government and Private only Primary Schools

	Govt. only Primary		*Private Only Primary*		*Percentage Growth in Govt. Primary Only*	*Rank Govt. Primary only*	*Percentage Growth in Private Primary only*	*Rank Private Primary Only*
Districts	*2002-03*	*2014-15*	*2002-03*	*2014-15*				
Almora	63587*	32428	6471*	11034	-49.00	13	70.51	8
Bageshwar	12536	15534	1889	6860	23.92	1	263.16	3
Chamoli	43513	23547	4510	6133	-45.89	11	35.99	11
Champawat	27306	16970	3997	10024	-37.85	8	150.788	5
Dehradun	63383	48014	11490	33917	-24.25	3	195.19	4
Haridwar	101035	85918	33999	59189	-14.96	2	74.090	7
Nainital	59484	40616	16528	21463	-31.72	5	29.86	12
Pauri Garhwal	55865	34453	199	10959	-38.33	9	5407	1
Pithoragarh	42840	23440	4415	7713	-45.28	10	74.699	6
Rudraprayag	24369	15277	752	6113	-37.31	7	712.898	2
Tehri	75808	39632	18240	14274	-47.72	12	-21.74	13
Udham Singh Nagar	108440	80546	39498	67040	-25.72	4	69.73	9
Uttarkashi	33455	21667	6217	8667	-35.235	6	39.41	10

Source: DISE and Authors' calculation;

*Since data for Almora only was not available for 2002-03, it has been substituted by figures 2003-04.

Except the district of Bageshwar, all the districts showed a decline in the total enrolment in government schools primary (Table 20.9). This decline was highest in the district of Almora at 49 per cent followed by Tehri at 47.72 per cent and Chamoli at 45.89 per cent. Only Bageshwar district witnessed an increase in enrolment at the growth rate 23.92 per cent which is explained at a later stage in this paper.

On the other hand all the districts had an increase in the number of private primary only schools, except for the district of Tehri (-21.27 per cent decline from 2002-03 to 2014-15). The increase was highest in the district of Pauri Garhwal where the private only primary schools increased from 199 in 2002-03 to 10959 in 2014-15.

Table 20.10: Total Enrolment in Government and Private Primary with Upper Primary Schools

	Govt. only Primary with Upper Primary		*Private Primary with Upper Primary*		*Percentage Growth in Govt. Primary with Upper Primary Only*	*Percentage Growth in Private Primary with Upper Primary only*
Districts	***2002-03***	***2014-15***	***2002-03***	***2014-15***		
Almora	1222*	23	1431*	10274	-98.12	617.96
Bageshwar	0	0	1404	2510	00	78.77
Chamoli	1303	60	4796	8868	-95.39	84.90
Champawat	30	-	593	1415	-	138.62
Dehradun	2871	82	14673	48723	-97.14	232.06
Haridwar	1245	81	21007	-	-93.49	--
Nainital	1319	191	3495	21940	-85.52	527.75
Pauri Garhwal	36	17	374	13377	-52.78	3476.7
Pithoragarh	1780	283	1569	11223	-84.10	615.29
Rudraprayag	469	-	143	3668	-	2465
Tehri	1512	320	2912	9522	-78.84	226.99
Udham Singh Nagar	1828	-	1645	43692	-	2556
Uttarkashi	2318	222	2268	8437	-90.42	272

Source: DISE and Authors' calculation; *Since data for Almora only was not available for 2002-03, it has been substituted by figures of 2003-04.

As shown in Table 20.10, all the districts showed a decline in growth of government primary with upper primary schools. However, all the districts showed an increase in percentage of private primary with upper primary only. The increase were noteworthy in districts US Nagar, Pauri, Pithoragarh, Almora etc.

It is also to be noted at this juncture that district Udham Singh Nagar, showed one of the highest percentage increase in the private primary with upper primary schools. The district being in the plain area of the state has shown trend of increase in migrant population and hence this expected increase in demand for private schools.

Table 20.11: Total Enrolment in Government and Private Only Upper Primary Schools

Districts	*Govt. only Upper Primary*		*Private Only Upper Primary*		*Percentage Growth in Govt. Upper Primary Only 2002-03 to 2014-15*	*Rank in growth of Govt. Upper Primary only*	*Percentage Growth in Private Upper Primary only 2002-03 to 2014-15*	*Rank in growth of Private Upper Primary Only*
	2002-03	*2014-15*	*2002-03*	*2014-15*				
Almora	11375*	5735	1778*	1412	-49.58	12	-20.58	13
Bageshwar	3360	4313	628	1106	28.36	3	76.11	5
Chamoli	11285	6120	839	1455	-45.76	9	73.42	7
Champawat	6739	4330	1013	2098	-35.75	8	107	3
Dehradun	10476	15848	1227	6535	51.28	2	432.59	2
Haridwar	9841	17516	7811	13553	77.99	1	73.51	6
Nainital	18273	8564	4558	4842	-53.13	13	6.23	10
Pauri Garhwal	15923	8180	38	2850	-48.63	10	7400	1
Pithoragarh	10712	5415	803	932	-49.45	11	16.06	9
Rudraprayag	4599	3999	721	1298	-13.04	5	80.03	4
Tehri	16052	13396	3516	3098	-16.55	6	-11.89	12
Udham Singh Nagar	24381	18973	10514	13439	-22.18	7	27.82	8
Uttarkashi	7848	8466	960	953	7.875	4	-0.729	11

Source: DISE and Authors' calculation; * Since data for Almora only was not available for 2002-03, it has been substituted by figures of 2003-04.

According to Table 20.11, only the district of Bageshwar, Dehradun, Haridwar and Uttarkashi showed an increase in the total enrolment in governmemt only upper primary schools. The highest increase was observed in district of Haridwar (77.99 per cent) followed by Dehradun (51.28 per cent) and Bageshwar (28.36 per cent). The rest of the 10 districts witnessed a decrease in the number of government upper primary schools. The decrease was highest in the district of Almora (49.58 per cent) followed by Pithoragarh (49.45 per cent) and Pauri Garhwal (48.63 per cent).

The 10 districts observed an increase in the number of private upper primary only schools. The increase was highest in the district of Pauri Garhwal where it grew from 38 in 2002-03 to 2850 in 2014-15. This was followed by Dehradun and Champawat. The remaining three districts demonstrated a decrease in the number of private upper primary only schools with the highest decrease in the district of Almora (-20.58 per cent), followed by Tehri (-11.89 per cent) and Uttarkashi (-0.729 per cent).

It is also to be noted here that Pauri Garhwal which ranked amongst the lowest increase in the total enrolment in government only primary schools (-48.63 per cent), showed the highest increase in enrolment in the private upper primary school (38 to 2850) during the reference period. Thus at large the demand for private school is clearly visible.

Table 20.12: Total Number of teachers in Government and Private only Primary Schools

	Govt. only Primary		*Private Only Primary*		*Growth in Govt. Primary Only*	*Rank Govt. Primary Only*	*Growth in Private Primary Only*	*Rank Private Primary Only*
Districts	*2002-03*	*2014-15*	*2002-03*	*2014-15*				
Almora	2213*	2593	57*	846	17.17	6	1384.2	2
Bageshwar	678	1053	124	394	55.31	1	217.7	6
Chamoli	1792	1947	342	505	8.65	9	47.66	11
Champawat	777	1111	202	616	42.99	2	204.95	7
Dehradun	2276	2256	797	1790	-0.879	11	124.59	9
Haridwar	1791		1258		---	---	---	--
Nainital	1829	2057	351	1414	12.47	8	302.85	5
Pauri Garhwal	2725	3436	10	688	26.09	3	6780	1
Pithoragarh	1862	2216	135	702	19.01	5	420	4
Rudraprayag	979	1056	36	456	7.87	10	1166.67	3
Tehri	2670	3061	511	1162	14.64	7	127.39	8
Udham Singh Nagar	2009		1065		---	---	---	---
Uttarkashi	1236	1494	418	659	20.87	4	57.65	10

Source: DISE and Authors' calculation;

* Since data for Almora only was not available for 2002-03, it has been substituted by figures of 2003-04.

As per figures of Table 20.12, all the districts except the district of Dehradun witnessed a decrease in the number of teachers in government only primary schools. The highest increase was in the district of Bageshwar (55.31 per cent) followed by Champawat (42.99 per cent). Dehradun district showed a decrease in the percentage of teachers in government only primary schools, a decrease of -0.879 per cent.

All the districts demonstrated an increase in the number of teachers in private primary only schools with the highest growth observed in district of Pauri Garhwal where it grew from 10 in 2002-03 to 688 in 2014-15. This was followed by Almora which increased from 57 in 2002-03 to 846 in 2014-15 and Rudraprayag from 36 in 2002-03 to 456 in 2014-15.

Table 20.13: Total Number of teachers in Government and Private Primary with Upper Primary Schools

	Govt. Primary with Upper Primary		*Private Primary with Upper Primary*		*Growth in Govt. Primary with Upper Primary Only 2002-03 to 2014-15*	*Rank in growth Govt. Primary with Upper Primary only*	*Growth in Private Primary with Upper Primary only 2002-03 to 2014-15*	*Rank in growth of Private Primary with Upper Primary Only*
Districts	***2002-03***	***2014-15***	***2002-03***	***2014-15***				
Almora	40*	5	27*	512	-87.5	6	1796.29	5
Bageshwar	0	0	59	110	-		86.44	8
Chamoli	72	6	327	584	-91.66	7	78.59	10
Champawat	6	0	41	76	-100	9	85.36	9
Dehradun	172	5	1002	1758	-97.09	8	75.45	11
Haridwar	43		622		---		----	---
Nainital	64	10	28	1140	-84.37	4	3971.43	1
Pauri Garhwal	10	5	18	668	-50	3	3611.11	3
Pithoragarh	53	28	25	725	-47.16	2	2800	4
Rudraprayag	20	0	6	226	-100	9	3666.67	2
Tehri	45	24	90	609	-46.67	1	576.67	6
Udham Singh Nagar	50		57		---		---	---
Uttarkashi	68	9	137	463	-86.76	5	237.96	7

Source: DISE and Authors' calculation; *Since data for Almora only was not available for 2002-03, it has been substituted by figures of 2003-04.

Figures in Table 20.13 show that all the 13 districts witnessed a decrease in the total number of teachers in government primary with upper primary only schools. On the other hand all the 13 districts showed an increase in the number of teachers in private primary and upper primary school. This increase was highest in the district of Nainital where it grew from 28 in 2002-03 to 1140 in 2014-15 followed by Rudraprayag where it increased from six in 2002-03 to 226 in 2014-15 and Pauri Garhwal from 18 in 2002-03 to 668 in 2014-15.

It is also to be noted here that on one hand a decrease of teachers was observed in all the districts in government primary with upper primary only schools, significant increase of teachers were observed in all the districts in private primary with upper primary only schools category. The first was due to government policy while the second was due to larger market demand especially for English medium schools.

The district Rudraprayag which showed 100 per cent decrease in the number of teachers in the government primary with upper primary only schools demonstrated the second highest increase in numbers of teachers in private primary with upper primary only schools. Thus, growth in opposite direction of government and private schools are very much visible in the state.

Table 20.14: Total Number of teachers in Government and Private only Upper Primary Schools

	Govt. only Upper Primary		*Private Only Upper Primary*		*Growth in Govt. Upper Primary Only 2002-03 to 2014-15*	*Rank in growth of Govt. Upper Primary only*	*Growth in Private Upper Primary only 2002-03 to 2014-15*	*Rank in growth of Private Upper Primary Only*
Districts	***2002-03***	***2014-15***	***2002-03***	***2014-15***				
Almora	595*	481	23*	132	-19.16	8	473.91	2
Bageshwar	229	380	50	88	65.94	1	76	9
Chamoli	694	710	53	136	2.305	6	156.6	6
Champawat	352	352	38	158	0		315.79	4
Dehradun	786	918	109	386	16.79	4	254.13	5
Haridwar	239		209		--		--	--
Nainital	1001	713	126	317	-28.77	10	151.59	7
Pauri Garhwal	1527	1149	5	234	-24.75	9	4580	1
Pithoragarh	621	695	30	142	11.92	5	373.3	3
Rudraprayag	434	433	54	99	-0.23	7	83.33	8
Tehri	977	1472	175	221	50.66	2	26.29	10
Udham Singh Nagar	778		335		--	--	--	
Uttarkashi	652	791	50	54	21.32	3	8	11

Source: DISE and Authors' calculation; *Since data for Almora only was not available for 2002-03, it has been substituted by figures of 2003-04.

The districts of Bageshwar, Chamoli, Dehradun, Pithoragarh, Tehri and Uttarkashi witnessed an increase in the total number of teachers in the government upper primary school as evident from Table 20.14. The district of Champawat showed no change in the number of teachers while data when retrieved was not available for Haridwar and Udham Singh Nagar district for the year 2014-15. The remaining four districts viz. Almora, Nainital, Pauri Garhwal and Rudraprayag showed a decrease in the number of government only upper primary schools. The highest increase was observed in the district of Bageshwar (65.94) followed by Tehri (50.66) and Uttarkashi (21.32). The maximum decrease was observed in the district of Nainital (-28.77 per cent) followed by Pauri Garhwal (-24.75 per cent) and Almora (-19.16 per cent).

All the districts demonstrated an increase in the private upper primary only schools. The highest increase was observed in district Pauri Garhwal where it increased from five in 2002-03 to 234 in 2014-15 an increase of around 4580 per cent.

Table 20.15: Districtwise GER and NER (Primary and Upper Primary)

	Primary		*Upper Primary*		*Primary*	*Upper Primary*	*Primary*	*Upper Primary*
	GER				*NER*			
Districts	***2002-03***	***2014-15***	***2002-03***	***2014-15***	***2002-03***	***2014-15***	***2002-03***	***2014-15***
Almora	84	93.03	87.1	93.85	70.8	78.84	62.3	69.3
Bageshwar	45.3	97.36	47.5	91.75	36.2	84.74	31	69.50
Chamoli	93.9	96.25	112.9	95.07	73.7	80.09	80.9	71.33
Champawat	84.6	100.28	81.5	92.83	63.9	87.38	49.5	66.58
Dehradun	45.3	114.23	26.7	94.90	35.8	97.79	19.8	71.57
Haridwar	68.8	111.71	41.6	70.98	63.3	95.55	38	52.30
Nainital	70.9	106.21		92.40	60.2	91.68		70.17
Pauri Garhwal	54		37		47.9		26.3	
Pithoragarh	71.2	97.19	76	94.88	61.3	82.26	55	72.90
Rudraprayag	74.8	102.35	44	95.75	54.7	88.74	28.5	73.64
Tehri	105.9	98.98	100.7	91.03	90.5	83.27	88.8	68.85
Udham Singh Nagar	79.4	124.67	60.3	85.67	63.9	-	41.1	63.91
Uttarkashi	96.7	108.11	88.3	87.82	77.1	85.61	66.1	63.41

Source: DISE.

From Table 20.15 it is observed that all the districts except Tehri showed remarkable improvement in the GER (primary) from 2002-03 to 2014-15, all the districts were able to achieve more than 90 points in the GER (primary). The maximum GER was observed in the district of Udham Singh Nagar (124.67) followed by Dehradun (114.23) and Haridwar (111.74). However, only for the district of Tehri, there was a drop in GER from 105.9 in 2002-03 to 98.98 in 2014-15.

All the districts except Chamoli Tehri and Uttarkhasi showed remarkable improvement in the GER (Upper Primary) from 2002-03 to 2014-15. However, data was not available for the district of Nainital during the study for the year 2002-03 and Pauri Garhwal for 2014-15. The highest GER was observed in Rudraprayag (95.75 per cent) followed by Chamoli (95.07 per cent) and Dehradun (94.90 per cent). The districts of Chamoli, Tehri, and Uttarkashi showed a drop in GER from 2002-03 to 2014-15.

Even in NER (primary), all the districts except Tehri showed remarkable improvement from 2002-03 to 2014-15, all the districts were able to achieve more than 75 NER in primary level. The maximum NER was observed in the district of Dehradun (97.79) followed by Haridwar (95.55) and Nainital (91.68). However, only for the district of Tehri, there was a drop in NER from 90.5 in 2002-03 to 83.27 in 2014-15. One primary reason may be rehabilitation and resettlement in the area due to the construction of Tehri dam.

All the districts except Chamoli, Tehri and Uttarkhasi showed remarkable improvement in the NER (Upper Primary) from 2002-03 to 2014-15. The highest NER (Upper Primary) was observed in Rudraprayag (73.6) followed by Pithoragarh (72.9) and Dehradun (71.57). However, the district of Chamoli, Tehri and Uttarkashi showed a drop in GER from 2002-03 to 2014-15.

Where does the state really stand now?

How much the children going to school are really learning, is it just the report cards and the promotion to a higher class, certain policy restraints

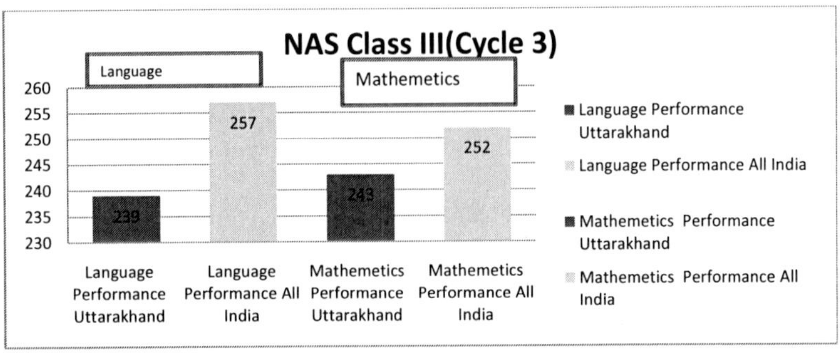

Source: MHRD, GOI.

Figure 20.1: National Achievement Survey (NAS Cycle 3): A comparison of All India and Uttarakhand for Class 3 students, 2015-16.

or is the knowledge imparted to them in a certain environment with teachers, facilities, curriculum, infrastructure etc. really enhancing their ability to understand their prescribed syllabus and beyond in this young Himalayan state is a major question in front of the well wishers, policy-makers and leaders of the state. To specifically get a broad idea about where does Uttarakhand stand at present in this direction as far as elementary education is concerned, the analysis in this section is made.

Figure 20.1 clearly shows that language performance for the State of Uttarakhand is lagging behind language performance of all-India Level for Class 3 students in the year 2015-16. Similar trend is observed in case of Mathematics where again Uttarakhand is lagging behind in the Mathematics performance of all-India level for class 3 students in the year 2015-16.

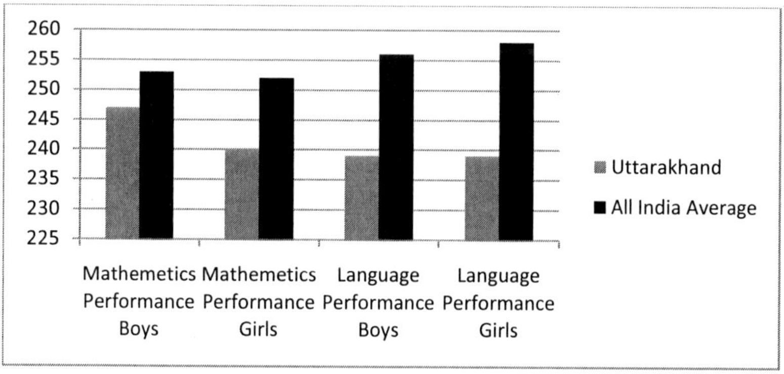

Source: Data from MHRD, GOI.

Figure 20.2: National Achievement Survey performance by gender (Class 3) for Uttarakhand and All India.

From Figure 20.2 it is seen that mathematics performance of boys (247) are behind all-India average (253 points), the difference of around six points is observed between the two. In the girls category, mathematics performance for Uttarakhand state is also behind all-India average, for Uttarakhand it is at 240 points while all-India average is at 252 points, a difference of 12 points in this indicator.

In language performance for Uttarakhand both boys and girls stand below all-India average. The difference being 17 points in case of boys performance (Boys Performance- 239 points and All India Average -256 points) and significant difference of 18 points in case of girls performance (Girls Performance - 239 points and All India Average- 257 points).

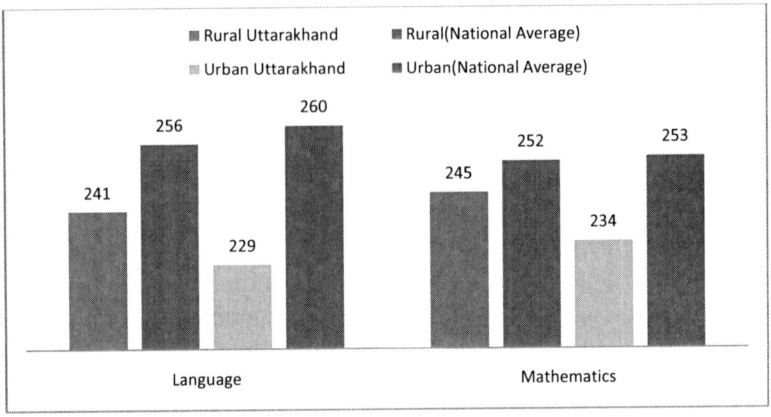

Source: Data from MHRD, GOI.

Figure 20.3: Rural Urban performance of Std 3 students in Uttarakhand and All India (2015-16).

Figure 20.3 reveals that in both the parameters i.e. language and mathematics performance of rural and urban students of standard 3 in Uttarakhand, the state stands below all-India average for the year 2015-16. It shows 15 points below in the rural language performance and below by 31 points in case of urban language performance.

In case of mathematics performance in rural areas it is below by seven points and below by 19 points in case of urban language performance.

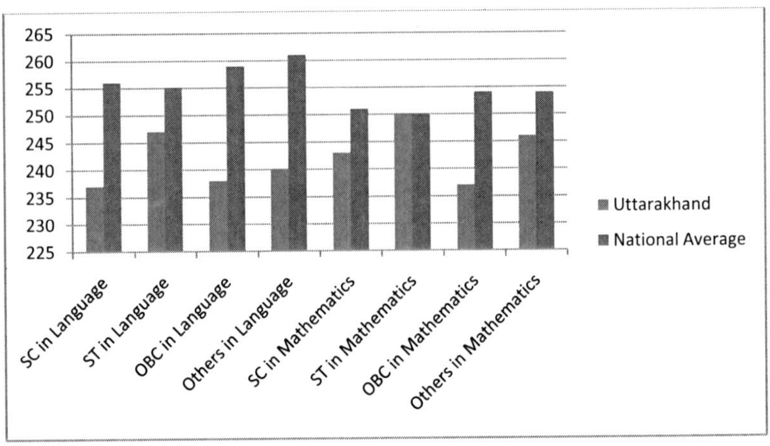

Source: Data from MHRD, GOI.

Figure 20.4 : Performance of Students by Social Groups in Uttarakhand and All India (2015-16).

Categories of social groups like SC, ST, OBC and others all show below the national average performance in language and mathematics. Figure 20.4 shows that the difference being significantly high in case of OBC category, SC category and other category students performance, in language the difference being 20 points in OBC category and SC category and 21 points in other category students. In case of mathematics, performance of OBC in Uttarakhand stands significantly below the national average, the difference being 17 points, the other category though stands below the national average but the difference is of seven points. However, the ST category performance is at par with the national average in case of mathematics but below national average in case of language.

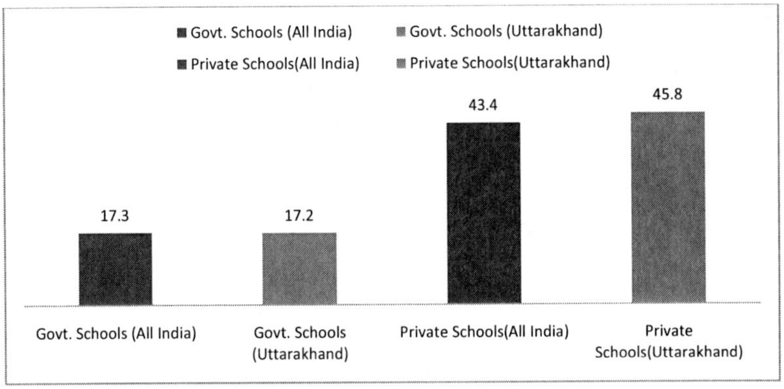

Data Source: ASER 2014.

Figure 20.5: Percentage of Children in Std III who can do at least subtraction by school type.

Figure 20.5 shows the students of standard 3 who can do at least subtraction by school type. The government schools of Uttarakhand are only 0.1 per cent below the all-India average, while the private schools of Uttarakhand show better performance than all-India average by 2.4 per cent points. Recent data from ASER 2016 reveal that percentage children in Std V who can read Std II level text is 56 per cent for rural government schools while 74 per cent for rural private schools.

According to Figure 20.6, both the school types of Uttarakhand (Government and Private) show better results than the all-India average in terms of standard V students who can do division. This performance being 0.7 per cent better in case of government schools as compared to government schools all India average and 6.8 per cent better in case of private schools as compared to all India average private schools.

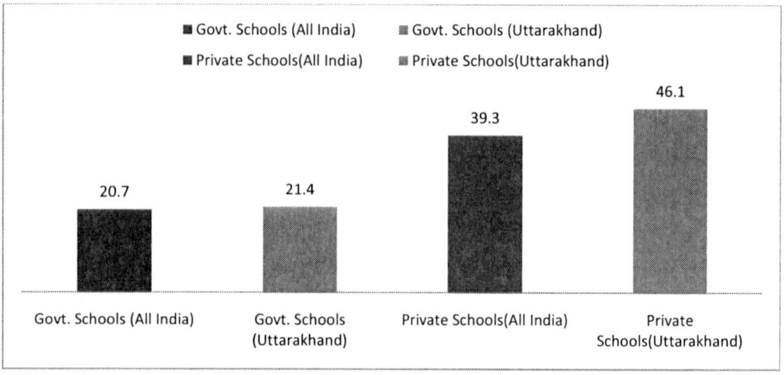

Data Source: ASER 2014.

Figure 20.6: Percentage of Children in Std V who can do division by school type

Recent ASER 2016 data for percentage of children in Std VIII who can read Std II level text shows that for rural government schools the percentage is 79.3 and 86.6 for private schools.

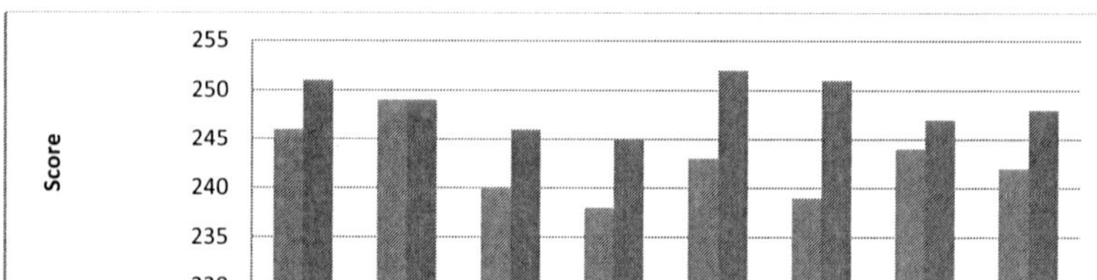

	Reading Comprehension Boys	Reading Comprehension Girls	Mathematics Boys	Mathematics Girls	Science Boys	Science Girls	Social Sci.Boys	Social Sci. Girls
Uttarakhand	246	249	240	238	243	239	244	242
All India Average	251	249	246	245	252	251	247	248

Source: Data from MHRD, GOI.

Figure 20.7: Performance by gender; NAS Class VIII.

Figure 20.7 shows that both the performance of boys and girls stands below the all-India average in reading comprehension, mathematics, science and social science for Class VIII except for girls reading comprehension, where it is at par with the all-India average (249 points). Performance in science shows boys of Uttarakhand are better than girls but overall performance in science for both girls and boys are below all-India average. In social science, the performance of boys and girls separately does not show much difference (the difference is of two points only with boys at 244 points and girls at 242) but if the performance of Uttarakhand boys and girls are compared with all-India average, the performance is poor.

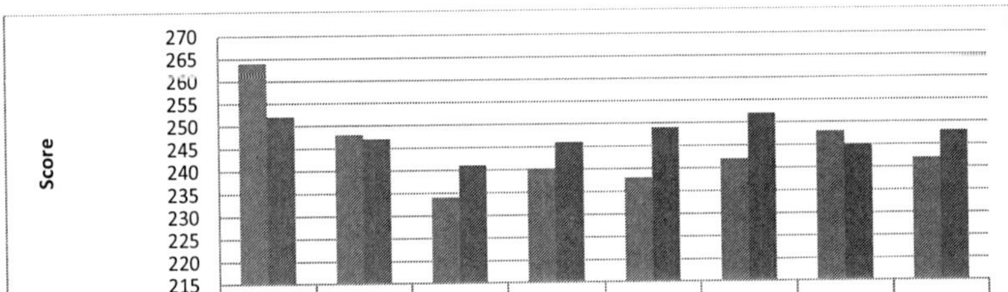

	Reading Comprehension Urban	Reading Comprehension Rural	Mathematics Urban	Mathematics Rural	Science Urban	Science Rural	Social Sci. Urban	Social Sci. Rural
Uttarakhand	264	248	234	240	238	242	248	242
All India Average	252	247	241	246	249	252	245	248

Source: Data from MHRD, GOI.

Figure 20.8: Performance of Class VIII based on rural urban category in NAS 2015-16.

Performance of Class VIII in reading comprehension both in rural and urban category illustrates better performance in Uttarakhand as compared to all-India average. But it stands below the national average both in rural and urban category in Mathematics, Science and Social Science.

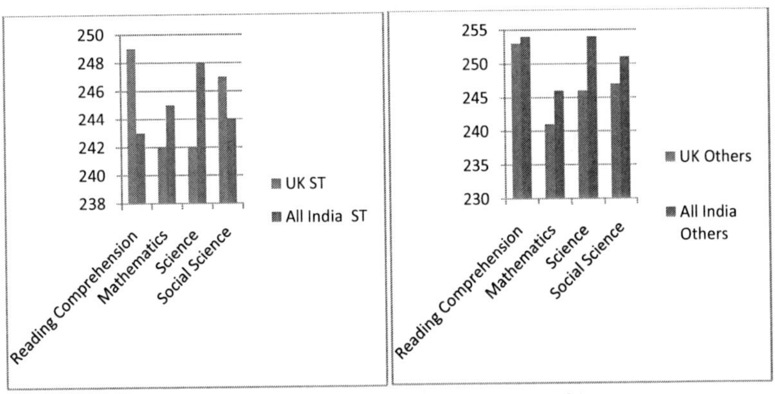

(a) **(b)**

Source: Data from MHRD, GOI.

Figure 20.9: Performance by Social Category of Class VIII in NAS.

Figure 20.9a reveals that the ST category students of Standard VIII in Uttarakhand performs significantly better in reading comprehension and social science when compared to all-India average. However, it is lacking behind in case of Mathematics and Science, the result being significantly poor in case of science performance in comparison to all-India averages. Figure 20.9b shows that students of standard VIII in other categories in the state of Uttarakhand is lagging behind in all the subjects viz. reading comprehension, mathematics, science and social science when compared to all-India average.

Thus in summary it may be concluded from the preceding two sections that though in general the inclusion in elementary education has improved in the state over the years but the 'learning outcome' indicators show that the Himalayan state of Uttarakhand is behind all India average in most indicators which is a serious issue of concern for the state.

Discussion

The study shows that over the reference period of study, growth of private primary schools have been at a very fast pace while growth of government schools are comparatively low. The general inclination towards private schools especially of low cost private schools in rural and semi-urban areas have facilitated in mushrooming of private schools.

However, the trend shows that GPS [Government Primary Schools] growth from 2002-03 to 2014-15 have been 16.05 per cent but in later years i.e. 2009-10 to 2014-15, it slowed down and the growth was negative (-0.65 per cent). This is a clear indication that either GPSs are unable to write the growth story in elementary education for the state because the larger market demand is diametrically different or the state has already established the schools in required numbers in most areas as per policy prescription or the government does not find it viable[18] to open new primary schools due to very less enrolment of students. In this respect it may be pointed out that the school education department of the state has a set of criteria[19] for opening up of primary and upper primary schools which reflects the provisions of opening schools in unschooled areas in the state.

Even the private primary schools growth has slowed down in later years (2009-10 to 2014-15) from 118.62 per cent in the period 2002-03 to 2014-15 to 6.47 per cent in the period 2009-10-2014-15. However, in rural sector, the growth of private primary schools in the reference period has been seven times more than that of government schools.This raises a question mark on the success of government schools and the major factors behind such a trend.

Percentage of single teacher school decreased in the state by around 7.2 per cent which is a welcome sign but yet this problem persists in the state and when coupled with teachers absenteeism becomes a major constraint for smooth teaching and learning activities and acts as a demotivation mechanism for students to attend school.

Though girls enrolment in primary schools have increased marginally in the reference period, in upper primary there has been a sharp fall in girls' enrolment. In most locations primary schools are available within one to five kms of radius of village, upper primary schools are not available near each and every village location. Therefore, while it becomes less difficult to send a boy for upper primary schooling in other villages or sub-urban areas, in case of girls, the basic social framework and the patriarchic understanding restraints the girl child to be sent to far off areas for upper primary schooling. A trend of fall in pupil teacher ratio in upper primary level is perhaps a clear indication of less enrolment in UPS.

The percentage of enrolment in English medium schools have increased over the period of study while that of Hindi medium schools have decreased. However, the rate of increase of English medium primary schools have been more than upper primary schools. There is a general attraction of parents towards English as a medium of instruction considering the larger market demand which is resulting in a disinclination towards government schools even if they are in the vicinity of the village. However, recently the state government has taken an initiative[20] in this direction.

Moreover in most of the GPS, there is a single teacher or two handling multi tasks - teaching multigrade classes simultaneously, maintaining MDM (Mid Day Meal) records, CCE (Continuous and comprehensive evaluation) records, enumeration of census, family planning programmes etc. Teachers have the burden of too much paper work in schools like filling of MDM registers, MDM sms, repeated information e.g. Students Profile, *Shalla Siddi*[21], CCE Register etc (according to RTE Act teachers are supposed to stay in schools for extra two hours after classes but due to teachers union pressure this could not be implemented in most parts of the country). Responsibility of other departmental works (which a child's family should do themselves) also lies with the teachers e.g. making of Aadhar Card, caste certificate, income certificate, RTE admission certificate, scholarship documents. In many cases the non-teaching activities occupy so much of time that the very purpose of teaching–learning activity gets diluted.

Moreover as the larger general behaviour and conduct goes, most of the teachers are reluctant to serve in the hills especially if those are in remote rural areas. In such cases transfer policy in the state is a major issue and it has been politicised over the years. Even after sixteen years of state formation, the scenario has not changed much.

Teachers absenteeism, especially in the hills availing almost all forms of leaves is a major constraint of performance in government schools. Availing long period of CCL [Child Care Leave] to skip from the remote area posting for some time has become a problem for the government and its officials to deal with female teachers.

Admission in government primary schools start from Class 1 or Standard 1 whereas in most private schools they start from Play Group, Nursery, Kinder Garten and even pre-primary, as a result it affects the enrolment in government schools as parents prefer to enrol the child at an earlier age and wants continuous education in the same school.

Lack of appropriate infrastructure in government schools discourages parents to enroll their children in government school especially in circumstances where private school are available. In this context it may be noted that recently in a landmark judgment[22], Uttarakhand High Court has directed the state government to provide infrastructure and other amenities to the government and aided schools in the state within three months.

A new tag for government schools that has come up after implementation of MDM is "*daal bhaat school*". There is an immediate need to come out of the tag by substituting it with quality education. Non-compatibility of teachers in use of technology even if infrastructure is provided is an area of concern e.g. computer literacy, using of LCDs etc. Failure of teacher to deliver the best in many cases even after undergoing trainings etc is another major issue, however it seems that in most of the cases the pertinent reason is that the profession is seen as a source of livelihood only but not as a profession that builds the nation.

Primary with upper primary schools (government) no more exist as per government law. They exist in private sector. Hence in some cases, to have a continued education in a single school, parents prefer not to enroll their children in government schools.

A special case study is found through research from the results of Bageshwar [as shown in Table 20.6]. One of the reasons for the figures could be that all the private schools recognition were cancelled in last few years by an education officer which led to re-opening of many Government Schools in Bageshwar and also increase in number of students in Government Schools of Bageshwar (Government Primary and Upper Primary.)[23]

As far as GER and NER are concerned, GER is very good at primary level while NER is comparatively lesser in primary level. The GER of Upper Primary level which was only 51.3 in 2001-02 has increased to 85.53 in 2014-15. NER in upper primary level was only 39.2 in 2001-02 which increased to 64.07 in 2014-15. This is a clear indication that educational inclusion in elementary level in the state has increased over the reference period however still there is lack of enrolment in the class according to the correct age for that class which is evident from the GER figures.

In terms of number of government primary schools, highest growth is seen in Bageshwar and lowest is observed in Chamoli. Among private primary schools, Pauri shows the highest growth while Chamoli shows the lowest. In the category of primary with upper primary, the significant decrease is evident as the state government has closed this category of school. However, among private primary and upper primary, Dehradun, Pauri and Pithoragarh shows a very significant increase. Bageshwar shows a significant growth even in Government UPS. This is a special case study and it has been discussed earlier that in Bageshwar, all affiliations/ registrations for private schools were strictly controlled in order to promote education though government schools.

Bageshwar has also shown a significant enrolment growth of students in government schools which is an indication that outmigration for elementary education did not take place in Bageshwar and the only option of studying in government schools was accepted by the people in the region. Among the districts, Bageshwar and Dehradun shows very high increase in NER which is a very good indication. These two districts are very distinct in their characters as Dehradun is basically a plain district and Bageshwar a hill district. Moreover Dehradun being the capital of the state has certain advantages by default.

Indicators like GER, NER, growth of teachers etc gives an apparent view of educational inclusion at elementary level but to what extent the students are learning in real terms is a very important question that needs to be addressed. From the analysis, it is observed that the performance in both language and mathematics in Uttarakhand is poor compared to all-India level. If the situation is analysed with respect to gender differences, both boys and girls performance are poor compared to all-India average, however boys perform better compared to girls in mathematics. As far as regional disparities are concerned, rural Uttarakhand performs poorer compared to all-India rural performance. Even in urban performance,

Uttarakhand is behind national average in both language and mathematics. The difference in urban performance of Uttarakhand, compared to all-India average is much more than rural differences. This firstly explains that Uttarakhand is lagging in 'learning outcome' of education as far as elementary education is concerned. Secondly, the poor performance of urban Uttarakhand is a very clear indication that Uttarakhand is not only behind in rural performance but it is not even at par with all-India average in performance of average of urban India. Hence this raises a huge question on curriculum content, teaching methodology, ability and /or motivation of teachers and also teaching learning environment.

Not much significant difference is observed in the performance of government schools in Uttarakhand and all-India or among the private schools in Uttarakhand and all-India. The only significant observation is that in both the cases, government schools are behind private schools as far as performance indicators are concerned. All these broadly specifies that Uttarakhand has not been able to demonstrate its growth in performance indicators in government as well as private schools in general. This is a great threat to the state and in depth diagnosis and prescription is the need of the hour.

Way Forward

This section is based on secondary data presented in the paper and the observation of the authors in various parts of the state during field surveys and administrative visits on a number of occasions and discussion with education officers.

In most cases learning has become a burden for students as teachers have a specified syllabus to be completed in specific time through traditional teaching learning process. In government schools after the SSA, RTE, MDMs etc the workload of teachers in paper work related activities to record keeping etc has increased a lot with an undesirable impact on teaching learning process. In private schools especially the low cost ones, retention of teachers is a major problem and the job is often referred to a 'time pass' before getting a regular government job. Hence in both the cases the students are the victims of the situation. There is a huge need to move towards more flexible teaching learning system where the thought process, the reasoning ability, the logical thinking of the students are developed. However, the supply side needs to be equipped for such a strategy. In rural and semi urban areas, a biology teacher should have flexibility to take the students to the forest nearby and help them to identify the Himalayan species of flora and describe their characteristics or a geography teacher can take the pupil near river or strem and show how erosion of rocks take place or show the types of rocks in the mountains in their area. Keeping the basic structure same, education in elementary level needs to be region oriented implying that for a hill state, the students first has to understand hill characteristics, nature of natural disasters, how to combat with such disasters etc. At a matured stage he/she can understand the other kinds of terrains and can compare with his/her own. Learning can be more spontaneous if such a method is adopted. We need education that opens up the mind where new ideas flow, not the one that burdens the mind.

Preserving the cultural heritage of the region through curriculum is also important. Scripts, folk songs, dance forms, fairs, festivals, folk art craft etc should be a part of the curriculum to understand the regional culture first. Himalayas have rare collection of medicinal plants in this region which if not made a part of the curriculum will not be known to the present generation learners as these are the indigenous knowledge of the people of the villages in the region. These needs to be documented and made a part of school curriculum so that the present and future generations can understand the worth. Himalayas have their unique indigenous practices of agriculture. The knowledge has to be transferred to the new learners though their curriculum with hands on experiences. Perhaps the need of the hour is not myriad of policies and provisions in education but changing the orientation.

If students are promoted from one standard to another just because the policy wants so, in the long run it will be nothing but intergenerational transmission of unskilled labour force in the market and hence the jargon of 'demographic dividend' will gradually lose its meaning. Monitoring of learning achievement should be properly scaled, time specified and regularly evaluated with suggestive measures. Though in this direction the state government carries out CCE but post-diagnosis treatment is poor.

GER or NER no doubt are good indicators to show enrolment but there is a need to find the correlation of enrolment and attendance. This can give a better picture of the real situation. Teachers absenteeism especially in government schools of rural areas with all forms of leaves that one can avail is a major issue of concern. In many cases those long absenteeism are only because of the backwardness of area where he/she is posted. This has a huge impact on students learning process. Strict policy related to station leave etc. and other forms of leave are required to be implemented. However, if the teachers are posted in stations near to the hometown or village through policy prescription strictly, some improvement in situation is expected.

Uttarakhand government needs to have a different model of elementary education taking into consideration various regional factors like terrains frequent natural disasters, accessibility issues, education through environment and natural resources, usage of technology and above all very effective monitoring and evaluation mechanism. It is high time that the state and the nation at large stops aping the western models of education and restructures it based on the need, capacity, constraints and ideology of the nation. A nation gets destabilised when the unawareness of the people about their own roots increases, or when it is not proud of its history and culture. Actually that is where real deterioration of a nation starts. There is a great need to revise the curriculum, methodology and set goals for education. Elementary educatoin being the plinth, demands prior reshaping.

It is high time for the state to move from 'inclusion in education' to assessment of 'learning outcome.' A 'state character' for building the future of the state through education of the children has to be imbibed among all the stakeholders- the parents, teachers, policy-makers, political leaders and administrators. Relevance of the present educational provisions and its impact needs to be diagnosed with policy prescription. Hence to save the Himalayan state from intergenerational deprivation of quality education, it is high time that the policy-makers start thinking in different dimensions with a "Himalayan Model of Education with Global adaptability approach" which can be implemented in other peer Himalayan states and Uttarakhand will have the opportunity to claim to be the pioneer in this direction. The history of educational development of Indian Himalayan states will acknowledge and honour the state in the future for crafting the new beginning of educational journey of Himalayan states and voice the concern of education in Himalayan region.

Acknowledgements: The authors are immensely grateful to Integrated Institute of Himalayan Studies, Shimla and Central Library (Himalayan Studies), HP University to allow to use the library for referring to some rare collections for this study. The authors also acknowledge with thanks all the agencies like DISE, Pratham, MHRD for the statistical figures used in this paper. Dr Datta is thankful to the principal DBS PG College, Dr O.P. Kulshrestha for providing a congenial atmosphere is the college. The authors are also thankful to the education officers and teachers whose comments helped to enrich the paper.

Bibliography

Atkinson, E.T., The Himalayan Gazetteer first published by Government Press, 1882, reprint Cosmo, Delhi 1981, Volume II, part I and II and Volume III, part I and II.

Barro, R.J (2001), Human Capital and Growth, American Economic Review 91 (Papers and Proceedings): 12-17.

Dabral, Shiv Prasad (1968), Uttarakhand ka Itihas, Vol. VIII, p. 91.

Drèze, Jean, and Mrinalini Saran (1993), Primary Education and Economic Development in China and India, Development Economics Research Programme Discussion Paper 47. London: London School of Economics and Political Science.

Drèze, Jean, and Amartya K. Sen (1989), Hunger and Public Action. Oxford: Clarendon Press.

Education Commission (1966), Education for Development: Report of the Education Commission 1964-66. New Delhi: National Council of Educational Research and Training [Reprint 1971] *Garhwali,* November 1913.

Jodha, N. S., Banskota, M. and Pratap Tej (1992), Sustainable Mountain Agriculture: Perspective and Issues, Vol. 1, Oxford and IBH Publishing Co., New Delhi.

Jodha, N. S., Banskota, M. and Pratap Tej (1992), Sustainable Mountain Agriculture : Farmers Strategies and Innovative Approaches, Vol. 2, Oxford and IBH Publishing Co., New Delhi.

Nevill, H.R. (1904), *"Nainital A Gazetteer being Volume XXXIV of the District Gazetteer of North Western Provinces of Agra and Oudh,* Allahabad, Government Press.

Ozturk, Ilhan https://mpra.ub.uni-muenchen.de/9023/1/MPRA_paper_9023.pdf

Rao, V.K.R.V. (1964), Education and Economic Development. New Delhi: National Council of Educational Research and Training.

Raturi, H. K., Annual Administrative Report of Tehri Garhwal State 1909-10, p. 4

Report on Monitoring of the Financial Management And Procurement Relating to Sarva Shiksha Abhiyan in Uttarakhand; Institute of the Public Auditors of India, http://ssa.nic.in/financial-mgmt-docs/ipai-review-phase-2/Uttarakhand%20Report-IPAI.pdf

Rawat, A. S. (1983), Garhwal Himalayas-A Historical Survey; Eastern Book Linkers.

Sen, Amartya (2000), Development As Freedom, New Delhi, Oxford University Press.

Sen, A, Drèze J., India: Economic Development and Social Opportunity. Oxford: Clarendon Press; 1995, pp. 14-15.

Schultz, Theodore W. (1961), Investment in Human Capital, American Economic Review 51 (1) March: 1-15.

The Framework Education Programme for Elementary Education, Research Institute of Education, Prague, 2007.

Tolia, R.S (1996), *British – Kumaun – Garhwal An administrative History of A Non-Regulation Hill Province Gowan, Lushington and Batten Years (A.D 1836 to 1856),* Almora, Shree Almora Book Depot.

Tilak, 2005, Post-Elementary Education, Poverty and Development in India, Centre of African Studies, University of Edinburgh.

UNDP (2000), Overcoming Human Poverty: Poverty Report 2000. New York.

Walton, H. G. (1910), British Garhwal A Gazetter, Allahabad, p. 106.

Websites of

Ministry of HRD, GOI: mhrd.gov.in

ASER: www.asercentre.org

DISE: www.dise.in

Notes

1. MHRD.
2. Report on Monitoring of the Financial Management And Procurement Relating to Sarva Shiksha Abhiyan in Uttarakhand; Institute of the Public Auditors of India, http://ssa.nic.in/financial-mgmt-docs/ipai-review-phase-2/Uttarakhand%20Report-IPAI.pdf
3. Jean Dre'z and Amartya Sen, 1995, pp. 14-15.
4. Ozturk, Ilhan https://mpra.ub.uni-muenchen.de/9023/1/MPRA_ paper_9023.pdf
5. Tilak, 2005, Post-Elementary Education, Poverty and Development in India, Centre of African Studies, University of Edinburgh.
6. The Framework Education Programme for Elementary Education, Research Institute of Education, Prague, 2007.
7. Based on Jodha 1992.
8. Based on R. S. Tolia, Indian Mountain Initiative 2014.
9. Tharu and Boksa are among the five major tribes of the region.
10. Based on H.R. Nevill 1904.
11. Walton, H. G. British Garhwal A Gazetter, p. 106.
12. Tolia, R.S. 1996.
13. Dabral, Shiv Prasad-Uttarakhand ka Itihas, Vol. VIII, p. 91.
14. Garhwali, November 1913.
15. Raturi, H. K. Annual Administrative Report of Tehri Garhwal State 1909-10, p. 4.

16. The primary gross enrolment ratio (GER) or primary GER indicates how many children, regardless of their age, are enrolled in primary school, relative to the population of primary school age.

$$\text{Primary GER} = \frac{\text{Enrolment in primary level}}{\text{Population of official age group for primary level}}$$

17. The net enrolment ratio (NER) in primary education is one of the official indicators for the Millennium Development Goal of universal primary education. The primary NER is the share of children of primary school age that are enrolled in primary school.

$$\text{Primary GER} = \frac{\text{Enrolment of the official primary school age}}{\text{Population of official primary school age}}$$

If all children of primary school age are enrolled in primary school, the primary NER is 100 per cent. A primary NER below 100 per cent means that not all children of primary school age are in primary school; some may be out of school, some may be in preschool, in secondary school or in other forms of education. By definition, the NER cannot exceed 100 per cent. On the other hand "Gross" enrolment includes students of all ages. In other words, it includes students whose age exceeds the official age group (e.g. repeaters). Thus, if there is late enrolment, early enrolment, or repetition, the total enrolment can exceed the population of the age group that officially corresponds to the level of education – leading to ratios greater than 100 per cent.

18. For better understanding regarding viability refer to the letter dated 12th May 2016 [No. F 1-13/2016-RMSA-III from MHRD to Secretary (Education), Uttarakhand referring to the minutes of the meeting held on 28th April 2016.

19. In the hill region, a new Primary School is opened if there is no access to Primary Education within one km and the population of the served area is above 200. For the plain region, the distance is 1.5 km and the population should be above 300. An upper primary school is opened between two primary schools if there is no access within 3 km to upper primary school classes.

20. Uttarakhand has drawn up an ambitious plan to shift the medium of instruction from Hindi to English in the approximately 18,000 government schools in the hill state.The state's education minister, Arvind Pandey, told TOI the project [That the state plans to shift the medium of instruction to English in approximately 18,000 government schools] would be rolled out in a phased manner, beginning with the introduction of English as the medium of instruction in Class 1 from the 2018-19 academic year. [Times of India, June 30, 2017].

21. The National Programme on School Standards and Evaluation (NPSSE), known as Shaala Sidhdhi is a comprehensive instrument for school

evaluation leading to school improvement. Developed by the National University of Educational Planning and Administration (NUEPA), it aims to enable schools to evaluate their performance in a more focused and strategic manner and facilitate them to make professional judgments for improvement. The programme's objective is to establish and refer to an agreed set of standards and to provide clear pathways for each school for self evaluation, by focussing on key performance domains and their core standards for school evaluation.

22. Kindly refer to the Judgement dated 19th November 2016 of the Writ Petition (PIL) No. 201 of 2014 of a division bench comprising of Justice Rajiv Sharma and Justice Alok Singh for detail.

23. This fact was revealed during discussion with some Education Officers.

Index

I

J

K

R

S

T

U